FROM SINGLE TO SCALE

HOW A SINGLE PERSON, SMALL BUSINESS, OR AN ENTREPRENEUR CAN GROW THEIR BUSINESS TO PROFIT

Michael Killen

Apress®

From Single to Scale: How a Single Person, Small Business, or an Entrepreneur Can Grow Their Business to Profit

Michael Killen
Honiton, United Kingdom

ISBN-13 (pbk): 978-1-4842-3813-4   ISBN-13 (electronic): 978-1-4842-3814-1
https://doi.org/10.1007/978-1-4842-3814-1

Library of Congress Control Number: 2018956407

Copyright © 2019 by Michael Killen

This work is subject to copyright. All rights are reserved by the Publisher, whether the whole or part of the material is concerned, specifically the rights of translation, reprinting, reuse of illustrations, recitation, broadcasting, reproduction on microfilms or in any other physical way, and transmission or information storage and retrieval, electronic adaptation, computer software, or by similar or dissimilar methodology now known or hereafter developed.

Trademarked names, logos, and images may appear in this book. Rather than use a trademark symbol with every occurrence of a trademarked name, logo, or image we use the names, logos, and images only in an editorial fashion and to the benefit of the trademark owner, with no intention of infringement of the trademark.

The use in this publication of trade names, trademarks, service marks, and similar terms, even if they are not identified as such, is not to be taken as an expression of opinion as to whether or not they are subject to proprietary rights.

While the advice and information in this book are believed to be true and accurate at the date of publication, neither the authors nor the editors nor the publisher can accept any legal responsibility for any errors or omissions that may be made. The publisher makes no warranty, express or implied, with respect to the material contained herein.

    Managing Director, Apress Media LLC: Welmoed Spahr
    Acquisitions Editor: Shiva Ramachandran
    Development Editor: Laura Berendson
    Coordinating Editor: Rita Fernando

Cover designed by eStudioCalamar

Distributed to the book trade worldwide by Springer Science+Business Media New York, 233 Spring Street, 6th Floor, New York, NY 10013. Phone 1-800-SPRINGER, fax (201) 348-4505, e-mail orders-ny@springer-sbm.com, or visit www.springeronline.com. Apress Media, LLC is a California LLC and the sole member (owner) is Springer Science + Business Media Finance Inc (SSBM Finance Inc). SSBM Finance Inc is a **Delaware** corporation.

For information on translations, please e-mail rights@apress.com, or visit http://www.apress.com/rights-permissions.

Apress titles may be purchased in bulk for academic, corporate, or promotional use. eBook versions and licenses are also available for most titles. For more information, reference our Print and eBook Bulk Sales web page at http://www.apress.com/bulk-sales.

Any source code or other supplementary material referenced by the author in this book is available to readers on GitHub via the book's product page, located at www.apress.com/9781484238134. For more detailed information, please visit http://www.apress.com/source-code.

Printed on acid-free paper

*This book is dedicated to my Mum, Miranda.
Thank you for teaching me my love of writing and
using the English language to help others.*

*And my partner, Olivia. Thank you for making coffee
at 5 a.m. and listening to me dictate at 2 a.m.*

Contents

About the Author vii
Acknowledgments ix

Chapter 1:   Why You Need to Scale 1
Chapter 2:   What's Stopping You From Scaling?. 25
Chapter 3:   Types of Single-Person, Scalable Businesses 43
Chapter 4:   Developing a Scalable Product from What You've Got. . . 65
Chapter 5:   Creating Content for a Scalable Product 91
Chapter 6:   Building a Larger Audience 111
Chapter 7:   Connecting More of That Audience to a Scalable
             Product 131
Chapter 8:   Why Process Is the Key to Scale. 153
Chapter 9:   Outsourcing the Scalable Process 169
Chapter 10: Growth Optimization 185
Chapter 11: Profit and Money Management to Scale 203
Chapter 12: Scale and Growth Are Just Around the Corner! 213

Index 215

About the Author

Michael Killen currently runs his own consultancy, where he coaches businesses on money, scale, finding customers, and making sales. In 2017, Mike sold his first business to a larger media agency. He has a background in digital marketing, having worked for a large global corporation as a lead, developing digital marketing strategies for small to medium-sized businesses that fit their business needs.

Acknowledgments

I'd like to give special thanks to Anita Henderson (www.i4design.nz), who edited the first ever draft of this book. I'd also like to thank my Mum for working through the first edition with me and helping me clarify my ideas.

A massive thank you to Laura, Rita, and Dulcy at Apress for helping me bring this book to market and for putting up with my embarrassing lack of knowledge as a first-time author. Also, thank you to Shiva who reached out to me to talk about a book deal—that was awesome.

Thank you to everyone at Sell Your Service, both members and colleagues, who believed in my blog content enough to help me put it in book form!

A huge thank you to the team at The Generator co-working in Exeter, my office, who let me talk their ears off about writing the book and then keeping dozens of copies around the office. And not minding when I forced people to take home a copy!

Thank you to my fiancée, Olivia. She helped me get up early to write and stay up late to write some more.

Finally, thank you to you the reader for taking a chance on a new book from a new author. I know your time is precious and it means a huge amount to me that you've read my first book. If I can ever help you, please email me michael@sellyourservice.co.uk and I'll answer anything I can.

CHAPTER 1

Why You Need to Scale

I want to give you a better quality of life. There are many lies and preconceived ideas that consultants and freelancers tell themselves. All of these are killing your business and perhaps even making you unhappy. In this chapter we're going to explore why scale isn't just about a bigger office; it's about helping more people and giving you more freedom.

Recurring Revenue

Growing businesses are allowed to exist because they generate recurring revenue. It's as simple as that. If you want your business to grow, you need recurring revenue. Recurring revenue is a specific type of income that not all businesses can create. It's not necessarily related to offering a product, service, or craft; instead, it's about how your customers use your products and how you sell them.

For example, a car manufacturer makes a sale and it's a large lump sum of income. That's a one-off sale and chances are that same customer isn't going to buy again anytime soon. Also, with the manufacturing costs and staff costs, that one-off sale probably doesn't provide much profit. Manufacturers realize that recurring revenue comes from repeat customers, so servicing, maintenance, and check-ups are how most garages and retailers generate recurring revenue. However, that can only grow with staff and space. If you had 1,000 people ask for servicing today, chances are they'd have to wait or you wouldn't be able to service them at all.

So you also need a scalable product: things you can sell that can always keep up with demand. When it comes to your consulting or coaching business, or if you build web sites or one-off solutions for customers, you're selling the car at the moment.

The job of this book is to get you to a scalable position with your business. Often, as entrepreneurs, we're trapped in a cycle of project-based income and then months of nothing. Growth comes from recurring revenue, sold with scalable products and services. Recurring revenue gives you more than these two options:

Work more hours or charge more money. When your business needs to generate more income, you can be left with limited choices as a solo, micro, or small business. You have two options: Either increase your fees per project or increase the number of projects you take on. Both of these are double-edged swords. In one respect, it makes sense and it's easy to increase your fees. If you're working per hour, just increase the number of hours you work.

However, how easy is it to increase your fees? Surely there's a saturation point. When it comes to adding more hours to your working day, aren't we trying to work less? Besides, there are only so many hours in the day you can work; you still need to eat, sleep, and relax.

This is the fallacy that so many micro and small businesses fall into, that there are only two options when it comes to generating more income and revenue. Surely the answer is just "get more customers," right? Wrong. Your best option is a third choice that hardly any small business goes for, the option to generate recurring and scalable income.

Sure, we could move customers onto retainers and monthly packages. Coaching and consulting is a great way to build recurring revenue, but it's not scalable. All we're doing there is guaranteeing our income, not scaling and growing it. I want to show you how to *scale* and *grow* your income, rather than just securing it (and yes, you can do both). I want to show you how the opportunities are larger than you think:

The market is bigger. The first mind-shift you have to get over is that you think your market is small, because you're only able to service a small area. It becomes a self-fulfilling prophecy. If you're only able to work with 10 clients a month, it leads you to think that there are only 10 clients a month out there. If you're working on project-based income, there is a finite and limited number of clients you can service per month.

When we look at scalable and growth-based products and services, our market becomes massive. It becomes so much larger because we're able to sell, deliver, and interact with so many more clients in the exact same space of time. Think about one-on-one coaching. If one person wants to hear you talk, why wouldn't 100? If you could get 100 people to pay the same amount and be in the same room at the same time, doesn't that sound more profitable?

There's a myth that if you scale up the number of people listening, you need to drop your prices. This is not true. If one person is willing to pay, then everyone else who attends can pay that, too. If anything, what you'll find is a select few people want to pay more just for the opportunity to sit one-on-one with you. I know some coaches who keep bumping up their prices for one-on-one time (because they don't want to do it), but people still keep offering to pay.

In summary, the people that you're helping now exist all over the world. There are hundreds of people in the exact same position as your current clients who also need help. You've got an opportunity to sit with all of them in the same space of time.

Scaling is easier than ever. The beauty of the Internet is that it brings technology, power, and community to a laptop. You have access to all the communities out there who can automate and execute for you.

There are powerful and free cloud apps and software that let you create products and content and easily distribute it to people you've never met. Finally, there is an infinite amount of knowledge available from social groups, search engines, and blogs. This gives you the power of all those resources; all that research and all that experience are right at your fingertips.

Single-person businesses can set up a blog and drive thousands of visitors to a page in less than a day. We can capture leads and e-mail addresses within minutes and automate every single e-mail that gets sent to customers. PayPal handles payments and WordPress handles pages, memberships, and sales. Google lets us get in touch with drop-ship businesses, manufacturers, and suppliers. We can ask fulfillment companies to deliver goods and all we have to do is drive traffic and write content.

With e-mails, Slack, Facebook groups, and post comments, you can reach out to an enormous audience and put awesome content in front of them. It's so exciting to me that we have this huge potential for reach with our content. We can use simple screen capture and writing apps (Google Docs, PowerPoint, Camtasia) to create content and products that last forever. The beauty of those types of sales are that the supply never runs out.

Is it hard work? Of course it is, but it scales and grows so much faster than any other type of business. Even the best bakeries in the world have a queue of people lining up who can only be serviced one at a time, assuming there is enough supply. We're going to build a business that can scale, serve as many people as it needs and be run with just one or very few employees.

Limited options. Well, the options seem limited. Whatever you've seen as a large scaled business might seem way out of reach for you. You're only one person and all the ideas and examples that I've given or you've seen just look way too massive.

Amazon is a really bad example of a large, scalable, and growth-focused business. It has 230,800 employees and it's well known for "growing rapidly and at pace."[1] However, this was only possible because it had millions in funding, investments, and financial backing. Jeff Bezos has done an outstanding job turning high-street and shop-based retailing on its head, but his is not the model we're going to follow.

On the other side, it seems hard to imagine a business outside of the type of service that you're providing now. For example, if you're building WordPress sites at the moment, and you love doing that, what on earth could you provide?

This *isn't* a book about creating a business from your hobbies. You could do that if it has a market, scalable product, and sales process, but we're not going to suggest that this is your only option. It helps to be in the market you're servicing, but that's not a requirement. It definitely helps if you enjoy the product or industry you're in, but that again is not necessary.

As an example, I have a friend who makes around £750 a day selling sports drinks bottles and simple sports leisure equipment. He does this entirely through drop-shipping. However, he started as a sports coach. He was a personal trainer for amateur athletes, but he could only exchange his time for money. He literally could only book eight clients a day and it was stifling his growth. As soon as he let go of the control of being the only personal trainer his clients would see (or the idea that he's the only one they see), he realized he could still help them with physical products, workout plans, and therapy guides.

Now his full-time business is selling foam rollers, skipping ropes, and other inexpensive sports products. He doesn't design, build, or ship them. Amazon (sorry to mention them again) ships and delivers all his products. Here's the truth: Your options aren't at all limited. You've got a wealth of potential ahead of you and we're going to discover exactly how to create a profitable, scalable business using everything you've got at the moment. You need to stop trading time for money.

Eating up profit. Have you've ever noticed that your overall revenue grows, but you never seem to have more profit left at the end of the year? I noticed something happening repeatedly throughout my business. My revenue was

---

[1] See https://www.statista.com/statistics/234488/number-of-amazon-employees/

growing every year, and I had the cash flow ledgers to prove it. I never seemed to have any more money, though. I never seemed to grow my profit. All my profit, year-in, year-out, remained roughly the same (and it wasn't great amounts, either).

I couldn't figure out why, even though the projects I was getting were bigger. Even though the budgets were better, I had more customers and I had a small team. It seemed that even though everything else was growing, my profits weren't. I kept thinking, "I just need one more big client, one more big project, that'll sort it all out." Whenever that bigger project and a bigger client came in, though, there was no change.

At first, I always blamed the project. Something must have happened that made it difficult and ate into the profit. Then I started to think that because I was growing, I was having to spend more money on tools and team members. I needed those things to deliver the projects, which kind of made sense. Then how could I get out of that cycle? If I need more tools and team members to make the same amount of profit, what's the point in having them at all? It seemed that no matter how much money I had, the universe seemed to know exactly how much to take away from me.

Here's what happens. If your business relies on one-off projects from customers, no matter how large they are, you're essentially trading time for money. We hope that, as time goes on, the projects get larger and we're earning more per hour. Remember when we said you had two options? Work more or charge more? Most people hope they can grow to charge more. Instead of those projects turning into profit, however, they simply pay for the costs of running the business. As you grow, it costs more per month to keep the business afloat. The projects do grow in size, but so does the cost of keeping the business alive.

Figure 1-1 displays what most single and micro businesses see in their cash flow and profit. The red line represents the costs of running the business: tools, staff, subscriptions, rent, overheads, loans, and so on.

Chapter 1 | Why You Need to Scale

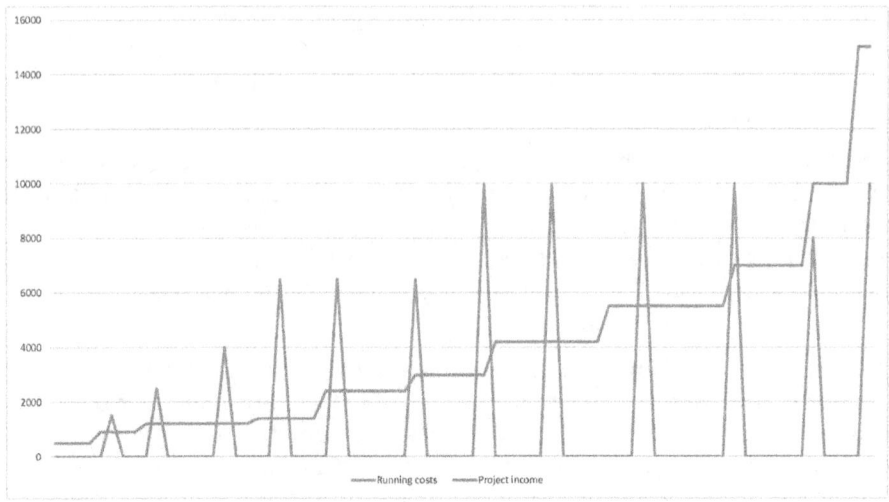

Figure 1-1. Running costs to project income

These costs continue to go up, and always will. Even the most frugal of business owners can't escape necessary costs to the business. They have to invest to find the very projects that pay for them. The gray line in Figure 1-1 shows the project income, each new project with progressively larger and larger budgets. Eventually they reach nice big fat project budgets. All the profit (the gray spike above the red line), though, ends up being used during the periods under the red line, to pay for the business costs. How does this look to you? Recognize it? Well, we're going to change this graph, and it's easier than you think.

Trade time for money. I can hear you say, "Mike, you told me that I shouldn't be trading time for money." Let me ask you a question: Have you ever had a job? I have. It was awful. I'm going to clearly state this: I don't like working in a company. I don't enjoy being employed. I don't enjoy having a manager. I don't enjoy trading time for money.

The truth is, though, that there are thousands of businesses and entrepreneurs who claim to run or own businesses who still trade time for money. They still have jobs, but they have 10 managers instead of one, and their income isn't guaranteed. Here's what most people do. They set up a web site or WordPress business or consultation agency and look for customers. Clients sign up and say they want a project delivered in two months and they'll pay throughout the project. Even if you're doing all that right,[2] you're still trading your time

---

[2] I know of many many businesses who design, build, develop, and deploy entire web sites without receiving a penny first. Then, they send an invoice. If you're doing this, stop immediately. Ask for 50% up front for any work you do.

for money. You're delivering the project, building and doing whatever it is the client needs in exchange for money. This is a first-generation profit business. The concept relies on ignoring the graph we saw in Figure 1-1, expecting larger contracts to build up, but still relying on you, the owner, delivering the goods.

It fails to answer the first rule of profitable, scalable businesses: Do I have to do it or can someone else do it? This applies to these areas, just as an example:

- Web site design and development
- Construction
- Building
- Plumbing
- Consulting
- Coaching
- Social media businesses
- Digital marketing
- Blog writing
- Content creation

These are some businesses that rely on a "time for money" exchange. Typically, 90% won't even break even. Most just about stay afloat. Businesses that do manage to increase prices still trade time for money. Their situation doesn't much change.

A second-generation profit business knows that exchanging time for money isn't profitable. They'll hire other people to deliver the goods and services that they're selling. Some people call this outsourcing, or contracting. It doesn't really matter what you call it. When you're so busy that you can't deliver the work yourself, you need to get others to help you, even if it's not the same work you do. For example, a web site designer might get someone to build and develop the site, someone else to do the social media, and someone else to provide the search engine optimization (SEO).

This certainly allows for larger projects to be undertaken. Typically they're more profitable as you share the workload and, provided that you're all able to communicate, larger projects can be delivered. The problem is that you're essentially still trading time for money. The scale is larger, but working in a team just splits the revenue between more people. Although we've managed to get other people to do some of the work, we can't scale it. This second generation of profitable business can't answer the second rule of profit: Can it scale? I couldn't get 1,000 orders in today using this method of outsourced work and still handle it.

Finally, a third-generation profit business knows that a truly profitable business can be outsourced, scaled, and repeated. Some products or services can't be automated, processed, or repeated with the same results. These are typically very hard to build profit from, as the parameters for the project always shift. Almost everything can be documented. By this, I mean that whatever you deliver to your clients can usually be documented and written up or recorded as a process. That means other people can execute the actions without you.

Often, when I am running these exercises with consultants and coaches, they tell me they believe that what they're producing can't be replicated. To an extent they're correct, but that simply means they might need to look at other options if they want scalable, profitable products.

In summary, we need to develop products and services that aren't time for money. They need to be executed and sold without you physically being there or doing the work. They need to be able to get 1,000 orders in and still get the same results and they need to be repeatable so you can train other people to deliver.

No work on. All businesses have quiet periods. We tend to think of businesses growing and filling up those quiet periods as time goes on. In truth, all businesses face lulls in income. Sometimes it's seasonal or sometimes it's just the nature of your business. For example, I know of a team that sells French Alps ski holidays. During the winter, they're crazy busy. People typically book their holidays while on their previous break or leading into winter. Spring and summer are usually very quiet, which makes sense because of when their customers use their product.

Businesses like marketing consultants and web site designers have quiet periods, too. Some of that might be seasonal (Christmas is notoriously quiet) or due to the fact that working on a project is the worst thing for your business. Here's what typically happens. After a couple of months of quiet (remember Figure 1-1?), you find a project and some work comes in. Maybe you spent the quiet time wisely and went looking for customers. However, as soon as you've got customers and you've got work, you now can't spend time finding more customers.

It's a vicious cycle and often means that you're eating into the revenue and profit from your projects. Every day you're not making money, from new or current customers, your money is being used up. During quiet periods, we tend to work on our businesses. This is often more productive than we realize. We write content, attend networks, and build contacts. At the same time, though, those quiet periods cost us money.

Most businesses want fewer or no quiet periods, but without that time spent working on your business you might never have the busy periods. So how can we get the benefit of quiet periods where we can work on our businesses, while experiencing the income that comes with busier periods?

Flat out. On the other side of the coin, we have busy periods, those times when work rolls in, almost to the point of breaking. "That sounds awesome!" I hear you say. Although they can be great for your bank balance, busy periods unveil two crucial problems.

First, during busy periods you're not working on your business. You're spending time working for the customer, as opposed to growing and scaling your business. Second, busy periods mean you're still trading time for money. Again, your bank balance might thank you, but if you're working 16 hours a day is that really better?

Anyone can be busy. I'll often hear consultants and coaches talking about how busy they are. If we probe a little deeper, asking about new products or developments, they'll often say, "I haven't had time for that because I'm so busy!"

It's tough, I know. We have bills to pay. If we're not working on ways of removing ourselves from the transaction, or ways to make the business busy and ourselves less busy, however, then we'll never grow. Typically, people who would describe themselves as very busy aren't profitable. They spend so much time working on projects and working in the business that they never have time to work on the three rules of profit:

1. Do I have to do the work or can I outsource it to someone else?
2. Can I receive 1,000 orders tomorrow and handle it?
3. Is the process or delivery repeatable so anyone can do it?

If you're flat out with work, really take a step back and ask yourself if this is growing your business, or just providing an income. Income alone won't grow your business.

Single to scale. It's absolutely not impossible to grow a single-person business. Many entrepreneurs have done a great job being the only person in their organization, and have grown. However, it is much harder to grow a single-person business. The most common objection I hear to this is, "I can't afford a team or to employ a load of people." This isn't about saving hard and employing someone. Just because a company has a team of staff doesn't mean it is profitable.

What I mean by single-person business is how much of the work you are doing yourself, versus having virtual assistants, part-time outsourced work, a referral network, and a couple of good friends. For example, a graphic designer I used to work with does everything from logos to leaflets. This is pretty standard stuff. I would pay her and she'd run the discovery session with me, design the logo, choose the font, create a color palette, build branding guidelines, and deliver all the files herself. It would take about four weeks and during that time she wouldn't be working on anything else. What happens when larger, better, and more profitable projects come along and she'd have to turn them down? Worse still, she might put mine off and chase the larger work. It happens to all single-person businesses and it means that small single-person businesses are harder to grow.

Working in the Business

My graphic designer friend worked so hard in the business that she never had a chance to work on the business. Snappy motivational quips like that (work *on* the business not *in* the business) might sound trite, but they are true.

Scaling your business means giving up control (we'll get to that) and taking a cut in income for a bit (we'll get to that, too). What this means is that you can focus on running a business. You have to ask yourself, are you a web designer or do you run a web design business? We all love saying we run a business, or own a business, but often we're the ones doing the work, too. To me, that's like being employed but not knowing where your next paycheck is coming from.

Running a business means working on finance, marketing, product design, processes, business development, and more. I will admit, 100%, that the idea of tax, banking, insurance, and writing hours of documentation doesn't inspire me at all. I became a marketer so I could help people.

That's the beauty of the world today. By setting up our business in a way to scale and run as a business, we can focus more on the work we want. We can get people to do the stuff we don't want to do. There are services and products that let us work while others run the day to day. However, it has to come with giving up control of certain other parts of the business.

On the other hand, many business owners end up enjoying running a business. They find skills in areas they wouldn't think of or they discover practices that they didn't even know existed (I, for one, love income investment and splitting my money across various accounts). You know you want to scale. You know you want to grow and spend less time working. This is the start of how you do that.

Not the only one. I'm going to really upset a few people here. No matter how unique or special you believe your product or service is, you're not the only one who can deliver it. This sounds awful, I know. Part of that is because of the education system we set up. It teaches us as children to find a speciality and narrow down on what we can deliver. The idea is that if we're the only person who can deliver it, we're more valuable that way.

Unfortunately, the real world doesn't work that way. For a start, unless you're Muhammad Ali or Jackson Pollock, you aren't that special. Not many people have skills so unique that other people are willing to pay thousands for them. Bill Gates didn't even write MS-DOS, the first operating system that made him rich. He bought it and marketed the hell out of it.[3]

Businesses and people do want unique, sure, but when it comes to buying something that they actually want, what they mean by "unique" is a unique delivery for them, on something that is entirely standard. Take web sites, for example. WordPress as a platform powers 25% of the world's web sites, including the sites for BBC, CNN, eBay, and other big players, too.

Now, if I offered two web sites to a customer, unique in design and content, but powered by one of two options, which one would they take? Option 1 is my own proprietary content management system (CMS), which means I work really well with it, but only I can work on it. That means if I go missing or if I leave, no one else can fix it. Option 2 is a platform used by 25% of the Internet where if you decide to move on, there are literally hundreds of thousands of developers and designers who can help with the site.

Even in coaching and consulting, sit-down sessions where you impart your wisdom to others can be taught. They can be documented, processed, and delivered by other media, from books, courses, videos, team workshops, and downloadable PDFs.

If you're really as good as you say you are, you can document the process you're going through. Often that's the problem: Businesses who want to scale face documenting processes. They don't know how, so they don't do it at all, but if you can't help other people do what you do, then you're not going to scale.

Hold onto control. One of the main reason single-person microbusinesses fail to grow and scale is relinquishing control. It usually starts as a bootstrap approach. As a single-person business, you just don't have the resources to employ or outsource. We get used to doing our own things. We build our own web sites, do our own marketing and finances, and, of course, we deliver the services ourselves.

It's important to note that there are two types of activities that we could give up control of: running our business and delivering services or products. Often we fool ourselves into thinking that we don't have the money or resources to get others to help us. The truth is that we don't really want others to do it because we're happy with things the way they are. If you don't accept that you need to give up control of every aspect of your business, it'll never grow. It's very simple. Of course, we're going to cover how to give up that control, in a constructive, economic manner, but you need to understand that one person can't do everything.

---

[3]See http://electronics.howstuffworks.com/tech-myths/5-myths-about-microsoft4.htm

Chapter 1 | Why You Need to Scale

It's how it's always been. The reason people don't expand their income streams and options is because it's hard work, it's scary, and they're worried about what others will say. There are two decisions you need to make before you decide to scale and increase your options. First, do you want to explore other options for income, even if it means going against the crowd? Second, are you willing to work hard and work through the initial fear (it only lasts a day or two) because you know you're expanding your options? An interesting thing happens when you decide to open your options for income and revenue. You wonder why more businesses don't do it.

Budget and location. You're also limited by budget (both yours and those of your customers) and location. Let's take a physical therapist, for example. If our physical therapist needs to treat patients, he or she will have to visit their location or have them visit him or her. Treatment and therapy are perfect examples of freelance style businesses that look very similar to profitable, scalable businesses, except they're not.

Our therapist (and the same goes for consultants, coaches, freelancers, designers, and mercenaries) needs to exchange time for money. Further still, his or her time is restricted to location and budget. Would it even be worth spending $10 on fuel to see a $35 customer?

Absolutely, there are limitations in outsourcing staff. For example, many therapy businesses couldn't just train anyone to perform the therapy. Aside from the years of training, there are insurance and legal reasons, too. That's also confining the product to the older style of thinking, though. It's assuming that being there and performing time for money exchange is the only option. Even with 100 staff, could our therapist deal with 1,000 orders in a day? No. What if there are thousands more potential customers in other locations but, for very practical reasons, we can't meet them?

What we're trying to do here is understand that the delivery of your product and service might need to change. It's so important to know and remember that the results and benefits are largely the same. We're just changing the method in the way it gets to your customers. Think about medicine and how we used to deliver benefits. When the first inoculations for smallpox were discovered by Edward Jenner in 1796, the old method of vaccinating someone was by taking old cowpox scabs and inserting them under the skin. This proved so successful that they traveled the world with the cure. Over time, the method for vaccinating became more and more sophisticated. The delivery method doesn't need to be tied to the benefit.

Gas station sandwiches. This is one of the largest contributing factors for me in deciding to scale my business. I was forever traveling from customer to customer, eating gas station pasties and sandwiches. I needed to see so many people that I had hardly any time to sit down and eat properly. I'm sure someone much smarter than me can work the math out, but essentially I was spending hundreds of pounds a week on gas, food, and shelter just to cover the costs of a new project.

The more projects I took on, the more income I needed to sustain a relationship with my customers. I had to spend more money to make just a fraction more. On top of all that, petrol station food is awful, particularly English gas station food! Can you imagine? It's terrible. I remember on one particular consulting session near Plymouth, I sat in my car, eating a pasty, the rain pouring down as motorway traffic sped past me. "This doesn't really feel like I'm an entrepreneur," I thought. "This is basically my old sales job, except I can't claim expenses." No more, I decided. How could I get the same results (or better results) to customers without eating another chicken mayo sandwich?

Free freelancers. This leads us to a very important point. Most freelancers aren't as free as they think they are. "Yeah, I work my own hours, choose my clients and best of all, I don't answer to a boss." Here's the truth: You have three bosses—your bank manager, your mortgage or rent officer, and your customers. There are even more bosses and managers if you have several of each.

Your bills, expenses, and outgoings really piss off your bank manager when they're not paid. What's worse is that we often don't have personal relationships with managers anymore. At the time of writing, despite being a Barclays customer of four years, I've just been told that I don't even have a business manager. We're held accountable to computer systems and customer service representatives, which is fine, I guess. In fact banks are a great example of businesses scaling and automating (although losing the human touch, some might argue).

The notion of freelancers working from beaches and coffee shops might sound appealing, but it's often not true. When we have to deliver the work ourselves, we're stretched to then fit other obligations into our lives. Running the business, managing the finances, seeing friends and family, sports, hobbies, eating, cooking, and cleaning—they all have to fit in somewhere.

The concept of working 9 a.m. to 5 p.m. in an office is both antiquated and, paradoxically, a relatively new idea when compared to human history. The problem comes from our perception of what "work" is. I believe our idea of work, employment, or jobs is incorrect and even unhelpful. We're trapped in the idea that even running a business means we have to work the same hours our old jobs required.

It wasn't until the Victorian period that large offices or factories with salaried employees was even a "thing." Most people were self-employed or ran small businesses before that. However, it's also foolish to believe that we can live a life of beach writing and carefree travel just because we call ourselves freelancers.

Chapter 1 | Why You Need to Scale

Running a business is hard work, sure, but it means that we can have more of that freedom that we were promised. We're just not going to do it the same way everyone else is.

> "My main problem, Mike, is that I don't want to work on this business anymore." Mark sighed and looked down at his laptop. Money was rolling in, around $10,000 a week. But they weren't making any profit.

This is unfortunately a very common problem. More and more businesses feel trapped in a business model that doesn't really work. If they take their foot off the gas, they feel everything else will collapse. Typically, this is because we can't see a way past what we're delivering now. How on earth do you scale a consultancy business? It physically needs you to be there. You're the only one who can get customers those kind of results.

Your customers aren't interested in Internet learning or e-books. Most of them don't even have the budget for the work you're doing now. Getting them to commit to a time, date, and location is difficult enough. None of it seems to work, so it becomes a self-fulfilling, negative cycle. We have to keep fighting for work that isn't profitable and eats into our time. The income doesn't give us more freedom, but it does pay the bills. Most of those bills are just expenses, designed to keep the business running.

Tell me you don't recognize this. You have to pay for hosting, banking, subscriptions, business expenses, and bills, just so you can work some more tomorrow. This scenario seems a little broken to me. That cycle can be broken. We can break the pay for work cycle of money for time. We can discover new ways to give you back time and pay the bills. It does not require capital investment or loans. It doesn't require employing staff. It just needs two things: swallowing your fears and sticking to the rules.

1. Do I have to do the work or can I outsource it to someone else?
2. Can I receive 1,000 orders tomorrow and handle it?
3. Is the process or delivery repeatable so anyone can do it?

Yes, you'll have to make sacrifices, but I can assure you, once you start cutting back the fat, you'll find it tough to stop. It's liberating when you stop paying for the gym. It's liberating when you stop paying for satellite TV (that you never watch anyway). It's liberating firing clients that suck up your time. We're going to switch from being resentful about our business to euphoric and full of ideas. First, though, we need to get over one massive fear.

Afford the time. "I can't afford the time to grow. I barely have enough time as it is. I'll have even less time if I have staff, outsourcing, processes and organization management stuff." If I told you that we could get you more time back to run your business or even do some hobbies and go out, what would you say to that?

Don't worry about what you think growing your business does. What we're going to create is a system that gives you time back. Even small items like social media posting, customer support, and e-mail correspondence can take up hours of your day. Let say you work on your social posting for an hour a day. That's 5 hours a week and 20 hours a month. How much is 20 hours a month worth to you? What could you do with almost another full day per month? Create new products? Write an e-book (1 hour a day = 6 pages, 20 hours = 120 pages)?

Growing a business is about giving time back to you. Even if you run a small shoe store in the middle of nowhere, there are things that you need to do to grow, and there are things holding you back.

Often I hear that business owners and entrepreneurs don't have time to grow. It's the classic case of taking your foot off the gas. If you stop doing what you're doing, everything will crash down around you. This is seldom actually the case. More often than not, we find that all the plate spinning we do doesn't crash down around us if we take a day to organize our growth and systems.

Your scalable product. Here's the single biggest reason you need to start scaling your business. You've already got a product that you can scale. If you're a coach, freelancer, consultant, designer, developer, chef, entrepreneur, or anything else that has you at the center of your business, you can scale. I'm not going to tell you to write a book (although you should), but let's look at the model of an author.

As a chef, I can maybe teach 12 people at once. I could actually deliver to maybe 40 or so people a night. With a book, however, I can reach as many people as there are (1) books in production, and (2) people willing to buy. We can flip that model and reach even more people, with lower overhead costs, using a digital book model.

No matter what your skill, trade, or profession is, you have a checklist or a way of doing things. You might think it's more fluid and organic than that but, trust me, you've got a process. When you have a process, you have a product. There are an almost unlimited number of ways to turn a process into a product to sell, such as these:

- Outsourcing the process and having others execute them to deliver the goods to your customer.
- Documenting the process and teaching it to others for a fee.
- Writing up the process and creating a series of books.

- Presenting the process via a webinar and charging for materials.
- Systematizing the process and releasing it as an app or cloud-based app.

I could go on.

You might think, "But if I teach other people to do it, they won't need me anymore." Nonsense. If that were true, why would we still have teachers? Why do we have managers? If you honestly have no desire to help more people and sell more products and services, stop reading here. The key to successful, growing businesses is helping more people at scale, more than you could help just by yourself.

We're going to be giving away the cow, the farm, the milking equipment, and the delivery truck. Businesses that hoard their skills and experience to charge customers will always face scarcity. Businesses that share their knowledge are rewarded with an abundance in return. When we learn how to scale, we're rewarded at scale, too.

Bigger Businesses Don't Buy (at Scale) from Single-Person Enterprises

I've always been fascinated with the idea of consultants being hired by larger businesses. The idea that one person could have the answers to an entire organization's problems intrigues me. Here is the fundamental, undeniable truth about large businesses hiring external consultants. Larger organizations hire external consultants to tell them what they already know. The reason someone from the outside is hired to tell them the exact things they already know is because internal teams value the opinions and words of external people more than their own managers.

I wish this weren't true, but it is. How many times has an external consultant come into a business and led a really energetic workshop, only for things to go back to normal a few weeks later? The consultancy model is broken and it's not doing itself any favors. Deep-rooted shifts in an entire organization's model don't happen overnight. They especially don't happen after one person has told them to change.

Consultants brag about how much a single day costs, but when businesses don't get the results they're expecting, the consultant model is damaged. "But I'm not like that, Mike. I get results and my clients love me. I'm not a con artist." I hear you, but you are in the minority. You know as well as I do that most consultants are cowboys. On top of that, deep down, be honest with yourself: How many customers have been disappointed not because of your results, but because of their expectations?

I've been a $3,000-a-day consultant and I've hired $10,000-a-day consultants. There is often a disconnect between managers and external staff, and between expected results and actual results. Here's the kicker: Larger organizations don't buy repeated and at-scale products and services from single-person enterprises. They just don't. There's an image associated with single-person businesses, rightly or wrongly, that they're more "mercenaries" than "army." They are something to be hired when and if needed, not something that provides value every day.

The beauty of today's digital, high-tech world (the most 1999 sentence of all time) is that a single-person business can appear genuinely larger and more sophisticated. It can offer services and products that are needed by larger organizations, while remaining small and agile. We're not talking about expanding to become a multiteam agency. We're talking about building a system that supports 1,000 new orders every day, without you spending hours on e-mails or in conference rooms. It's not just about scaling our delivery, though.

Grateful to customers. I think this is the top reason I wanted to move away from the traditional model of consulting and coaching. Despite my attitude of not acting desperate, every time a customer bought from me, I felt utter relief that I could pay that month's bills. It's exhausting running from job to job, acting like you don't care when a lead turns out to be a dud. I'm not saying we shouldn't be thankful or appreciative to customers, but it needs to balanced. Too often the balance is stacked against us as businesses. Larger customers often know this, too, feeling like they're helping out the little guy.

I remember one particular client (which was a turning point for me), after I thanked them for the opportunity. They replied with, "Don't thank me, help me." They were absolutely right: They should have been thanking me, grateful that I had got space in my calendar to help them with their work and grateful that there was a solution to their problem.

As one person, it's hard to make that shift, from "lucky to be chosen" to "they're lucky we're free." We have to strike a balance between customer service and well-positioned service. If something was so valuable that customers didn't care if your customer service was terrible, you're in the best position you could be. You'd just have to work at your service. Typically, we're on the other end: friendly, accommodating, and they can contact the owner.

The only problem is that our product and service isn't "crawl over broken glass to get it" valuable. As single-person businesses, we're rarely seen as that important, but larger, scaled businesses can be, even if you keep your team small or even just to you. At its core, customers buy process. They're not buying hamburgers and fries at McDonald's; they're buying a convenient location, predictable delivery, and repeated packaging.

On the other end of the spectrum, when we have customers, our greatest fear is that they'll leave us. We used to have "quitting policies" in our contracts that stated if customers left our hosting, web delivery platforms, and other services, they would have to pay to release their web site from us. I can hear you screaming at me now. I totally agree that it was the wrong thing to do. However I didn't want customers leaving me. I was trying to make it difficult for them to leave so they would stay. That way they'd be happy.

Quickly, though, I realized that this was how utilities and telecommunication companies ran their businesses. It's disgusting when I think back: I shouldn't be threatening to punish customers who want to leave. I should be rewarding customers who stay. At the front of my mind, during every customer meeting, I thought they might fire me. Part of that was because I knew their expectations were too high. The other half was just because they might get bored and they just could. They were in charge and, honestly, most of us aren't delivering anything that someone else couldn't do.

Part of our new growth strategy will be (1) mitigate customer turnover with new customers always coming in, and (2) provide so much value to customers that they just don't want to leave. On top of that, we're going to provide a process for dealing with customers who do want to leave, turning it into a learning experience so that we can reduce the number of customers who do actually leave. All this time spent delivering to customers, means you're missing out, though.

You're not developing. You need to scale because, as we've explored, your business doesn't develop when you're delivering. Business development is talking to customers, exploring opportunities, and developing the business. It's usually something that results in a tangible benefit to you and the business. Take networking, for example. It's about balance, remember, so if you attend seven networking events a week it's counterproductive.

Often, though, we feel we don't have time to network because we need to deliver the products and services that other customers have bought. It's the old cycle of halting work on the business as soon as you're working in the business. Delivering products and services halts the progress of developing the business when we're the ones delivering. Ultimately, that's because we're trying to do both. If you had a dedicated business development manager you could focus on delivering the goods. Realistically, though, delivery is much easier to document and systematize. That means we can leave delivery to other people and processes while we're exploring other opportunities.

Imagine knowing that when you're networking, when you're running discovery workshops, or when you're working on content, your products and services are being delivered and paid for. You can be in two or more places at once. We have to scale before we start to see the benefits, however. The good news is that you aren't limited in your methods of growth.

Infinite ways to grow. There are infinite ways to scale your business. You're restricting your growth in general if you're not open to the various methods of scale. What we're going to look at is not just getting more customers or making more money. Scaling your business for growth is about looking at what you're delivering to the customer.

What is it about working with you that other people would value? Don't worry about the deliverables yet, and don't worry about creating the product. When we start to think about what the customer gets after working with us, we stop thinking about delivering a product and we start thinking about methods to scale. If we can deliver a benefit and value to one customer, why wouldn't another want it? Why wouldn't that same customer want those same results again?

Our options for growth are infinite. Once we see past what our business delivers now, we begin to see what customers could get in the future. We dissect how they feel after working with us, over what we deliver to them. So, if we know that customers, after working with us, have more time to spend with their families, and if we know that customers have higher page rankings on Google, or if customers generate more revenue after working with us, then why does our current product or service have to be the only thing that delivers that?

If I want to run a marathon faster, is it the trainers I buy that do that? The sports running top? The bamboo socks? My gym membership? The results I get and the results I seek are what helps other businesses to scale. It's not what I'm looking to buy that scales; it's the results I want. Once we can see how results are what drive growth and scale, we stop blinding ourselves to what we think is possible. We start seeing what is possible with our growth and scale.

Break Free from the Feast and Famine Consulting Project Income Cycle

The single most draining lifestyle I know of is the feast and famine cycle of projects for consultants and digital creative professionals. All the freelancers, consultants, and solo businesses that we interviewed said that their number one wish, if they could wave a magic wand, would be consistent and regular income. We all know how consultant projects come in, with a huge lump sum payment. It's a massive relief because we need to pay two-month-old bills and settle a few invoices.

Some of that cash will go to a new purchase or two, maybe a plug-in that'll help. Some will go to the main bills. Most, though, is eaten up over the course of the slow months because we have no other income. It's a vicious cycle as the times we're quiet cost us money no matter what. We look for work during those times and when work comes in we spend our time delivering.

Because we're working on projects, we have no time to look for more work. Plus there are always quiet times anyway, and so on and so on.

It becomes exhausting having to try to keep hold of money over three months. Rather than having income regularly make its way to you, we have to stockpile and spread it out. It's almost impossible to plan when your finances run like that. Scaling your business, growing your business, is the way we're going to solve that. We're not going to go after bigger projects. More lump sums haven't helped anyone (just ask 70% of all lottery winners).[4] We're going to look at business and income that's more manageable, scalable, and recurring.

Hot desking everywhere. "It's okay, I have a few e-mails to send. I'll perch myself over here." It wasn't true, of course, I just couldn't hack the idea of driving back for two hours after a 15-minute meeting. Also, I wanted to look cool. I wanted to look busy, saying I had work to do and I would do it anywhere. I'm a mobile worker right? I'm a millennial who believes in being productive wherever I am. Working from a coffee table in Basingstoke just outside the office door wasn't exactly what I imagined, however. I was thinking more like a beach in Thailand, or from my couch on snow days.

We're fed the idea that a laptop, Wi-Fi, and e-mail means we can work from anywhere, which is absolutely true. Since taking scale and growth into our business models, I've worked from coffee shops in Budapest, a zoo in Melbourne, and on a remote island called Urupukapuka in New Zealand. The problem is that when we work from anywhere, we often still have to deliver a large chunk of the work face to face. Have you ever tried to consult anyone over Skype? It's exhausting. Absolutely there is a stage where customers offer to fly us to their office abroad. This means we have to work remote, but we're still delivering something to them in person.

What if we delivered products, services, and made income from anywhere in the world? It doesn't always have to mean while trekking K2 or running the Inca trail. Sometimes I just want to be at home with a green tea watching Netflix. Growth and scale means we set up systems and processes that deliver while we're wherever we want to be. As consultants and freelancers we think that working from a service station in Bracknell is working remote. It is, but I've worked in nicer places. Truly working remote means working where we want to be. Scale and growth is going to help us do that.

Take a look back at Figure 1-1. It shows the running costs of our business, over time, if we stick to a feast and famine cycle. The costs go up to maintain what we're building. Although our income spikes grow, they're quickly eaten into for operating costs.

---

[4]See http://www.cleveland.com/business/index.ssf/2016/01/why_do_70_percent_of_lottery_w.html

From Single to Scale

Scaling and growing your business solves this problem. Figure 1-2 shows running costs in a dashed line, still rising as we grow. The dotted line shows our income spikes—the projects that add sudden and irregular income to the business. However with the long dash/dot, we have regular income, products and services designed to pay for the operating costs of the business.

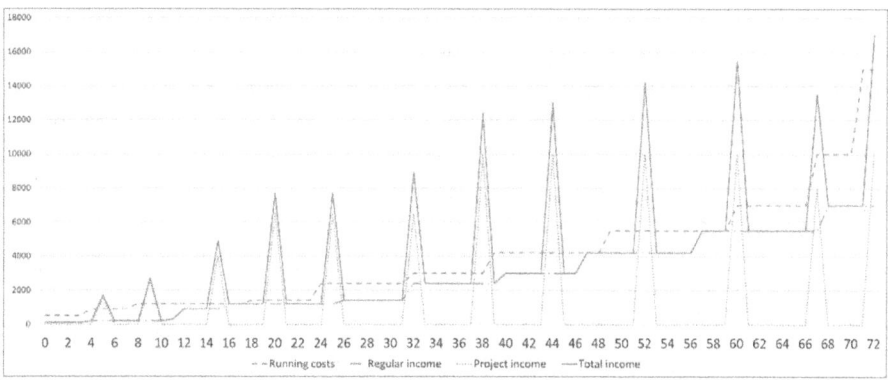

Figure 1-2. Income chart with recurring revenue

They're easy to scale and they're easy to grow. They don't cost us time to deliver them and, most important, it means that the spikes become profit rather than paying for operating costs. Scaling and growth allows us to build this model, rather than run from income to expense.

Chicken and egg. "Okay, Mike, so to get regular income, I need to scale my business. But now you're telling me to scale and grow I need regular income? Sounds a bit like the chicken and the egg. Which do I do first?"

Growth, scale, and income aren't a sliding scale. They are a cyclical process. Imagine a massive hamster wheel that we can climb inside. We have to take those first steps to get the wheel moving. We have to exert more energy to get it moving than we do to keep it moving. Starting to scale and grow your business is the effort needed to start the hamster wheel. It's hard and takes time, but once it's going, once you start to see regular income make its way into the business, it's 100 times easier to grow with regular income.

It's controversial or even offensive to some businesses to talk about income and money, profit, scale, and growth. These are all terms that many people shy away from.

> "I'm happy as one person. I only need to pay the bills."
>
> "I don't want loads of staff, I don't want to be a manager."

I hear these objections all the time. In truth, some people are just detractors and they're never going to get it, so I don't worry about them. Next, I never said you're going to hire staff. Are you 100% positive that you couldn't use a bit more cash? The reason people use these excuses is because they don't want to make a change. People don't like to change because it sometimes feels like they're admitting failure.

It might feel like you're not good with money or that you don't have the mindset to grow and manage a business. If you're still reading, I'll assume you're happy having a few skeletons from the closet come out. This is not a "holier than thou" book. Certainly some aspects of my business are a shambles (eight e-mail addresses? Really, Mike?).

By looking at our business model and finances we can see where we need to grow and where we need to cut back. It's as simple as that. Once you've started, you'll wonder why everyone doesn't do it. Imagine what your business needs to look like in a year, or two years. Maybe it involves some part-time virtual assistants. You spend nine months a year working and three with the kids. Perhaps you go on surf breaks.

You're hardly "at the office." Products come naturally to you and you want to find ways of getting them to customers. None of this happens by accident and all too often we are so busy working in our business that we can't work on it. Growth and scale gives us time back to work on our business. The dirty secret is that this business has far more potential than you're capable of delivering, especially how you're running it now.

I love the idea that a business is bigger than me. It takes the pressure off my shoulders. I start to think about what else I need to do to help the business grow, rather what I'm capable of within the business. We can reach more people. We can help more customers and we can deliver more value if we stop doing what we're doing now.

I don't doubt you're an epic designer, or 'a genuine consultant. I don't doubt you're a great programmer or you really can get me to the top of Google for some killer keywords. My point is that if you're only delivering what you are now, it's not going to scale. You need to start doing some uncomfortable and squeamish things to start growing. The beauty is that this book is exclusively designed to help you do just that. Even as one person, I'm going to show you how to grow and scale your business. We're going to move from a single-person business that chases work and income to a regularly profitable business that gives you more time back.

Summary

Your business has so much more potential than you're giving it credit for. Here are some key takeaways from this chapter:

- You must start working on the business, rather than delivering to customers and working in the business.
- Scale isn't about just growing your business size; it's about serving and helping more people.
- Scaling your business leads to a better quality of life.
- You already have the tools to scale your business. You just need to let go of control and the ways things were.

CHAPTER 2

What's Stopping You From Scaling?

In short, there isn't anything stopping you from scaling. In this chapter, we're going to see exactly how to start scaling, as well as why scaling becomes exponential—meaning the the more you scale, the more you find ways to scale in future. The biggest roadblock stopping us from scaling, though, is often seen as money.

Money to scale. There's a catch-22 when it comes to scaling your business. It usually revolves around money or budget: "I can't grow my business because I don't have the budget to grow. But I'll never have more money unless I grow." The school of thinking that it takes money to make money is old and outdated, though.

> "I often hear people say, 'It takes money to make money.' This is not true."
>
> —Robert Kiyosaki

It takes determination, discipline, and a willingness to learn and try new things, but most of all, it takes time. When we think of scaling and growing, the archaic ideal of having more staff, a bigger office, and a private jet are what we've been conditioned to think of. Scaling and growing your business is not about buying more things. Having more staff and a bigger office aren't helping you scale; they're the results of growth.

Scaling your business is about helping more people. That's all. In your current state, how many people can you help a day? Ten? Maybe even one? Scaling your business is about looking at your resources, what you know, and who you can help, and then multiplying the methods and ways you can reach those people and help them. If you're smart and dedicated, disciplined, and you have a plan, you can start to scale your business in a few days. It doesn't need a huge budget, but it does require a shift in understanding what your business can deliver. This is critical when regarding the growth of your business, for example.

Scaling a consultancy. Deciding that you want to scale and grow your business is more important than knowing how to scale it. Freelancers, we're covering you in the next section, but you still need to read this, as you share common walls with consultants.

If you're a consultant, you're exchanging your time for money. It can be hard to see how to scale this business. You barely have the time now to talk to customers, so what's it going to be like when you've got 100 more customers? That's part of the problem. You don't know how to scale a consultancy because you're focusing on the wrong part of growth. Growth and scale aren't in the delivery. It's about the systems and processes you use to run the business. It's about the variety of products you have to help people.

Having said all that, the most common objection I heard when researching this book was, "No one else knows what I know and no one else can deliver this." If that were true, and I mean *really* true, this book can't help you. Let's be honest. It's probably pretty unlikely that you developed your own unique and completely new consultation process. You probably learned a few different skills and exercises from a variety of people.

If what you do can only be delivered by you, then how do people remember it and implement it in their life or business? What happens if the advice and exercises you give become a part of their business process? How do they teach it to their new staff or colleagues? Don't get trapped into thinking that you're the only person who can deliver results because you're not. Besides, the methods we have for growing a business don't really rely on getting other people to deliver the work.

Scaling a freelance business. "I'm the only designer/developer/chef I trust. I haven't found results like mine and it's important to my brand that things stay consistent." See, consultants? You're not the only ones who think this. Also, don't skip this part. You share a lot of commonalities with freelancers.

Freelancers, I want to ask you a question. Have you ever looked at other people's work, in the same marketplace as yours, and thought, "I'll never be as good as that. He/she is way better than me?" We all have. I compare myself to others every day. It's human nature. If you think that, I can say with utter confidence that you're a better designer and developer than me. You really are.

If that's true—you do have peers in your network who you think deliver better work than you—why then do you believe you're the only person who can deliver work to your customers? We call this the *freelancers paradox*: I'm the only one who can do it … but I'm sure there are better people than me out there. Usually what people mean when they say this is that they can't afford to hire someone better than them. Even those they can hire, wouldn't know how to ensure consistent results.

This is a two-part problem because it highlights that what we really want is consistent results, with which I totally agree. It's imperative that your customers get the same experience and results from your business. It also shows that we feel our only options are to spend money to get other people to help. It does take time to ensure reliability and consistency with results. It's not going to happen overnight. Your own results might not be that consistent either. What if we could develop a system to make sure that everyone delivered the same level of work and you had more time to work on your business? Sounds good to me.

Here's the really scary part: I know full well why there are excuses about growing and scaling. At its core, we're usually afraid of surrendering control. Humans crave routine and control even over small aspects of their life. Not everyone wants to become a tyrannical dictatorial overlord (although personally I wouldn't pass up the opportunity). Nevertheless, we do all have control over certain aspects of our lives and businesses. The idea of letting other people have control over that seems terrifying.

On the other hand, the thought of having to take more control and more ownership of a business is equally scary. Maybe you don't think you want the stress of more responsibilities, or maybe you feel no one else can quite get it right, just how you do it. Both are untrue. Scaling and growing your business is not the Industrial Age idea of being a big boss manager, sitting behind a Cheltenham desk. It's about giving you more breathing room and autonomy in your business so you have more time and resources.

Scale and growth are also not designed for micromanagers. Every micromanager I've ever worked with has always said, "I'm not a micromanager." One manager I had used to constantly refer to himself as "a hands-off kind of guy." He would always be inspiring us to take ownership of tasks and grow our own experiences. Yet when someone presented a solution to him, or a series of ideas, he ended up having his own and we'd do those. It was utterly

Chapter 2 | *What's Stopping You From Scaling?*

demoralizing. The reason he was never happy is because he failed to provide details and specifics on the results he wanted. Therefore, when people came to him with their idea of "ownership of a task," he'd always be thinking, "Yeah, but that's not how *I'd* own it"."

People unwilling to give up control are so inclined because they're not willing to explore the systems, results, and process behind what they're giving up control of. If I just threw over a web design project to someone on a feelancing site, without any details, of course the results would be disappointing. If I document and set a path that I need people to follow, the results become a lot more consistent.

It can be hard to even think about what you need to change when you don't know what your options are. Where do you even start? New products? New systems or payment methods? How much does that all cost? I've got some examples here.

- For me, and the rest of the team at Sell Your Service, it always starts with the question, "What results does the customer want?"
- What results does your audience want? What do your customers want to change and do?
- If you're a social media traffic consultant, would it make sense to help your customers get more traffic from social media? Then let's start there.
- We'll work backward from the product, looking at scaling our audience, money, and profit management and managing outsourced labor.

By the end of this book, your problem won't be thinking of what to change; it'll be deciding, from among all your ideas, what's the most important to change.

How do you change? It's all well and good knowing that you need to change the payment process, or you need a new online course, but how are you going to make those changes? It's tough knowing that you're going to have a lot to learn again. It's exhausting making mistakes and growing your business. This book is specifically designed to alleviate some of the pain, but I know the effort of change and learning is hard work.

I provide examples of what to change and how businesses need to create those changes. It's not always about large flashy products and services. It might be as simple as streamlining your blog conversion process. If we don't know how to deliver a change, in this book, specifically designed to help people scale a freelancer or single-person consultancy, then we'll know someone who can. Don't let "how" stop you from exploring a better business and life.

No Spare Funds

One of the most frustrating aspects of growing a business is the funds. We've already explored why having no funds isn't necessarily a roadblock in growth. However, there are realities that some projects will require fiscal injections. There is usually one of two scenarios played out. First, any income is quickly eaten up by bills and other expenses. There doesn't seem to be anything left to put into future projects. We'll cover profit and money management later, demonstrating the reasons why you've got no money to invest. It's easier than you might think, too. It's not about scrounging or buying cheap. Second, you're concerned that growth-based projects need subscriptions to other services and products. If you're barely scraping by now, though, how are you going to be able to afford repeat payments for new products? The answer to this lies in pricing. Your price to cost model needs to be able to cover the products you're using or offering to customers. We'll cover this later, too. You're not going to go into debt for this growth. It's designed to help scale your business and make it profitable.

Marginal Gains

Dave Brailsford is the current Team GB cycling coach. *Freakonomics* author Stephen Dubner interviewed Dave (he doesn't like to be called Sir David) about what he calls "marginal gains."[1] The concept is that by making small, deliberate, and habitual changes to projects, teams, people, and work, the outcomes exceed those of people who stick to one type of training. A specific pillow for each cyclist, antibacterial cleaners on the bikes and clothes, and routine in the diet and exercise: Will each one of these by themselves win a Tour de France? No, but together, they create a mighty outcome.

Imagine a granite mountain face, with us and a rival at the bottom. We both want to get to the top. One the one hand, we might chip away at the rock, removing chunks at first, but trying to create step after step. Progress will be slow (unless an injection of cash gives us staff, more tools, etc.), and it won't look like you're making huge gains, but the heavy-handed symbolism should be obvious. Our rival on the other hand, is repeatedly trying to run hard and fast up the face. It's easy at first but, as the terrain gets steeper and the rock more slippery, he'll end up at the bottom again.

Slow progress is still progress. Our industry and hemisphere are obsessed with "quick wins" (one of my most hated terms). We should embrace slow, deliberate progress, even if we don't appear to be making significant gains. Everyone else is running up a mountain while we're chipping away. One other

---

[1] See http://freakonomics.com/podcast/in-praise-of-incrementalism/

Chapter 2 | What's Stopping You From Scaling?

thing about slow, deliberate gains is that it's lonely. Everyone else is either going to be at the bottom of the mountain, or halfway up, slipping up and sliding back down. Lots of businesses are going to talk to you about making faster gains. Looking back, though, even over just three months, you'll see just how far you've come. The difference is that our slow chips turning into steps gives us everything that profit needs. It's scalable, because 1,000 people could climb those steps as easily as you. It's able to be outsourced. If we need time off, other people can chip the steps. It's repeatable and can be automated. It's the same work time and time again. Don't get sucked into fast wins. They look great and you'll feel excited when you're running up the side of the mountain, but you're not making it easier for yourself in the future.

A huge contributing factor in scale is the result. What do you want the business to give to you? All too often we work hard on our businesses, giving it life and an identity, but we fail to understand what the business is going to give us. That's why we set these up, right? Our businesses were supposed to give us freedom: more time at home with loved ones, less time in meetings with managers, and more freedom with customers. All too often, though, as freelancers and consultants, we end up working hard just to keep the business going. We'd love to scale and get more time back, but what would we do with that time?

> *For all their bitching about what's holding them back, most people have a lot of trouble coming up with the defined dreams they're being held from.*
>
> —Tim Ferriss, *The 4-Hour Work Week*

It's a fundamental flaw in our path to success when we don't know how to define success. If we're scaling and we want to scale, what is going to happen when we're there? What does success look like? No, there is no final wonderful goal, no shining light, no Xbox achievements. Do you want to pay the bills? Invest more for retirement? Take a three-day weekend? We need to know what the ultimate goal is before we can truly scale. Creating a business that serves 1,000 customers a day might sound great but, if you're working 14 hours a day to do it, maybe it's not such a great idea.

Try this as an example. I'm scaling my business, because:

1. I want to work four days a week. On on that extra day I'm going to …

2. I want to put 10% of my personal income into retirement investing, which means I need to earn X more a year.

3. I want to spend more time growing my business. At the moment I spend X hours a day delivering work to clients. I want this to be only Y hours instead. With my new time per day I'll …

Figure out why you want to scale. Why put this effort in, and what are you going to get out of it? Also, make sure you're focusing on the business end goal.

Business end goal. Often we're told, "If you have a get out plan for the business, you don't have a business." The thinking is that if you have an escape plan, you're not committed. Personally I think this is a little Machiavellian. If I had someone approach me and offer to buy me out for $10 million plus 5% in revenue shares, you bet your bottom dollar I'd sell. There are two types of escape plans and often we only envisage the negative one. If everything went south today, if I lost all my work, my clients, and my skills, could I survive? The short answer is yes, you could. It would be depressing, sure, but you could survive. People have endured much worse.

That isn't the only end to the business, though. For example, I have a customer who knows they want 1,000 members in their business. At $100 a month from each member subscription, that's a $1 million a year business. Her end goal is not to sell, but be in the position to sell. By building her business to be in that position, she can start to assess her next goal. However, she had to structure her business in a very specific way to reach that goal. She knew what she was doing to get there.

What is your end goal for the business? It's not always about selling or going public. Maybe you want to build something that you can pass on. Maybe you do want to sell. Where is your business going, though, and what happens when you're there? Let's take, for example, my membership growth agency. My ultimate end goal for that business is to sell it for $10 million. The income from that business will allow me to work on future projects. Lofty? Maybe. Whatever I'm aiming for gives me direction on what I'm doing, though.

Do People Want You?

"But what if no one wants what I'm putting down?" Ignoring the fact that you should already know if people want what you're selling (market research, smoke tests, previous customers), we're going to structure the growth and scale of your business to only sell what people want. Usually, we'll build a few products then create sales pages, pitches, and e-mails to try and get people to buy. It's an expensive route to take, particularly if you're not making income while making these products.

We're going to sell only what people want. We won't have created anything before talking to our audience. If you're struggling for sales now, scaling your business opens new doors and opportunities. However, you must be willing to try new things. There's a sunk cost fallacy where we believe we have to keep working at a business even if deep down we know it's failing. It's hard to "quit," so to speak, but it doesn't mean you've failed. Your business's most valuable asset isn't your projects or skills—it's your audience. Until that dries up, you've got options.

Let's take Devon Digital Design, Ltd. In 2014 we had our worst year ever. I was sued (but won), we were losing customers, and income was drying up. I had nothing else to do other than create content and write e-mails. I did webinars, recorded courses, and talks. All this was seemingly free stuff I was doing just to fill my time. Part of the failure was down to not defining my customers, as even "local businesses in Devon" was too broad.

More and more of my content skewed toward membership businesses: gyms, courses, and subscription businesses. I was getting to know more and more of them. My audience was growing but no one wanted what I was selling. Very simply, I had a disconnect between my message and their wants. As soon as I listened to what my audience wanted, I started helping with that. My blog post on accountancy-based web design had 100 visits. My blog post on how members could capture more e-mail subscribers had 1,000 visits a day. We're building an audience and, if we listen, they'll tell us exactly what they need.

If you've hardly had any repeat sales or regular income from your business, why bother trying to get getting bigger? I agree, the idea of growing to a large business doesn't make sense if you don't need to grow. How often have we heard of startups with no income stream getting nice offices, staff and scaling with investment, only to go under within 18 months.

#1 Cause of Startup Death? Premature Scaling[2]

That's not what we're going to be doing. The reason you're not scaling as a freelancer or consultant is because you're restricting your time and efforts. A business with a team and investment fails after scaling because their bubble grows faster than their income. Investment keeps them breathing, but no new blood is pouring in. Single-person, microbusinesses fail to grow because so much of the business relies on the owner executing the work.

Let's say, for example, there was a magic, free clone of yourself. Can you already see how much easier it would be to scale? You version 1 could spend your time building the systems that gets customers in. You version 2 can do the work. What about a you version 3, where the original you develops new ideas and you version 3 goes and finds customers? You're struggling to find sales now because your efforts are misplaced. You'll grow naturally after that. We're going to grow with sales, not to find them in the future.

I don't know if it's stubbornness, ego, or fear, but freelancers and consultants, in the same space as you, will tell you that scaling isn't possible.

---

[2]See http://www.forbes.com/sites/nathanfurr/2011/09/02/1-cause-of-startup-death-premature-scaling/#6a7a461415aa

It's not possible. They won't know anyone who's done it. If it was that easy, everyone would do it. "You don't want to get too big." Unfortunately nothing we can explore, and nothing I can tell you, will stop this from happening. Your best option is to keep your plans to yourself. I've given talks and workshops to groups of designers and freelancers, consultants and microbusinesses, and there is always one person who challenges me on the ideas. Of course, I'm deeply hurt by this and retreat, often not coming out for a few months. Joking!

Challenging the steps in this book and questioning what's right for you is so important to growth. If you took everything at face value, you'd be pulled in every direction. A "Zed" (coined by Al Ramadan in *Play Bigger*) is someone who only wants to detract from progress. It's either fear of change or ego shock. Often, if people are told there is another way, they'll feel personally attacked, as if you're telling them their entire history has been for nothing.

Most businesses (and our industry of freelancers and consultants, particularly in the digital creative space, are particularly bad at this) don't like the idea of other businesses succeeding, as if the business that does well will suck up all the work and leave nothing for others. I've been called selfish, arrogant, and delusional. One competitor (and his business partner) took to e-mailing me every day, telling me how childish and naive I was to have plans like I did. What's funny is that I even offered to show them how I planned to grow or what I was doing now, and they turned their noses up at it. What gives you power over people who tell you it can't be done is being open and willing to show them how you're going to do it. "Stealing" ideas is harder than it looks and you should be proud to demonstrate your learning journey. If you'd rather just keep quiet and find people who want to know, though, that's cool, too.

If you don't have a blueprint for growth, which seems like a very grand term for a one-person business, have no fear. That's what this book is. It's nothing more than a plan on how we're going to develop into a more profitable, stable business. A blueprint doesn't have to be for a huge house or building. Smaller items need blueprints, too.

The reason we use the term blueprint, rather than strategy or plan, is twofold.

1. A blueprint can be repeated and is annotated and has a key. We can pick and choose the areas to work on.
2. It can be understood from a high level and the details can be focused on later.

This involves no long business plans and no multipage documents, just ideas and "how-to guides" for your business. There are no initial public offerings, no board-level executives, and no water coolers. Large businesses have those. Corporate juggernauts have those. Small, agile microbusinesses don't have those. Does your business need growth? Sure it does. Growth and scale are more applicable to small and microbusinesses. From small acorns, right?

Chapter 2 | What's Stopping You From Scaling?

Large businesses don't have scale, they have momentum. They don't have growth, they have bloat. If you've ever tried to change the direction of a company with more than 200 employees (still considered a small business by many governments), you're in for at least an 18-month exercise. I've joined companies that have started the brand change and direction before I joined and haven't completed them until after I've left (maybe it's me).

Growth is a scary word, sure. It's hard work. It needs constant energy and nurturing. It's also been hijacked by massive multimillion-dollar startups. Startups are not always the $100 million valued tech-social businesses run by 23-year-olds. They don't need growth. Believe me, their problem is not growth or scale. Their problem is income management (or even just generating any income). Our businesses are small and agile, as one to five people work at most startups. I am focusing on amall businesses working from laptops, in coworking spaces. Don't be put off by growth when you see numbers like $150 million flying around. We're not making those businesses.

If you need to outsource work, where do you start? The hardest thing to do is find good work. Typically, people with bad experiences of outsourcing have those bad experiences ffor two reasons.

1. They went cheap and didn't hire the right people for the job.
2. They didn't write out the process properly and gave vague instructions.

We all have had bad experiences with outsourcing, but most of the time it can be narrowed down to the hiring party not giving clear enough directions. The reason we use the profit triangle is because it covers all our bases. It's created from the three profit questions:

1. Do I have to do the work or can I outsource it to someone else?
2. Can I receive 1,000 orders tomorrow and handle it?
3. Is the process or delivery repeatable so anyone can do it?

Before we outsource, we create the process. We make it repeatable, then we get someone else to do it. This is for most manual tasks, like data entry, e-mailing, content creation, and so on. When it comes to hiring, you need to vet people and interview. I'll give you this process and plan later. Don't worry about where to hire people and what for. It's about giving yourself time back, and you have to measure whether a $15 an hour VA (virtual assistant) might be cheaper than a $5 per hour VA if you're spending time fixing what the cheaper hire did. On the other hand, manual data entry or data gathering can be done for $5 per hour when you've got a well-documented process. Why do we do this? Give yourself more time.

"Well now what do I do?" Like I mentioned earlier, for all their whining about being held back, most people don't know what they'd do if they had more time. Let's assume you've cut two hours a day from your workload using outsourcing and automation. What are you going to do with that extra 10 hours a week? Do you have long-term goals? Do you have a hobby you want to pick up again? What about a new product or calling in to see a customer?

I agree that you shouldn't plan to scale or grow unless you know what your ultimate goal is, but don't let the very scary thought of more time on your hands stop you. Most people like to be busy, even if it's unproductive. They feel if they're moving then they're making progress. If something is being taken care of, it can be scary to feel like you've got spare time. We've been conditioned to think that if we're free we're being lazy or unproductive. Don't just fill the time with more busy work. Start working on something that makes you happy, business or otherwise.

Busy or Effective?

If you're working on customer projects, if you're delivering the work, or if you're already at maximum bandwidth, then sure, you don't want more work, but it's a downward spiral. We've covered this already, but if you're working to deliver the work, then you can't work on the business. You're working in the business, not working on the business.

Scale and growth are about removing work from your plate and giving you space to grow. If you're finding you're spending less and less time at home, or less and less time with loved ones, then my goal is not to give you more to do. I want to give you time back. Scaling your business is the way to do that. Following the three laws of profit and growth is the way to reclaim more time. You'll do more work, get more done, be more productive, and be more effective, but you'll be less busy.

You deliver the work to the client or you're a designer who works freelance for other businesses. Wouldn't scaling remove all the customers you've got now? I understand how you feel. A lot of independent and microbusinesses felt the same way, but we've found that our customers are delighted that we scale in the way that we do.

We're not becoming a faceless business or a corporate entity. We're looking for more ways to deliver work and value to customers. We're becoming more responsive to their needs. Besides that, you owe it to your customers to be profitable. If you're not there in two months' time, that's going to annoy them a lot more. You're still going to show personality and your brand isn't going to change, but we're making sure that you can reach more people. We're going to grow the network of paying customers that you have and we're going to delight them all.

Can My Business Scale?

It can. I'm telling you it can. I've seen lawn care, insurance, paper notebooks, productivity software, management consulting, branding agencies, web designers, app developers, and others scale and grow. If you've got a niche (and I mean a well-defined niche), then your chances of growing and scaling are infinitely better. If you don't have a niche, or maybe you're struggling to identify one, then we'll work at that.

The reason businesses fail to grow is often because they fail to identify a specific market and stick with it. They're worried about being too narrow and missing out on work. The weirdest thing happens when you're targeting a niche market. Let's say you get just two clients in your niche under your belt. For example, let's say we're a marketing consultant who only works with paper notebook retailers. All your content is geared toward finding those customers. Remember also that we're building recurring revenue into our business model. If you get two customers under your belt and you get results for them, do you think that's more appealing to all the other notebook retailers? Absolutely. Will furniture manufacturers ask you if you can get the same results for them? They most certainly will. Rather than thinking that your niche can't scale, then, understand that your niche is the key to scale. If you don't have one, we're going to get you one. We're not, however going to look at complicated systems.

Complicated systems. Doesn't everything get very complicated when you've got all these systems and processes: Zapier, ActiveCampaign, MailChimp, WordPress? What about supplier chains, outsourcing staff, virtual assistants, payments, and manufacturers? Managing multiple systems is complicated when you first start. The good news, though, is that you'll only start using systems and processes when you need them. We're probably not going to jump straight into multiple systems like Zapier and Infusionsoft, but like any skill, it gets much easier with time. You'll learn what to manage and how to support systems that go wrong.

Finally, the systems and processes that you set up are always supposed to make your life easier. We're not just talking about cloud-based apps like MailChimp. We're talking about the steps people have to take to work with you. Examples include the lead qualification process, the first e-mail sent with invoices, and digital product sales and downloads. They're all designed to give time back to you and show customers that you've got a process. People want to buy from businesses that have a process. It builds trust. If you need proof, Google "hired coach Mike because he has a process."

Quitting Your Job

You don't need to quit your job yet. This book is not a "follow your dreams and love life" book. If you have a full-time job and you've bought this book to boost your "side hustle" (cheers Nathan from Foundr), that's perfect.

We often find that a lot of freelancers and side hustlers have a full-time job. We all started there.

You don't want to quit your job until your side work can support you, right? This book is designed to help you scale and grow to the point that you can quit your full-time job. Isn't it a catch-22, though? You surely can't grow and scale your business if you don't give it more time? To get more time you need to quit your job, but you can't quit your job until your business pays more, and on and on. Here's the deal: We're going to switch what you're working on so that you spend less time on the business, but it scales faster. The only investment is that you will need to work a few late nights to get the system set up.

Investing your time is the new cash. Time is what runs out every day, because we have a finite reserve of it. If you spend 20 hours setting up a scalable business, using what you already know, you must make sure that it gives you back more than the initial time investment. The fear of quitting your job is still a big deal even if you're making money. We're taught to believe that jobs provide security and a predictable future. Unfortunately this isn't the case. I don't have time to explain in this book why that's the case (and I'll also sound like a tinfoil-hat-wearing conspiracy nut if I do).

Long and short, retirement funds, paid with your salary aren't as secure as you're being led to believe. Work and jobs aren't as predictable as you're told. You're fearful of change, which is fine, but every business owner in the world will tell you that once you quit your job and fully work on your business, you'll wonder what all the fuss was about.

As I've mentioned, sometimes we think we don't have the time to grow a business. We are busy with kids, housework, jobs, gym visits, and more. Whatever your time sucks are, it's tough to find time to grow your business. It boils down to priority and whether you want it enough. We find many consultants and freelancers do have spare time. It's not where you'd think, though. Sure, for a few weeks you might have to give up a few extra hours a day, but most of the time we find people have tons of time when they stop doing busy work on their business. You need to prioritize what you want to do. Prioritize and choose the number one project to focus on. Doing work for clients often fails to build your business when you don't already have the systems in place to handle growth.

Answering e-mails, browsing Facebook, or Googling WordPress plug-ins: None of that builds growth. It's all a time suck that depletes your most precious resource. If you don't think you have time to grow your business, then you never will. You can find time; you just need to prioritize what's more important. Finally, working on something that takes time away from you, if it's about growing your business, should give you time back as a return on your investment. If you're serious about growing your business, and if you're serious about scaling your income and profit as a single-person microbusiness, consultant, or freelancer, find the time to work on it. No one is going to give it to you. What about doubt, though?

Doubt. Are you even capable of growing a business? Isn't that more of a thing for investors who have fancy offices and business college backgrounds? When we see movies and TV shows about successful, growing businesses, it's always a montage that we see. They move into a nice office, sit down, and have epiphany visions of creating ultimate products. That's absolutely not how it works. The common perception of growing businesses is so far removed from reality that it might as well be business porn, which I'm certain is a category.

If a fancy office, dedicated team of hard-working geniuses, and "big break" moments with customers is your idea of a growing business, you're never, ever going to see that. Running a business is a slow, deliberate process, like chipping at our mountain to make steps. The truth is that running a business can also be more exciting than the sexy encounters in the movies. You get to decide on video content, logos, product names, and processes. It's 100 times more satisfying to get a desk at a coworking space and watch sales roll in.

If you want the office, high-rise views, and young team (which you have to pay for), go for it. You could get that today if you wanted. There is a reason that high-rise offices and technical business parks are losing customers. Large, multinational, billion-dollar businesses are leaving them because it's unsustainable. Don't aspire to be anything like those businesses. You can be better than that. I'm 100% confident that you can do it.

Too much money is often as big a problem as not enough money.

—Robert Kiyosaki

How? How can having too much money be a problem? Honestly, if you're scaling properly, this will be a problem sooner rather than later. Have you ever wondered why over 70% of lottery winners are now broke? Of the 30% that are solvent, most of them are left with less money than when they started, let alone the rest of the winnings. Growth to the size you want to be is like training for any skill: How far do you want to run? How much do you want to bench? How much are the bills you want to pay?

To work all this out, think long term. Take into account kids, school, holidays, retirement funds, and investments. What do you need to make per month? What do you want to make per month? It might sound arbitrary. "Well, $10,000 a month would be nice." Okay, that's not going to be a problem. What happens with that money, though? Are you prepared for taxes, emergencies, or other expenses? Growing to the size you want isn't a problem at all. I know that I want $1 million a year income, 5% profit growth year on year, and 30% profit margins.

I also know what is going to happen with every penny of that income because it gets divided up already. The book *Profit First* by Mike Michalowicz taught me exactly what to do with each penny as it comes in. If you can't do that now, then your problem will be too much money. Grow to the size your systems allow. So many businesses fail because they scale way too quickly and their systems can't handle it.

Give yourself the goals of time: "I only want to spend 10 to 4 at the office," or "I don't want to check e-mails past 5 p.m." Once you start creeping over those goals, it's a sign that your processes and systems can't handle how big you are.

Scaling and growth require a big change in your attitude. Even if you're raring to go and start working on a new business, it needs a few skills that aren't taught. Discipline, attention management, and "internal true North" are all somewhat linked, as are the ability to say no to low-value e-mails and the confidence (even if you're not internally confident) to stick to the path. Our attention is being dragged in 100 different directions every second. It wants to suck our time, and if the activity you're working on isn't directly going to help you grow, drop it.

This is tough because our boredom–attention muscles have weakened with smartphones and 4G data. You might think it's harmless to check your phone or play a game when waiting in line or browse Facebook when watching Netflix. What you're doing, though, is listening to that little lizard brain inside your human brain, the ancient part of your anatomy that fixes for dopamine releases every few minutes. Changing our attention to something novel and new gives us a little high and our tolerance for focus is slowly diminished. When you sit down to do some real work, it'll feel like agony because you're now punishing your brain. It'll tell you to check your phone, answer an e-mail, or like something on Facebook instead.

You have to remain strong that your work is more important. Does that mean you can't reward yourself after a work slot? Of course not. Studies show that 90-minute blocks for work, even if it's only three times a day, yield better results than slogging through for the sake of it.[3] Do you want to spend that free time on Facebook, though, or do something genuinely rewarding?

Finally, you're going to become a pariah, and quickly, too, because other freelancers and consultants are notorious attention drains. "I just want to pick your brains," can turn into an hourlong waste of time. It might even seem rude to turn people down, but your internal true North knows that you need to

---

[3] See https://blog.hubspot.com/sales/ultradian-rhythm-pomodoro-technique#sm.0000uri934ifzcu9v6j19wz4pfdbj

do something else. Don't be swayed to what other people want. They're not against you exactly, but they're for themselves. Be disciplined in your approach to your time. Manage your lizard brain when it wants dopamine and stick to your true North when others steer you toward their goals.

Never Run a Business

This is a big one. What if you've never run a business before? It's not as clear cut as you're thinking. Self-employed people and consultants might say they're not running a business, or never have. Other people have jobs and work full time, running a side hustle that isn't a real business (hint: it probably is), and there are people who have never done anything like this before. Does running a business sound complicated? Maybe it is, it certainly can be. Is it scary? It definitely is. Well, at least the first time is.

If you've never run a business before, what's stopping you? Even if you're already making your own income, what's stopping you from being a real business in your eyes. Is it the office? We've covered that. Is it a business name or a web site? That's not how businesses start. It's tough because there are so many books, blogs, courses, and resources out there on running a business, it can seem a little overwhelming. Do you really need to learn all that's out there? No. You certainly do not. Some stuff is going to stick and some stuff is going to pass you by. Don't worry about it. Stick to your true North and develop what works for you.

Even if you never consider yourself a real business, don't worry about the labels that come with it. Focus on helping customers, building an audience, and delivering processes that work. Focus on the results that you need to be happy. Think of it like this: We're building a process and a system that gives you more time and money and you get to wake up later. Who cares if that's a business or not. Call it a philosophy or a blugherthmen for all I care. What really matters is running or owning.

Running or owning. Are you a web site designer or do you run a web site design business? Maybe there doesn't sound like a difference there, but there is. Typically, a lot of consultants, freelancers, and single-person microbusinesses don't want to become owners or managers. Maybe you think you're no good at finance or marketing. Maybe you hate sales or don't like talking to suppliers and staff. Here's the deal: This book is going to help you scale your business and grow the results you're getting. We're not a management book and we're not a business book. I'm going to show you how to scale your business from where it is, to give you more back in return.

What we are going to learn and discover along the way will result in you being a better manager. It will make you clearer with money management and marketing. All the things we sometimes shy away from, because we think we're bad at them, are going to seem easy. You're not even going to notice that you're running a business. It'll all be designed to make your life easier.

There is an inescapable rule of running a business: The bigger you get, the less work you'll do for the business. That means if you're a graphic designer, you'll do less graphics work for customers. However, we don't have to sacrifice the reason you set the business up. We can look to other business areas to take care of money, payments, and marketing. You need to design the process that those sit on, however. Who knows, you might even discover a skill for something you didn't know existed.

Other Businesses in My Network Have Told Me It's a Bad Idea or I Can't Do It

Forget them. Move on. Are you ready to change your business? What's going to happen if you do? What are your excuses for not changing your business? If you keep doing what you're doing, you're going to keep getting what you're getting. If what you're getting now isn't working for you, then maybe it's time to change. We tend to swing between what we want and what we want *now*.

In the long term, I want to be more fit and run a marathon. Unfortunately, I love doughnuts. In the long term I want to change my business and work at a new system, but right now, I want to *not* do that. I've got family to look after, I need to clean the house, and I have to get to the gym. Also, I'm a little scared to change because I don't want to fail. What if everything goes wrong? I have to choose whether I want to be scared or if I want the final results.

That's what it breaks down to: What do you want more? There's never a perfect time, never a great time. However, if you want it now, and you'll want it tomorrow, then go for it. Only you can decide if you're ready to change your business.

Summary

It's clear that there isn't anything or anyone stopping you from scaling business but yourself. Here are some key takeaways in this chapter.

- Although scaling might seem like hard work, it's more like repeated habits built over time.
- You can decide how you scale.
- It's got nothing to do with how anyone else has done it.
- Scaling is exponential. The more you scale, the more resources you'll have to scale further.

CHAPTER 3

Types of Single-Person, Scalable Businesses

When looking at scaling our business, growing profit, and giving ourselves time back, we need to look at three key questions:

1. Do I have to do the work or can I outsource it to someone else?
2. Can I receive 1,000 orders tomorrow and handle it?
3. Is the process or delivery repeatable so anyone can do it?

The products, services, and businesses I talk about later on all adhere to these rules in one way or another. Some are slightly easier to set up and to imagine working. Others require a longer commitment. All of these are designed to allow you, the owner, to create and then distribute with relative ease.

Later on we'll be going through the processes and systems we can use to build, set up, attract, and deliver these exact products. We'll talk about money management and profit, as well as the resources you'll need to grow this business. Whatever you can help people with now, whatever industry or category you're in, these next business ideas could suit you.

© Michael Killen 2019
M. Killen, *From Single to Scale*, https://doi.org/10.1007/978-1-4842-3814-1_3

Chapter 3 | Types of Single-Person, Scalable Businesses

I've decided to give examples of business, product, and service types first, as many people don't know their options when they want a scalable business model. The concept of many of these products will be new to a lot of people, so I want to share what's possible before we look at how to create and deliver them.

E-books from transcriptions. If you're a consultant, freelancer, or microbusiness, at some point you probably have to train your customers. Perhaps it's how to use the WordPress dashboard or how to define your market offering. Whether its consultation or coaching, you're sitting down with your customers to help them do something. One of the fastest scalable products you can create is an e-book, an electronic book rather than a printed one (although that's certainly an option).

E-books never run out of stock, can be bought on massive marketplaces like Amazon, or just downloaded via your web site as a PDF. The one drawback is that they need to be written, which can take time. However, you're delivering training all the time. Even if you're not, there's no reason you couldn't mock up a training session. Whip out your smartphone, record your training, and get the audio transcribed (I'll explain where and how later). This gives you all the copy you could need.

We've worked out that a one-hour presentation provides 8,000 to 14,000 words, which is more than enough for a short e-book on a specific topic. People like e-book content because they can reference it. They can print it out, make notes, and reread it.

Often people say to me, "But if I've delivered the training, they won't want the book," or, "If the book is cheaper than the training, people won't pay for the training anymore." At first glance these might seem like valid objections, but the truth is that e-books allow you to reach a wider audience among people who couldn't afford your training. The people who can afford your training will appreciate the extra content that they can reference.

Create a course. This requires a little more work, but no more than building any other product. Online courses, with video content, worksheets, quizzes, and online communities, are fantastic ways to deliver your results. Most of us are in the digital creative or marketing space, but I've seen courses in Muay Thai, carpentry, and defensive driving.

- You don't have to create a course that tells people everything you know. In fact, Rock Star Empires, who teach businesses how to create courses, recommend a broad topic within your niche.
- Six modules within that topic and six lessons within each module.

- Each lesson only needs to be 5 to 10 minutes long, giving you around 36 videos and between three and six hours of online course content.

The key to producing online video courses is structuring your content and delivery. Most of us have a process when completing work for a client. Whatever you do, write out the steps you go through with customers and make bullet points. For example, let's say you're a social media marketer. You want to teach customers how to generate more traffic from social media.

When you sit down with your customers, where do you start? Do you perform a traffic audit, or maybe look at their analytics? You then go through a process to help them get more traffic, explaining all their options and how it works. Break down your broader topic into six modules, maybe the four social major channels available, an introduction, and a summary. Each module then needs six lessons to cover what you know. Try to include a worksheet or resource template for each lesson so your students have something to do.

There's way too much course delivery to cover even in one book. My recommendation would be to check out Rock Star Empires (https://www.rockstarempires.com/) if you want to see how the pros do it.

Create a teaching course. We need to go deeper. Rather than a course teaching someone how to execute a social marketing strategy or a content plan, how about teaching someone how to teach others that skill? Other businesses are always looking for more strings to their bow. New skill sets and services are often required by other businesses to expand their offerings.

What if someone said, "I want to do what you do." Immediately, most people's reactions are defensive: "If I teach you, then you'll take all my business!" This simply isn't the case. Frankly, if we're being realistic, there are very few jobs that can't already be delivered by other people.

If you could find an entirely new market (bearing in mind that you already have contacts who probably do want to learn to do what you do) you could become an authority very fast (due to your experience). Now you're known as the person who is so good, you teach other people how to consult and coach. The structure behind a "teach what I teach" course share similarities with regular courses. The language and timing differs slightly, though, as you might need to include sections on answering customer questions for their customers or pricing and selling techniques.

When you teach others how to do what you do and encourage them to find customers, it elevates you above your competition. You'll become a vital resource for your students who want to deliver better results to their customers. It becomes easier to provide coaching to your students and you can increase prices for your own customers. It becomes very hard to negotiate with the person who teaches others to do it.

High-traffic blog. Advertising revenue from blog posts is a wonderfully simple model. However, you need a lot of traffic to pull in advertising. That's not to say it can't work, as you can even have promoted posts from larger brands who pay to be on your blog. What you need is regular, high-quality, and valuable content. It needs to be extremely useful, targeted at a specific market, and have constant work promoting its content.

Specific niche markets can draw large traffic numbers relatively quickly. If you can get others to share the content via social channels and e-mail marketing, you can draw a large regular audience. Advertisers want to see consistent, regular eyeballs to your content before they're willing to commit to paying you.

On the other hand, Google Adsense network, Sovrn, and Outbrain are all advertising networks that will happily provide you with code to start advertising straight away. It's a snippet of code that you install on your site and boom! You've got advertising revenue. Fair warning though: Although it scales and requires only content, you need a lot of traffic. Estimates to generate $100,000 in revenue per year from a blog mean you need $274 per day. That's close to $1 per day from 274 pages. There's roughly a 1% click-through rate on ads from blog posts. The cost per click might be $0.25 (it could be far higher), so that's four clicks per day, per post, which needs roughly 400 views per page. That is 400 * 274 to the site per day, which means 109,000 visitors per day, roughly.

For some sites, that's easily achievable. Also, you're not just using AdSense for your revenue. There are sponsored posts, banner ads, and products. Head to http://www.minterest.org/how-much-traffic-do-you-need-to-make-money/ if you want more information. Honestly, I love the blog and ad revenue model. It's a strong contender, especially if you have nothing but time and content. Nevertheless, you need to be serious about creating content for a specific market if you want those numbers.

Templated content. When you're working with clients, you probably use the same 5 to 10 templates for e-mails, web pages, worksheets, designs, and more. What's stopping you from selling them? Copistore.com was our exact answer to that. We were using the same basic e-mails and page templates for all our clients. We still use them today, but now we let other businesses use those templates to help their customers.

Release the fear of "If my customers and competition use my templates, they won't need me!" They will, they always do. First, just offering the templates does not necessarily show how to use them. That's your second product straight away. Second, you can reach so many more people online with template-based products.

Take Envato, for example. You can set up your logos and graphic templates to be sold on their marketplace. You'll have to lower your price, and I'm not suggesting that's your only option, but the proof is there that people want templates. There's no reason you can't provide a consultation template pack with support, forum access, and coaching calls, telling people how to use them.

If only there were 100 clones of me. Then I'd get so much done.

Training staff. If you've ever thought that, training staff might be the perfect route. Here's the deal: There are no employee salaries and no expensive benefits, just the staff and the results. If you listed the 100 things that you do with customers, I'd bet that at least 60% of them are repeatable, boring tasks like data entry, report crafting, e-mail support, invoicing, and so on.

When you have to do them, it's a chore, repeating the same task over and over. So why not get someone else to do that? Outsourcing has become a beautiful, viable model for so many business tasks. If you talk to a customer and offer them reporting, e-mail support, updates, and SEO work, there's no reason that process can't be documented and handled by other staff.

By charging a recurring fee each month, part of that goes to pay the staff and part comes to you. Document repeated and monthly tasks, write them up as a checklist in Process.st, and then outsource the job to virtual staff. By having a documented process you'll fare much better with virtual staff. You'll also keep costs down because they don't need to think, just act on your process.

Product reselling. If there's one thing we're not short of in the world, it's products. If creating your own and selling them seems like a lot of work, search for products to resell. You have almost infinite options when it comes to reselling products. You can find physical or virtual products, and services, too, with lots of agencies looking to take on more work, but giving you a cut.

Reselling is similar to affiliate products, but the model is slightly different. We'll get onto affiliate sales later. Google "digital reseller products" to see the range of products available to start selling today. For digital products, specifically we're looking for private label rights (PLR) products. These are products that others have built and created that are available for you to sell.

Rather than sign up to a huge reseller commitment straight away, buy a few products and see what kind of revenue you can generate. I'm a huge fan of using PLR products in funnels and as one-time offer sales. Typically I've had trouble selling them for over $100, but that doesn't mean it's not possible. It's all about how much time you're willing to put into it.

Successful reselling means getting your offer and message right. Reselling products can also mean finding product sellers and helping them sell. Phone cases, exercise equipment, audio gear: Almost everything needs a distributor. There are a lot of routes through to this market from drop-shipping to manufacturing.

Finally, talk to your local network about becoming a distributor for their services. Lots of designers, coaches, and developers are hesitant to sell, which is a real shame, but a great opportunity for you. Taking 20% of a project cost for passing on some details and a worksheet seems good to me.

White-label products. White-labeling products (again, focusing on digital products and services) means another team builds and develops an app, software, or product. You put your name and branding on top and charge per month. Support is often provided by the other company, and you maintain the customer relationship.

There are two main choices with white-labeling. The first is agency-based white-labeling and the second is app- or product-based white-labeling. Agency-based white-labeling means another agency (maybe even local) provides the actual work while you take a cut of the total cost. These can be one-off or monthly projects. Just Google "digital services white-label" and see what's on offer from other agencies. The customer only ever sees your name and brand. They interact with you. It's like an elastic team that only costs when you use it.

On the other hand, app and software white-labeled products are built by other businesses but sold and distributed under your name. The beauty of white-labeled app and software products is that the support is often carried out by the other company, meaning less time spent working on smaller issues. It's also often very elastic. You only pay for what you use.

Affiliate products. At this point I feel it should be noted that reselling and white-labeling products often get people very excited. However, you still need to market and sell those products. They don't come with messaging or sales copy. You need to understand what your audience wants and what you can provide. Often business owners who discover white-labeling or PLR go nuts at the idea of adding 100 products to their suite. As Seth Godin says, though, "Don't find customers for your products, find products for your customers." Make sure you're still providing what your audience wants and not what you think is an easy sell. For some reason, people seem to get a bit edgy about affiliate products. It seems to me that a few bad apples have spoiled the cart for everyone else.

The concept of affiliate products is that services or apps, for example, need more customers. They're willing to give a cut for every new signup. Typically, we're given a link that you have and your users click that link. If they sign up for the products, you'll get a cut. Most times, people are pretty up front about the links being affiliate links. It doesn't cost the customer any more than a regular purchase and it helps you out. However, some businesses have tried to pass off affiliate links as regular links, or even as their own product. Plug-ins and cloud apps provide great opportunities for affiliate sales and can help your revenue. However, you're unlikely to make millions from them.

E-mail courses. If you can help a business get more traffic, or maybe you're a branding guru and you want to create a course, don't think you have to create a high-investment course site to get course sales. We can provide e-mail courses to customers for a price, sending them a new lesson, video link, and worksheet for them to complete each week.

The beauty of e-mail courses is that you can set them up in MailChimp (or whatever system you use) and set the course to automate. With a few hidden pages on your site and a worksheet for each lesson, you can send customers a new lesson every week. Take the same concept as a course and focus on just one module. If you give six lessons per module, that's a six-week course.

E-mail courses make fantastic splinter products. They can be low cost, simple to create, and introduce you to your customers. Record a series of videos and transcribe the audio. Use the transcript in the e-mail and create a worksheet to help customers get more from the content. You could password protect the video, but there is no need to get too complicated.

People aren't going to steal your content. It's harder than it looks to rip off and sell or copy your work, especially content, as it's so easily tracked. Besides, if people really want to copy your work, they'll find a way. Deliver one e-mail a week (maybe the first lesson immediately and the second one that week, too) and try to have conversations with your customers. Ask them what they liked and what works for them.

Outsourcing content services. Web site customers need content, no question. Often, we take for granted that they're experts in their business or industry. However, that doesn't mean they're expert copy writers. In my experience, experts get bogged down in the heavy details rather than writing exciting and compelling content. If you can facilitate a content workshop, get a list of what they need to write about, and then find someone else to write it, you're onto a winner.

Use a service like Speedlancer (https://speedlancer.com/) or Upwork (https://www.upwork.com/) to find content writers and give them the brief and worksheets that you do with your customers. Keep content easy to produce: list articles, how-to guides, and embed posts. Don't overcomplicate the content that needs to be created. Now, deliver that content to the customer and talk to them about one new blog post a week. They could either decide the topic, research it, write it, edit it, and publish it themselves, or just hand it over to you and get new blog content every week. Combine that with a social media automation process and you've created a machine that costs you nothing but yields huge results for the customer.

Outsourcing administrative services. One of the largest drains of time for your customers is administrative work. Often, small and microbusinesses do all the admin work themselves. Outsourcing Angel and Brickwork can provide work for as little as $6 per hour. If you can systematize the work that your customers need to have done, you can outsource it to other businesses and take a cut. Data entry, e-mail marketing, and social media management are just some of the hundreds of options. Run a quick workshop with your customers. Ask what takes most of their time. For example, e-mailing customers might take two hours a day. That's 10 hours a week. What could your customers do with 10 extra hours a week? Document and record what they do to solve that problem themselves. Write up the process they use (there is always a process, even if customers think there isn't) and get someone else to do it.

Warning: There are always teething problems with outsourcing administrative work. It depends on how clear you are with instructions, definition of work, and documentation. Don't let that put you off, because outsourced admin work often becomes indispensable after it's running well.

Lead qualification. If you've seen a lot of coaching leads and clients come in, then you might be perfect as a closer. Closers have a bad rap as being middle men and an unnecessary step in the sales process, but the truth is that the link between someone interested in buying and someone actually handing over money can be very complicated.

Whatever industry you're in, if you have a process for qualifying and understanding what a customer wants, you're a valuable asset. Consultants and coaches would pay through the nose for qualified, suitable customers for their projects. The key to being a great closer is a high pitch-to- close rate, a network of customers, and a network of consultants or coaches.

Web designers, social media consultants, and business coaches all need clients, and rates can be as high as 30% of the initial project cost. For a $5,000 project, that's a $1,500 payment for finding and qualifying the customer. Closers work well because they can deal with far more customers and the process can be outsourced. By asking the right questions and giving the right presentation, you can pass over customers that sign up to another consultant.

The reason consultants will pay such a high cut is because they know they are getting a high-quality client. You'll have to work out yourself how the relationship progresses from there. Ongoing fees for future work are messy, unenforceable, and frankly, weak. On the other hand, you have an opportunity to train other people (e.g., consultants and freelancers) who take on your work how you would execute that project for that customer. Remember, closing is the first time the customer benefits from working with you. As soon as you close, you're delivering a result and benefit.

Automated manufacturing. 3D printing is rapidly becoming a viable option for small businesses and freelancers. Printers can range as low as £1,000 and allow you to print and build small items that your customers would usually buy. It's not your only option, though. Manufacturing both inside your home country and outsourcing from Eastern Europe, China, and India (to name a few areas) is also an option.

Consultants and coaches might be wondering why we're talking about physical products when we provide services. Sure, the model might not suit all businesses, but for those looking to scale, manufacturing is a great option. Try thinking about your customers as an audience rather than a transaction. As Seth Godin was quoted earlier, "Find products for customers, not customers for products."

One of my customers, a running therapy coach, noticed that a lot of her customers needed slight adjustments to the insoles of their trainers. I'm not much of a runner, but from what she explained, we all land on our feet differently. Some people roll their ankles in, some people have wide feet, and so on. Finding the exact trainer to suit was harder than it should be. Her customers can now buy the trainers they want and she can fit a small piece of plastic inside the shoe to help them run. She found a local university that prints 3D models and sends them the schematics. A local running shop helped her develop a method to determine the right fit for the plastic. For a customer to do this themselves would cost way too much. However, she can do it for a few pounds and charge £10 for the fit. Look at small products to manufacture (or even buy) as a part of your product suite. They make great splinter products and easily scale.

Coaching transcripts as blog posts. Stick with me on this one because it defies a whole load of commonsense ideas on running a business. If you're giving coaching calls, maybe –two or three hours a week, that content is recorded and sent to the customer as an audio or video file. Let's be honest: Those aren't really watched or listened to more than twice. Let's also be very, very clear about the difference between coaching and consulting.

Coaching is where we help the client get clarity on their goals. It's about asking questions and working out what they want to achieve. Coaching helps to bring out ideas and cement in the client's mind what needs to be done. It's often said that a coach "brings out the best in you already." Consultants are who you turn to for creating plans and strategy. They'll teach you skills that you don't know and point you toward new ways of thinking.

Both are equally important, but coaches will work through the concepts and ideas that you already have and help you implement them. Often they don't do the work themselves, but they do leave you with worksheets or checklists that cover what you've talked about. Think about sports coaches: They help you get better at what you're good at. If you're a swimmer, they help you swim better. If you're recording coaching calls, there is a ton of valuable content specific to that customer, which also means it's specific to that customer's market.

I tell my customers that all our calls are recorded and sometimes I take out excerpts and modify them to turn them into a blog post. I remove all names, brand names, and company details. I'll get the recording transcribed and talk about customers with the same attributes as this coaching customer. Usually it's a few months after the call, and when I publish the post I'll run it past that client just to make sure they're cool with it. I've never had anyone say no. Try it once and see what kind of content you get. Maybe take their goals and the roadblocks you've discovered with them and write up that part: How [type of customer] solves [road block] to get to [result]. That's your post and you only need a few minutes of content to write that up.

Consulting transcripts as blog posts. As mentioned earlier, coaching and consulting are two different products or services. If we're consulting, we're usually presenting a new platform or process to that customer. We'll cover strategy and action steps, getting the team involved in a workshop, too. There are worksheets (more on that later), group sessions, and whiteboard sessions. Occasionally I've had customers 100% happy with video recording the whole process and publishing it. Most, however, are happy for me to audio record it and send them the files.

However, we have started to record just me, presenting from the whiteboard. The clients are not seen on camera and we don't mention their name. We'll run through a strategy or process and transcribe the audio from that presentation. Workshops are the same, although we typically just record the audio. When we transcribe it, we sometimes publish it raw. People like the idea of raw transcriptions. After a time, we'll edit the copy and turn it into a "how-to guide" or case study.

You can direct new leads and clients to these posts and have them work through them. You could bundle up the posts into an e-book and sell it as an entire consultation book. The options are limitless if you're willing to think outside of what we're told about creating content. You're doing it every day, for free. You might as well start keeping it and repurposing it.

Worksheet content. All coaches, freelancers, consultants, designers, and others have worksheets or a process. If you think you don't have a process, because "all projects are bespoke," you'd be surprised at what we can see. For those who do have templates and worksheets, there is a business model in itself to help people get through that.

One customer of mine uses Asana to map out an entire project. They talked about how each project is custom built, so they don't have a worksheet. When we asked them to start at the beginning and go through the questions they ask a customer, we listed all the questions they go through for a new project:

- How much budget do you have?
- Who makes the decisions?
- How long before the project starts?

- What are the goals for the project?
- What kind of results do you have now?

When I asked them what questions there are for another customer, they explained that the starter questions are always the same.

> *There is a process behind how we work with clients, often the delivery isn't systemized (although again, comparing project to project, there are commonalities), but we can create worksheets that customers can run through.*

Turn your qualification sheets and discovery workshops into "how-to guides" and "Are you ready?" exercises. "The ultimate worksheet for furniture makers to see if an e-commerce web site will make your business money" is a very compelling title. If you write up those questions and create a short how-to video, you can help customers through a seemingly complicated process.

Coaching seminars. Can you coach one person? One-on-one coaching might seem easy: Sit down, have a coffee, and talk with your customer. Here's what I've found one-on-one coaching delivers. Customers often have the same problems and desires across industries, categories, and types. Most businesses want more customers, leads, and money. There are many ways to skin a cat, but if you can help one customer with that problem, there's no reason you can't help 100 customers with that problem.

If you had someone pay you $400 (our going hourly rate for coaching) for an hour, what about 10 people paying $200? Talking to multiple customers at once is key to growing a consulting or coaching business. You have a lot of options, from webinars to coaching seminars. Building up a list of potential customers can take a little longer, but the cut in price often makes it more accessible. Also there is absolutely no reason why you wouldn't be able to get more than 10 customers to a day's coaching.

Systematize the coaching and look to see how it works in a group. If it's all individual businesses and customers, group work is often hard (and not that valuable). Running them through worksheets and exercises for themselves, however, and giving them access to the course content recordings, is very valuable. Take the same pitch and sales process for one-on-one work and apply it to a group session. If you've got 10 previous customers, get just 5 of them to a hotel and talk through the session.

Group mastermind sessions. A mastermind session is like a perpetual motion machine. It requires a little energy and content to start the ball rolling, but eventually all the attendees provide all the content and momentum. For those who don't know what a mastermind session is, it's a group workshop where the group provides the answers. The problem in group workshops is they often succumb to the two biggest voices in the room. One or two people usually dominate the conversation and provide all the volume because "they have all the answers."

> **Pro Tip** They just like hearing their own voice.

A mastermind session flips the group workshop on its head. At a very high level, as long as you've got at least five people, you are facilitating the problem-to-solution journey. Some masterminds run all day, some run for a week, and some last for just an hour. What we do is ask for people to list their goals, problems, roadblocks, and so on individually. Then we ask them to show these to the group. The group votes on what they think the top goal, problem, and roadblock are. Once everyone has gone through their own list, every member has a vague objective list for everyone else in the group.

The group is then asked to brainstorm ideas, by themselves, for the other members. For example, if five people are in the group, I'll have five problems, five goals, and five roadblocks. I'll list all the ideas that can help each person (large pads of paper help) and brainstorm as many as I can.

Now, each member stands up again with the top goal, problem, and roadblock and writes down the suggestions from each other member. We build a list of potential ideas for a roadmap. Sometimes people will say the same thing, which is great. Just mark that down with a number and count the number of people who suggest an idea. After you've got ideas for all three objectives, the group then votes on what needs to be done first, second, and third in order. Just because something has been said five times doesn't always mean it's number one. The vote might mean other ideas get preference. At the end, you have a three-step roadmap for each goal, problem, and objective for each member and all you did was facilitate it.

Accountability calls. I have no idea why, but some people pay handsomely for the privilege of being held accountable. "I pay you to yell at me, Mike. Make me do my work. Reward me when I do it and punish me when I don't." Some people are into that kind of stuff I guess. Businesses like uGurus have scaled this model wonderfully. They ask you what your long-term, medium-term, and short-term goals are. On each live call (which you pay monthly for) they'll ask where you are with your goals, what you've been doing, and what you haven't done. If you want to run your own accountability calls, you can do it one on one. They only take 20 minutes each or five people in an hour if you're running a group call.

People will pay to be kept on track. You list their goals and hold them accountable on task. It's a fantastic move into project management, too. Accountability calls offer the chance for group mini-masterminds as well. Ask other people on the call to suggest an action to help callers with their goals.

There's no need for you to be the font of knowledge every time. In fact, being the center of the call and knowledge is unsustainable. Being a facilitator of other people's ideas and building it into constructive work is a valuable and scalable skill.

Webinar recordings. If you want to start looking at a scalable and repeatable process that involves relatively little work, look at webinars and recordings. Webinars are a wonderful source of audience, as you're not restricted to a geographic location. Even time zones are pretty flexible if you time it right. Think of the presentation or seminar you'd give to a group, maybe based off a killer post that you have. If people had to pay you to get the same results, what would you teach them?

Think about especially valuable and insightful content, with worksheets and case studies. The webinar only needs to be 90 minutes long:

- 10 minutes for an introduction
- 10 minutes for setup
- 40 minutes on the content, with screenshots, worksheets, and examples
- 20 minutes for Q&A
- 10 minutes for a wrapup

We charged $497 for our first webinar and couldn't believe the results. Our first ever call like this sold to 20 people. Although it didn't mean we could retire, we decided that webinars would be a core component of our model. Other businesses offer monthly webinars as a series, maybe for a year or a few months. You've got so many options. In addition (and this is killer), you can record the webinars and offer the recordings to customers for free. People love lifetime access. Your content can also be transcribed and turned into e-books and blog content. The recordings can be sold at a lower price on repetition and you can cut the webinars up into a course.

E-commerce supplier. Let's not think in old-school e-commerce ways, not just physical products. What about resources, graphics, images, photos, audio, and templates? The list goes on. Creativemarket, Warrior Forum, Envato, and copistore.com: There are hundreds of options for releasing a digital product onto an e-commerce platform that doesn't require you to build a store.

Admittedly, the rates aren't always brilliant. Up to 80% can go to the e-commerce store, but in terms of opening up your options, everyone should have a few items in a store to generate a few bucks. You can promote the products however you want. Get affiliate sales or drive traffic to the page. There's no reason your web site can't just be sales letter and product pages for your content, but when people go to buy, they buy from another store.

It's not going to break the bank, but it is going to show you multiple revenue streams, unlimited product stock, and if you want to sell things, people are going to help you do that.

E-commerce store with suppliers. The next level up is being an e-commerce store. If you can build an audience, there's no need for you to provide the stock. The products can be supplied by someone else. Other companies are always looking for platforms to sell their products. If you're absorbing the costs of setting up payments, e-commerce, refunds, e-mail notifications, and uploading content, there are plenty of businesses willing to sell their products on your store.

It's a beautiful model because you're not involved in the stock or product side. You'll have to pick a category and keep it fairly specific: There is no point having surfboards and PVC corsets on the same site. If you can build an audience or transition another audience to your site, people are always looking for "customer pools." Warrior Forum is a brilliant example of this. You pay to list your item and can pay extra to bump the post to the front page, and so on.

You earn cash every single time someone buys. If you're the e-commerce store, running this kind of operation can be complicated, but you're doing half the work. Other suppliers have to build the products, write the content, and get people to buy. You're facilitating the exchange, which is valuable.

Using Amazon to sell products. This approach might not be so relevant to consultants and freelancers, but there are other single-person, microbusiness professions that need this kind of revenue. Growth isn't just limited to those who sell consultation or marketing and digital services. I've mentioned sports therapists, but beauty workers, physical therapists, and anyone who has a kinesthetic (nice $20 word that means physical touch) teaching style means that physical products can make a huge difference to customers: foam rollers, yoga mats, wrist supports; the list is endless. Some suppliers will ship straight from their warehouse if you sell via Amazon. Again, you do pay Amazon per sale for the privilege of selling via their platform, but you can keep your site simple and full of content. This helps customers trust you and show them how to use these products to make their lives better.

You can then show them to the page to buy. Amazon is a trusted retailer so you don't have to work hard at how customers see that. Focus on helping your customers and showing them how to make their life better. Then use Amazon as a portal to let customers buy the items they need.

Video tutorials. The simple step-by-step tasks that you take for granted every day should be recorded, if not for anyone else, at least for yourself. When it comes to customers, the seemingly simple tasks of opening your e-mails, replying, and closing down Google Chrome might seem so trivial that it's not worth noting, but your customers might find those kinds of tutorials invaluable.

Skills vary wildly when we explore depth and length of expertise. Some people can build complex algorithms and development software; others are fantastic copywriters and message crafters. Your skill set, even the stuff you think everyone else knows, is extremely valuable to customers and your audience.

Take video user manuals, for example. They have a WordPress plug-in that teaches users and customers of WordPress web sites how to do very simple tasks on a WordPress web site. I'm talking about how to create a new post or upload a new image. We take for granted the seemingly easy tasks we repeat every day, things like installing WordPress on a new server, planning the week with tasks and meetings, or moving appointments in Google Calendar.

Write down a list of 7 to 10 tasks (it can be more if you like) that you do every day. It might look something like this:

- Post content to social media.
- Reply to e-mails.
- Write a new blog post and publish it.
- Save and back up important documents.
- Check my calendar for appointments and meetings.
- Check my investment account and bank.
- Talk to users in my Facebook groups.
- Open OneNote and write more content.
- Ask my team their progress on certain tasks.
- Clean out my Downloads folder.

Some tasks might need to be broken down into further steps. Writing and publishing a blog post is an entire course in itself, but talk yourself through each one of your steps (it's harder than it sounds). Be descriptive and explain why you're doing things in that way. Talk through how you craft an e-mail in your head before you reply. Talk about the tools that have made life easier and automate some tasks. Record the screen with Camtasia, ScreenFlow, or other screen capture software and talk into a microphone while you are walking through the tasks.

Even if you publish these for free on YouTube, they'll become invaluable to you and your customers. Let customers know that these are available. If you compile enough, there's no reason you can't publish them to Vimeo and charge people to access them as a library. Finally, your staff and team will want to see how these tasks are performed. When my virtual assistant understood why

I reply to e-mails in the way I do, she understood enough to take that off me for most tasks.

Publishing a book. Do what I did and write a book. You'd be staggered at how easy it is when you break down the chapters and tasks. When I suggest this to other businesses, their responses are split into thirds:

- One third say "Yes, I want to write and I've been meaning to."
- One third say "If I did, people would just read that and not need me anymore."
- One third say "I don't have the time or the knowledge."

If you're part of the first group, that's great news. Check out *You Must Write a Book* by Honoree Corder.[1]

If you're scared of people not needing your skills if they read the book, I need you to take a huge reality check. Are you saying that if you did write a book that you'd make yourself redundant? Does that mean your entire industry would be made redundant? If Stephen Hawking writes a book, do people stop working on quantum mechanics and astronomy? Of course not. If anything, publishing content makes the author more valuable. Publishing a book (or many books) is the key to authenticity.

Finally, if you don't know how to write a book or you say you don't have the time or knowledge, then I've got more good news. Rob Cubbon has written a book on how to write a book.[2] The key is splitting your book into manageable chunks. Writing an entire book from scratch is daunting. Writing six sections a day is easy. The way I wrote this book was I wanted to have at least one page per day in a calendar year for the reader, back when we had a different idea for the book. Sticking with that process, though, I wrote out 12 chapter titles (one for each month). In each chapter I wrote down 30 or 31 headings that would prompt me to talk about a specific subject or topic per chapter. For example, for Chapter 6 ("Building a Larger Audience"), I wrote out 30 ways to do just that, including these:

- Offer content upgrades on blog posts.
- Write long-form epic killer blog posts with a strong lead magnet related to that post at the end.
- Install Sumo to capture more traffic across sites.
- Grow your retargeting list with traffic driving from PPC.

---

[1] See https://www.amazon.com/You-Must-WriteBook-Go-ebook/dp/B01LBQ458E
[2] See http://robcubbon.com/amazon-kindle-bestseller-book-write/

Then all I had to do was write six sections a day (they're shorter than an A4 page) and I was done within 60 days. Within two months I had a big old book. Some days I wrote 10 sections, but I always did a minimum of six. First thing every morning, no e-mails, no texts, or checking Facebook, I sat down and wrote out the six sections I needed.

Web site maintenance plans. If you're a freelancer or web designer or developer, you probably have a list of clients that have web sites. How much time and money does supporting those clients take, updating plug-ins, backing up web sites, and restoring them when they break (because of the customer—we all know that)? Are you charging for that? Do you charge to support your customers and keep their web site running? You absolutely should.

Stop trying to justify why you don't charge for support. I've heard whatever excuse you've got:

- If I charge them they'll go to someone else.
- They can't afford support.
- I don't know how to support.
- Support should be free; they bought the web site already.
- They guilt me into doing it.

Ask yourself a quick question: "If this client left me, would I make less money?" Be really honest. Even if they pay for hosting, if they packed up and left, would you lose money? Most times, the answer will be no. Somehow customers hold leaving us over our heads, telling us they'll go to another provider. If you're not making any money from them, so what? Are they going to go to another provider and ask for free support from them, too? Maybe, but who cares. If they're not making you money, they can't make you less money by not working with you.

Gowp.com provides epic support packages for freelancers to sell to their customers. WP Elevation has an entire blog post on how to generate recurring revenue from maintenance plans.[3] Backups, security sweeps, and restoring if needed can be as little as $20 a month. Install Backup Buddy and make your life easier. Some clients won't go for it, but some will. I've found that most customers loved the idea of receiving support. The ones who left eventually came back when, and I'm quoting here, "My nephew can't fix the site, are your support options still available?" Look beyond the initial transaction and start to see how support makes sense to your business. Outsource it and it scales very well.

---

[3] See http://www.wpelevation.com/2015/04/selling-wordpress-maintenance-plans/

Splinter products. When we buy something, there is a pain felt in the brain when we hand over money.[4] Even if you are excited about the purchase, it can be tough for the brain to weigh up the benefits. If you're interested in reading more about neuromarketing (it is fascinating), check out *Brainfluence* by Roger Dooley.[5] At a high level, the "pain" to make a $10,000 purchase for a web site or consultation can be too much For a potential customer, even if we know we'd deliver and they'd get money back on their investment.

There is also a small amount of pain for spending $10, but it's much easier to rationalize and justify because even if it's a loss, you're not breaking the bank. Here's where it gets interesting. The difference in "pain" in the brain between one customer spending $10 and then spending $10,000 is much lower. The leap from spending nothing to $10,000 is so great that you need great sales copy, testimonials, guarantees, and time to bridge that gap. The gap from $10 to $10,000 is substantially less.

Sure, you still need sales copy and a sales process. You need trust and you must build a relationship. Too many businesses, though, are asking for marriage before they've even had a date. "But my products only cost $10,000. I can't give away consultation for $10!" You're right, but we don't want to use your core product, we want to use a splinter product. Sometimes this is also called a *tripwire*: We take a fragment or splinter of your core offering and package it up into a different delivery.

I often use "pick your brains" as the catalyst for creating a splinter product. When someone asks to pick your brain, or take you to coffee, what do you talk to them about? Usually we give away far too much for free when we have those conversations. What could you take someone through, within your core product, that costs as much as buying two cups of coffee and in the time it takes to drink them? That's your splinter product.

For example, let's *say* you're a productivity coach. You help businesses become more productive and give them more time back. If I ask, "Can I pick your brains and take you for a coffee?" you can reply with, "Look, I'm mad busy at the moment. To save us some time and the cost of finding a parking space, check out my Productivity Hack Guide. It's about the same price as buying us each a coffee and you can consume it in your own time. Then we can talk over what you want to achieve." Buying something small makes the user put skin in the game. They now have a vested interest in completing what they buy from you. The truth is that people don't really appreciate free consultation. They won't use it and you shouldn't give your time away for free.

---

[4]See http://www.neurosciencemarketing.com/blog/articles/the-pain-of-buying.htM
[5]See https://www.amazon.co.uk/Brainfluence-Persuade-Convince-Consumers-Neuromarketing/dp/1118113365

If we can package a splinter product (the sections before this give great examples on how to do this), we can not only increase our conversion rates of customers, but also we can provide a steady stream of income for smaller products. You'll increase your customer base and help yourself in the process: win–win.

E-mail list drops. There are two ways to look at e-mail list drops, but let's look at what they are before we decide which way to go. If you have a large e-mail list with active subscribers, you'll be pushing content and your own products to them (at least you should be). If your list is large enough, it's very attractive to other product providers to use your audience for their products. If I have 20,000 subscribers who are all entrepreneurs and small businesses, it makes sense to help them with other products. Maybe you don't have your own products and services to offer, which is fine. Lots of companies out there would love the opportunity to e-mail your list. Drop their product into your list.

Now, obviously we're not talking about abusing e-mail addresses and spamming them with sales e-mails every day. Appsumo.com is a fantastic example of how this works. They've got a mighty list and they don't have their own products (technically they do—Sumo.com, for example—but they're under different names). Appsumo helps users with new products and offers that they couldn't get anywhere else.

Working on the same model, you can charge a fee for promoting via your list or charge a cost per transaction. If you're discreet about your product choices the results can be very lucrative. The options are either create your own list and promote other products or find lists that are happy to promote your products. Offer an incentive to the list owner and talk to them about their customers. It's not just about making sales and finding customers: It's about positioning useful stuff in front of those customers and helping them. Just because they're buying doesn't make it dirty. It's a transaction for helping them.

Cloud-based applications. This might seem way too massive for a small section in a chapter about scalable products, but have a read anyway. Don't worry about being a developer, designer, or knowing how to build an app. When we talk about applications and apps, we don't just mean on phones. Any tool that helps people do something, via the Internet in their browser or on their phone, is an app or application.

Creating apps has become much more affordable. Creating cloud-based software used in a browser is more affordable still. Cloud-based applications are a great source of revenue because they scale really well. Your job becomes providing support and with a growing client base your revenue increases along with profit.

How do you come up with a killer idea? It's simpler than many people think. It isn't waiting for inspiration or a lightning moment of clarity; rather, it's about asking yourself, "What do I help people with now and how can I automate that? How can I make the results faster?" What would you use to make your life easier? Running coaches need training plans. Productivity coaches need time task lists. Web designers need landing page templates.

Don't worry too much if people already have software out there. Even Photoshop has competition (GIMP anyone?). Just think about how it would benefit you and then if your customers would want that. For example, a productivity coach might create a very simple task list per day and per week in a program she had built for herself. It then just notified her whenever she needed to start a new task and e-mailed her a brief everyday of what she needed to complete.

Very quickly she could scale that software, as it was all in her browser. She can sell it per month to new customers as her productivity tool and keep costs relatively low because it's very simple software. Talk to developers in your local area about the idea and find someone you connect with. Some developers are open to revenue shares, and some need investment up front. That's fine, too. If we're serious businesses we need to pay people for their services. A $10,000 investment for cloud-based software that allows you to charge $10 a month = $120 a year, so 84 customers and it's paid for itself.

Digital products. Halfway between splinter products and cloud-based apps, digital products are often used as template fillers. Take Funnelscripts.com, for example, or Digitalmarketer.com. Both have one- time-cost software downloads that have one specific function. They do that job insanely well (VSL builder and Freshkey, respectively) and are a one-time cost. Built in Unity, they're relatively cheap to produce and just sit behind a one-time cost paywall. It's just a `.zip` file that downloads and runs off Unity (a code engine like HTML). You can provide a small tutorial and help users go through the process, but most digital download products are simple to use.

For example, if we're a running coach, a small piece of software might ask us 10 questions: how often we run now, how far we want to run, time until goal, and so on. When the answers to those questions are entered, the software produces a running plan. What I love about digital download products is that customers then have your business on their machine. They're lightweight, cheap, and help produce results: "Hey, if you're serious about running plans and using this plan we created for you, you need to check out our bootcamp." This provides beautiful up-sell potential.

Summary

By now you should see that you have plenty of options to create scalable products. Rather than delivering one-off, single-project results, you're able to be in multiple places at once.

From Single to Scale

- You can create multiple products at a time, through recording and documenting your process or delivery.
- There are many ways to deliver the same results, some requiring more investment than others.
- Creating products is half the battle. We must also market and promote what we have.
- You already have plenty of products in your arsenal, it's just a case of letting them out the box.

CHAPTER 4

Developing a Scalable Product from What You've Got

The key to building scalable products, as a single person or microbusiness, is using what you've got already. Everything you do is already designed to be built and delivered by one person, usually to another small or microbusiness as a customer. Even if you consult for large companies, you're probably only dealing with smaller teams and a manager within that organization. This chapter is about taking what you've got and what you're selling now, and turning it into a scalable product. Half of these steps will be about doing what you do already and documenting it. The other half will be about using what you have already created and repurposing it.

Focus on the customer. Let's see what products and results you can deliver to customers. Be forewarned that when I do this exercise with my clients, they feel a bit queasy. For all our moaning about customers not "getting us" after doing this exercise, we see that lots of businesses don't really have a huge

© Michael Killen 2019
M. Killen, *From Single to Scale*, https://doi.org/10.1007/978-1-4842-3814-1_4

amount to offer their customers. Grab a piece of paper, turn it landscape, and draw two vertical lines down the middle, dividing it into three list columns.

If you want to use our worksheet template, head to singletoscale.com/customer and download your free worksheet. On the left column write "Products," in the middle column write "Results," and in the right column write "Benefits." In the Product column, write down all the things you offer to customers: web sites, courses, blog content, coaching, consultation, and so on. When I say products, I mean anything that you deliver that customers pay for: services, therapy, coaching, e-books, courses, whatever. Include blog content and lead magnets in that, too. People pay with their time to consume those.

If you feel your consultation or coaching is too broad, or maybe every customer is unique, feel free to write down a few topics that you coach on, such as mindfulness, physical therapy, or SEO. Even if you've only delivered something once, write it down. Anything that customers can take from you that they buy (or consume) is a product.

If there's room, write down a few of the featues that product provides. It's true that people don't buy features, but they are sold on them. Benefits and results get me in and help me understand what I'm buying. Features are where I make comparisons and cement the purchase.

Now, in the middle column, Results, write out the results that these products give. Try to be specific to each product. A result is something that's tangible, something that can be measured, and repeated, and seen. For example, a web site with a blog is a result. It's not brilliant, but it fits the result criteria. More traffic from Google is a result. If I then looked at the top 10 customers and the traffic they've got, I could say "a 200% increase in traffic from organic SEO in three months." The more specific and descriptive I am with results, the better.

It might take a bit of research. Maybe you need to talk to customers, get their testimonials. For example:

> "I can now run 10k without any hip pain." (Sports therapist).
>
> "3,000 unique new e-mail address leads in six months, 200 times more than last year." (Lead generation software).
>
> "I've applied for two interviews and got a call back for one." (Confidence coaching).

Explore the end result that customers get when working with you. Maybe you need to refer to the before–after list in the next section. Finally, in the Benefits column, list why that result makes them happier. Why does it improve their life? Why bother getting that result in the first place? Benefits are really what people are looking for. People don't want to run 10k for the sake of it. They want to feel healthier and have more energy.

Benefits are less tangible. They can't really be measured or recorded, but people sure know them when they see them. A benefit is a future that the customer wants. It's a future version or event that they want to see or have. Talking to customers and asking how they feel and how their life is is the easiest method for seeing benefits. What does more leads in our e-mail list mean? It means (benefit) that we can market our products to more people. What does getting new interviews mean? It means that we have more confidence to go after jobs that make us happy.

- More time with family.
- Less stress at work.
- Clearer identity with ourselves.

Almost all results, be they marketing or sales or sport or health or whatever, lead to personal and internal benefits. What's interesting is that we start from a wide range of products (or maybe not, but don't feel bad about that) and we narrow down the results. Our results repeat themselves because what we deliver is usually the same through different methods.

Before and After

Before we can start selling profitable, scalable products, we need to look at the "after shot" of the customer. When we see weight loss or fitness advertisments, they always start with a before and after shot. The secret is that (1) customers can envision themselves as the before and easily visualize the after, and (2) almost all fitness products are identical. They use before and after shots because listing the actual work required and what you have to do to get those results is not appealing.

We're going to make sure people can see our results and benefits before we start talking to them about what they need to do. Grab a piece of paper and draw a vertical line down the middle, dividing it into two columns. At the top of the left column, write "Before" and at the top of the right column, write "After."

If you want to use our worksheet template, head to singletoscale.com/before and download the worksheet. In the Before column, describe the customer before they work with you. This could be for your flagship product or your most popular web site type. List the ways they're frustrated, what their goals are, and what their problems are. Be as descriptive as possible while you explain where they are and what they're doing now. The more you write the better. It's hard at first, but don't stop until you've got 20 items listed. What does their average day look like? How do they feel? What do they have or not have? What do they want? What's their status?

For example, if you sell e-commerce web sites, before working with you, businesses:

- Have slow sales and no regular customers.
- Don't know how to market their products.
- Are frustrated at marketing and branding companies with selling logos.
- Are not spending enough time with families.
- Want to generate more than $100,000 in a year.

List as many as you can. Talk to current customers, look at their e-mails, and examine what they were like before they began working with you. Use emotions, feelings, and status as the most powerful before descriptors.

Now on the right side, under After, write down and describe what your customers are like after they work with you. Don't worry too much about the product or service yet, just look at how they feel and what they are after they have worked with you. Use the before list as a prompt, describing the opposite or preferred outcome compared to the before description. Do they feel frustrated because they can't keep regular customers? Now they're confident that customers will come back again and again. Our job is to make this before and after list appeal to our customers. They recognize the before list and they aspire to the after list.

The gap between the before side and after side is what people are paying for. They're not buying a web site or coaching; they're buying the journey from before to after. Or, as Al Ramadan said in *Play Bigger,* they're buying "from/to." The larger the gap we can bridge, the more value the customer sees. Therefore, the more we can justify charging. From "can't run up the stairs without feeling out of breath" to "confident I can run a 26.2-mile in a marathon in under four hours" is a huge value gulf.

When we boil it down and compare our before/after list and our products/results/benefits lists. The benefits we provide with the results we get are what customers receive in the value gulf. That value gulf is what we identified in the before/after list. Maybe it turns out you only really provide three benefits and five results from 18 different products.

Those benefits and results are what you're actually selling. Free up your preconceived ideas of what you can deliver. If you create a course or an audiobook with the same results and benefits, it's within your business. You have the skills and experience already and you probably already have the content.

Deliver the result. Take a look at your results column. Those tangible, measurable, and repeatable results come at the end of working with you. So far it might have only been you that has delivered these results to a customer.

Maybe it's something large like a web site, or maybe it's something ongoing like SEO traffic or marathon training. If we had enough time, money, energy, and documentation, could someone else deliver the same results? I do not mean the exact same process or coaching you do (although that is an option we'll explore later), but the results that someone could get working with you.

Work backward and look at the results you get customers. How could someone else deliver those same results? Think about what they can do afterward and how they feel, rather than what they do. Compare it to travel. Getting from London to Sydney is the goal. The result is to be in Sydney. Although most will opt to fly, some might try a cruise, or even travel via train and car to cross Europe and Asia. Others will stop off in the United States or search for cheaper connecting flights. If we boil down the goal of "travel," maybe to seeing somewhere new or going away for a few months, does Sydney have to be the only option? If you're traveling from London there are tons of destinations that will still let you be somewhere totally different.

What I'm saying is that the customers' goals and the results they want aren't tied to the process or delivery you provide. If customers need more social media followers, consultation and coaching aren't the only options. You've got courses, guides, e-books, and more—all the options listed in Chapter 3. If you can create a series of worksheets and video guides, there's no reason other people can't do the coaching for you.

Special and unique. I've mentioned this a bit and it's the result of an unfortunate by-product of our current purchasing habits. Business mentors and banks will often ask, "What's your USP?" Unique selling point (USP) is a hangover from the 1980s school of marketing. I'm still a big fan of what 1980s corporate marketing has done for our industry, but there are a few silver bullet ideas, like a USP, that reside in our business models.

If your USP exists within your business, it's probably you. You are unique, and most customers will buy from you just because they like you. Other than that, though, your business probably isn't that unique. In fact, even what you provide isn't that unique. You might have your own methods and styles, but most of the time the results you get are not that far from what others can provide. I'm not saying you're not great at what you do, or that your customers don't love you, but knowing that you can expand your business further than yourself is a liberating feeling.

You don't need a USP. What you need is scalable and profitable products. If it's about being first to a market, or unique to a market, I'd rather be first. You don't have to be unique; you have to be understood and trusted. You'd be staggered at how many businesses fail to be trusted and understood. They'd rather be unique. Different is enough, as unique isn't going to find customers.

Get off the tools. The largest roadblock to scaling your business is often the mental barrier of control. Giving up control is hard. We see other people do such inferior jobs we think we're the only ones capable of it. Maybe it's wrong, though, to charge money for a service that you don't have 100% control over. Does Colonel Sanders cook the chicken? Does Bill Gates write the code?

Businesses that succeed, even as small microbusinesses or single-person enterprises, succeed because they build systems and processes that allow them to get off the tools. You have to want to get off the tools, however. You have to want to build a process and start putting in place people and teams that can take care of things for you.

If you're worried about getting off the tools, it's because you're not confident in the instructions you've given to whoever is taking control. Maybe you don't know how to write the processes or can't think what needs to be done. We're going to cover this next. Often, when we worry about control, it's because our expectations are all over the place. We have what we believe we're capable of doing and we don't have confidence in the other party. If those expectations are written out and understood, it's much easier to hand over the tools. Let's look at how we can do that now.

Delivery process. We start off with a huge mind map, a big old journey plotting the process that we go through with our customers. This takes the most time to create, out of everything in this book. It'll go through several revisions. You'll add details and remap pathways. Have no fear, though, it's extremely rewarding to map out how your process works.

Take your before/after list and the products/results/benefits list. Take a large piece of paper or a whiteboard and choose one product or service, maybe your flagship product or the one you're most used to executing. At the top of the page or board, write the product or service that you're focusing on. For our example, it's a WordPress web site. At one end of the paper, the start, write a few of the before words and sentences, describing your customer. At the other end, the finish, write the result that the customer gets.

For example, if we're web site designers, the product is a web site. At the start, the client doesn't have a site, has few customers, and is new to digital online businesses. At the end, they have a web site that gets traffic. Now write down the broad activities that you go through with that customer from the first discovery workshop or the qualification worksheet they use. Run through each stage that you need to complete and in the order in which it comes. If you'd like an example, use the new web site process I use, shown in Figure 4-1. If you want to view a high-resolution version of this image, head to `singletoscale.com/process`.

From Single to Scale

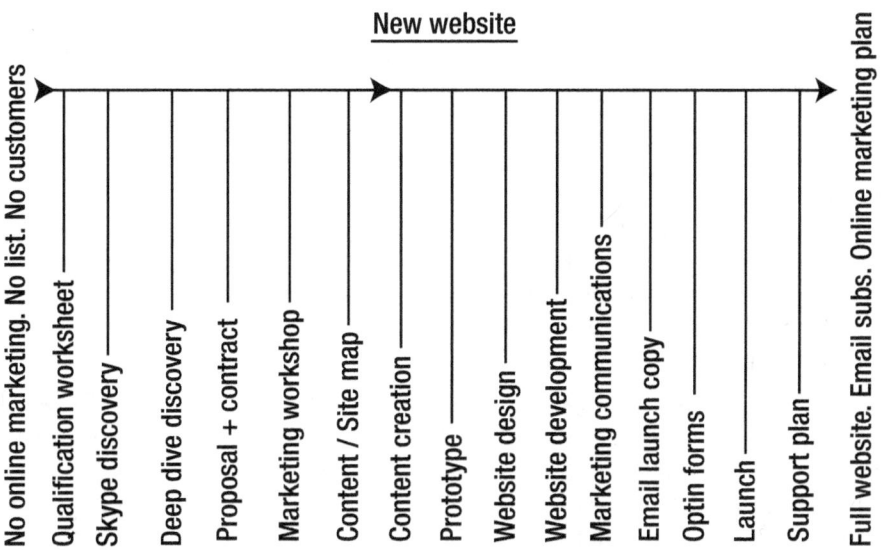

Figure 4-1. New web site process

At this stage, it's sometimes apparent that you either don't have as much of a process as you'd like or you think every customer is so unique, that they can't follow the process. Stick with the exercise and map out the stages that do happen for each customer. Sure, every client is different, but you will run through similar stages with most customers. Our job is to find the similarities and start systematizing what we deliver. Map out and list the stages of a project or coaching or consulting. It doesn't matter if this is a period of weeks or a period of months. What we want is a high-level overview of the process that you go through, the stages and system that you use to get your customers the results they need and want. We're not going into detail yet; that's in a later stage.

Templates and worksheets. When we look at your larger process or plan, think about the worksheets that you use with your customers. When we say worksheets, what we mean is anything that you use with customers to help them through a process, maybe your qualification questions or discovery questions. Maybe you have a questionnaire for starting a project, or a series of questions that you always ask new customers. Perhaps you use worksheets, forms, workshops, consulting sessions, marketing models, or anything that you share with customers when working on a new project.

For example, in our new web site process we talk about our qualification worksheet (qualification is qualifying the customer is right for your business with the right budget, decision makers, and project needs). We also have a marketing workshop, deep dive session, and opt-in forms. For each of these stages I have a set series of questions that I always ask. Sure, I might go off on a tangent during a call, but most of the time I'm following that set series of questions. Having these questions and repeatable steps in each stage is critical to scaling your business to profit. During this part of the book, most businesses realize they don't have as much documentation as they think. Most of it is habit and based on what they know at the time.

Spend some time to write down the steps and questions that you always ask or need to ask. Even if they're really broad and you have to go deeper with them, spend time to structure the way these questions are delivered, with templates and models, or worksheets (e.g., I run through a very basic high-level version of the CVO from Digital Marketer[1] with my customers during the marketing workshop).

The delivery is so practiced and rehearsed that if you played two recordings of it back to back, they're practically indistinguishable. For each stage in the project have your templates, questions, and worksheets written up and saved. The fastest way to look 100 times more professional than your competition is branded worksheets during a meeting. Keep all these templates and worksheets safe, as we'll be using them later in other products.

Map Out Each Stage

When you sit down with a new customer, what's the agenda for that meeting? Whether it is a project kick-off or catch-up calls, what are the main –five to seven bullet points that you'll discuss? For example, in our new web site process, we have a Skype discovery call. This is a 20-minute call that we book with people who have passed our qualification worksheet, and we want to know more about their project.

We have eight questions that we ask in a specific order. It allows us to uncover more about the project, understand their needs better, and go over their qualification worksheet.

- How many current customers do you have?
- How many leads do you have?
- How are you marketing your business at the moment and what's the marketing budget?
- What's the budget for the project?
- How serious are you about completing this project?
- What are your goals for the business?

---

[1] See http://www.digitalmarketer.com/customer-value-optimization

- What's the business revenue?
- What are your goals for the web site?

I send these questions in advance to the customers, as well as a brief outline of our agenda. Usually this is in an e-mail and I'll also confirm the meeting time, date, and Skype number.

Face-to-face meetings always have an agenda. It's very rare that they are just a "meet up." If you do the coffee thing and say, "Let's have a casual chat," I implore you to start reducing these interactions with people who aren't customers, because most of them just want free consulting and they'll waste your time. Write up your agendas in a document and save them. Again, you might only have three or four meetings that run like this, but keep the questions and agenda safe. First, it's now part of your process to send this document template as the agenda, and second, we've started writing some content for your scalable products and business.

Record all your interactions. Okay, so maybe not all your interactions but certainly the main meetings. I've never had a customer reject me when I ask them if I can record a meeting: "It's just so I can focus on our questions and helping you, rather than try to remember everything you say. I'll go back over the recording later so I can better understand your needs." This approach makes you look mad professional and it's extremely useful as a backup. I've left notes behind, had documents get thrown out, and one recording has even spared me a lengthy court process. It's simple: Get OneDrive or Dropbox and start automatically syncing your phone recordings to the cloud. Listen to them on the journey home and keep the MP3 as it's going to turbo charge your content creation.

Transcribe your audio. Since writing this book, Rev.com has released an app that allows you to record audio and get it transcribed in one sitting. With your new MP3, hop on over to Rev.com and get that audio transcribed, word for word. You'll get a professional and written-up document with every word said on that recording. Go through the document and remove any names and company details. Figures and lead numbers are okay; we want the content to remain anonymous, but still specific to a result or project.

Once we've got our edited transcript we can start to do amazing things with it later, but more on that in a bit. Transcribing is cheap, but $60 for every call is a lot. Instead, focus on one project and customer at a time. Read through the rest of this chapter and see what's going to become of all this when set up.

For example, with our new web site project, I might record the initial Skype call, only 20 minutes, which is about $20 with Rev.com. If I take the questions and agenda from earlier and map each question to the answers, I have an FAQ for web site design customers. If I take an hour-long presentation and record that, transcribe the audio, and keep the PowerPoint slides, I have a very in-depth blog post with slides and images.

Rewrite the transcript. With your new transcribed document, head over to Speedlancer.com and check out their content writing services. From $70 you can get a 700-word blog post written on any topic and content. They will even research it and write it for $100. Lead magnets, promotional e-mails, social media content, you name it, Speedlancer.com can get it written.

Use your transcription as the research material and foundation for a project. Write up a brief for the content and think about how you want that content to be useful to you. Try on smaller pieces first, like blog content. Your first stages of a project can often become FAQs, beginner guides, and must-know walkthroughs. If you've consulted a customer on healthy cooking over the Christmas period, that recording and transcription becomes just that: "The Ultimate Beginners' Guide to Healthy Food over Christmas."

Don't overcomplicate the subject. Just think about the results or what the customer now understands: Marketing funnels? Barefoot running? AutoCAD? Start with the end in mind and let Speedlancer do the rest with your content. While they're writing up whatever you need, you've got time to do something else. This is one of the core components to scaling your business. It's not always about employing people. It's about taking tasks off your hands and letting someone else do it. Speedlancer also has a 10,000-word e-book option. It takes about two hours to talk through 10,000 words on a presentation. If you present two-hour-long webinars on the same subject, that's an e-book right there.

Create Blog Posts

So we've got all this content and now Speedlancer can help us get it written, but how do we turn that content into a blog post? What brief would we give? If we're doing it ourselves (still a perfectly viable option), how do we restructure transcription content? Remember that we want to write as little as possible, taking copied text from the transcript and pasting that or even just removing speech-based text and making it look better to read. We have a few options.

First—and we've done this a few times—just release the transcript. This is meant not really for meetings or calls, but for webinars and presentations. We promote it as a raw transcript of our entire presentation. It's full of keywords, looks authentic when it's raw, and lets us publish content fast. If you want an example checkout the post at `https://sellyourservice.co.uk/2016/12/transcript-the-smartest-pages-you-can-create-on-any-website-and-why-you-need-to-use-them`.

Second, we'll take the questions, presentation points, or agenda points and use them as headings. Then just paste the bulk of the presentation text under those headings. For example, if one of the slides is on social media traffic, we'll take that as a title and paste the transcript for that slide under it. Pretty soon you have a few headings that you can promote as an FAQ or Should Ask Question series. Third, we might take the content and pick out –three to five main points. We'll then structure the content into a how-to guide or journal type post.

Typically, we use the same structure in our presentations as our blog content:

- Promise.
- Problem.
- Myth.
- What's changing.
- Main points.

Most of our presentation content goes under those headings. We'll name and promote the content as a how-to guide or regular blog post. Finally, if you've got a long presentation or a series of transcripts about a subject, think about creating an "ultimate guide," a piece of long content that goes into great depth on a subject. Killer content starts with a sales letter style introduction, really pitching the idea and method to the reader. By the end, they want the solution so badly they'd probably pay for it. Instead, you're going to give detailed help on that subject for free. If you have worksheets or handouts for that presentation, give them away, too.

Ultimately, the point is to take the copy and content that we've got and turn it into something else. It's not easy straight away. You'll think it's a huge waste of time compared to writing it from scratch, but stick with it. You're learning a new skill and it's never quick. Remember, too, that Speedlancer and other freelancer hiring sites (Upwork, Envato studio, people per hour, etc.) can rewrite a lot of content for you.

Create lead magnets. If you've got material that you've presented to customers or webinars or blog content, then you've got a lead magnet. What is a lead magnet? Well, if we're going to scale your business and make it profitable, you need leads. We really want to build a list of leads that we can contact, so we need their e-mail addresses. In exchange for that e-mail address and their name, we'll offer them a lead magnet.

A lead magnet is a specific piece of very valuable material. It solves a specific problem and can be used by someone to help them in some way. Most businesses used to give away e-books (fine, but not great). Now we can give away cheat sheets, checklists, guides, software, templates, worksheets, webinars … the list is endless. The key to creating a lead magnet that captures data and is genuinely useful is thinking about where someone will first see it.

For example, if you've taken your transcript and turned it into a blog post, maybe that blog post is about SEO for e-commerce web sites. Think about how that blog post helps someone. What can they do after reading that post?

What do they want help with? If they read that blog post, what can they now do? If they took every word and syllable from that post, they could do something by themselves. How can you help them get that result faster, or with less effort?

Offer a lead magnet that will give them clarity on the actions and steps they need to take. Checklists work wonders as lead magnets. List 10 to 15 steps that you talk about in the post to check off if they want the same results. Lead magnets work better when they're clearly related to the topic of the post or page that the reader is on. A lead magnet about creating a running plan in winter will convert much better if the post is also about running in winter.

The digital marketer's guide to lead magnets at `http://www.digitalmarketer.com/lead-magnet-ideas-funnel` is about as good a guide as you can get for creating lead magnets and the types available. At its core, if you were giving the same content away over a conversation, what would you offer next to get even faster results for that same person? Talking about social media traffic is great, and provides lots of ideas, but if you really want to get social traffic, you should use our social traffic cheat sheet.

At a high level, a cheat sheet is like a worksheet with the gaps filled in. Sometimes we use a table to let people reference things quickly, or we show them a high-level overview of a strategy. Resource lists are just that, a list of resources you use for that topic; think web sites, shops, books, tools, and blog posts.

Worksheets are where you lead the user through a series of questions. The answers are usually brainstorms or lists of ideas, to offer clarity and get them to write things down. There are hundreds of ways to create lead magnets, but make sure you keep it relevant to the topic or subject you're writing about. Keep it short and valuable (400-page e-books aren't that useful). Finally, think about if it can help someone get the same results they want and you can give.

Create an e-book. "But you just said to stay away from e-books!" I know, I'm a man of contradictions. There is absolutely nothing wrong with e-books, I just don't think they're the best lead magnets available. To offer an e-book to a qualified lead or even to create an e-book to sell, though ... that's a different matter.

Writing an e-book takes time, but it's a valuable investment. You don't run out of stock, they can be sold for profit, and they can position you as an authority within a niche. I'm going to let you in on a big secret, though. Serializing books has always been very popular. Alexandre Dumas, Charles Dickens, and many more authors used to publish chapters or parts of chapters in newspapers regularly. Then, once a book or serial was completed, they would collate the written work and release it as a full book. Can you see where I'm going with this?

Your blog posts, assuming they're all relatively related in subject matter and topic, can be collected together and published as a book. To lower costs and keep profit margins high, you can create an e-book and sell that instead. For example, let's say as a digital traffic coach we have 12 posts, roughly 1,000 words long each. That's a 12,000-word e-book. Assume the 12 topics are SEO traffic, PPC traffic from Google, content marketing, organic social traffic, automating traffic, PPC from Facebook, PPC from LinkedIn, YouTube traffic, conversion measuring, Google analytics, e-mail traffic, and remarketing. That becomes "The Guide to Getting Traffic to Your Web Site." That's a really terrible title for a book, but it's a start.

Now think about the niche or target you want the book to serve: Small business web sites over three years old? Under 12 months old? WordPress web sites? Small businesses without a marketing budget? By creating a result and market combination, you've got a very powerful e-book title and topic, something that becomes very valuable to an audience. It's also easier to get a number one bestseller the smaller your niche.

Something I've seen a few times is taking the different types of blog content and cutting that up across the book. Of 12 blog posts, let's say 8 are regular guides and blog posts. Of the remaining four, one is a resource list, one is a quote post, one is an interview post, and one is an ultimate guide. I've seen other businesses split the quotes across the 12 chapters, then take the resource list content and using that at the end of each chapter as a roundup. The interview post becomes its own chapter.

The ultimate guide becomes a final chapter that talks the user through how to complete a task. Very quickly we've got a varied and interesting book that we can sell. Create an introduction and a summary chapter and whip up an e-book cover. We're good to go. Try and sell the e-book via PayPal or sell it via Amazon Kindle. You need to market it and sell it like any other product, but it never runs out of stock and starts to become a recurring revenue pathway for your business.

Turn e-books into webinars. Webinars are a fantastic way to connect with an audience that you couldn't present to in person. Stretching across the globe, a webinar lets us help people from our laptops. If you've never done a webinar before, essentially, it's an online presentation. We might use software like Zoom or Google Hangouts to present the content, but the concept is the same.

Pick a date and a time and promote the hell out of it. Even if only 10 people arrive, the power of a webinar comes from being recorded and reusable. So how do we structure a webinar? It really depends on what you're trying to do with it. If you just want to demonstrate value and show yourself as useful, by helping people do something, then focus on content. If you're using the webinar to sell something, you need to have calls to action in the webinar.

At a high level, take the five main points from your e-book (or any content really, but presenting a webinar based on a book gives instant credibility and weight) and demonstrate them to an audience. Let's think of this webinar as just a valuable supplement to your audience. Based on your book, this is a high-level overview of what you can help them with.

This is how you should structure your presentation. Each point is one slide with very little text. Think headlines, not paragraphs. This structure, by the way, is taken from Oren Klaff's book, *Pitch Anything* (McGraw-Hill, 2011). It's brilliant.

- **Promise**. Make a promise right at the start of the presentation. What do you promise viewers will get from this webinar?

- **Problem**. What's the big problem you're helping them solve? What's the big issue that faces them?

- **Myth**. What do most people do with this problem? What's a myth that doesn't work when solving this problem?

- **Changing**. What's changing in the industry or world that makes things easier or harder for your customers? What's something they need to be aware of or take advantage of? The three areas to focus on are economic, technological, and sociological. Money, technology, and people all change.

- **Knife twist**. "And to top it all off ...": What's another thing preventing them from doing what they want? Another problem or a roadblock with the way people usually solve this problem? Cost, information, snake oil merchants: What is the final knife twist?

- **Solution**. Now we present the solution. In a value webinar we use an agenda here explaining what you're going to be talking about.

- **About you**. A common mistake people make is introducing themselves too early. By doing it now we're showing three things: (1) I just want to show you something cool. I'm not that important, the content is. (2) People who do want to know who you are will be desperate by now and this'll satisfy them. (3) We can show off what we've done and why we're right for this topic. Tell them one great result you have gotten (not two or three) and how you help people.

- **Results.** Very quickly go over one big result that they'll be able to get again. Affirm why they're here and what they'll be able to do.

- **Main point.** Now we get into the meat of the presentation. Teach them – three to seven useful points. Use screenshots or bullet points. However you want to explain the process, they need to get results.

- **Call to action (CTA).** It's always useful to add a CTA. Even if you don't have an automated product, give your e-mail or office phone number (no cell or mobile numbers, trust me on that) and get people to call you. Make it easy for them to contact you.

- **Dos and don'ts.** Wrap up with dos and don'ts. This is the easiest summary in the world. It retells clients what you've told them and wraps up the call. At this point as well, I like to open it up to questions and answers.

Promoting the Webinar

You cannot promote the webinar just once. I'm talking about repeat and constant promotion. You don't need to do the webinar live every time, maybe once a month for three months? That doesn't mean that you don't continue to promote the webinar recordings, though. Some businesses promote the webinar recording as a live recording and try to pass it off as live. Personally I don't do that, but some businesses have seen success with "green-fielding" their webinars. Be honest when promoting the recording. You don't need to trick people into watching.

The key to getting people to sign up to webinars, recorded or live, is worksheets. People love worksheets and checklists or cheat sheets when they attend a webinar. Use the same premise for lead magnets from your content as you do with a webinar. What would people need to do to get results faster and with less work? If you're going through a webinar, can you use worksheets live on the webinar? Offer the first one without a signup and offer the others after they're on the call. What we're doing is structuring the webinar to be productive and highly valuable, more like a workshop than just a presentation.

Have extra resources, guides, posts, and templates available to support your webinar. Once it's recorded and you've got all the worksheets available, go into promotion mode. Use Facebook advertising to create an audience and target people. Show them the webinar and advertise it to that audience. E-mail your list and drive as much traffic as you can to your webinar signup page. At first, it's going to be tough work. PPC advertising is a snowball effect. You're not going to get hundreds of signups overnight.

However, at Sell Your Service, for example, we can run webinars every few weeks and get around 500 signups each time now. That's for recordings, of course, and that's nothing compared to what some of the larger players are getting. Get other people to promote it, talk to attendees, and ask them to share it. You have the page and webinar now. You need to work hard at promoting the content. Treat it like a product and drive as much traffic as you can.

▪ **Note** Never, never buy cheap traffic from Fiverr or other cheap sources. They say you'll get 10,000 hits, but I guarantee that none of them will convert into a lead.

Creating a Course

Think about the results that your content can get people. From your before/after list and products/results/benefits list, look over the results and benefits you can give. You've got a webinar and blog content. Now we're going to look at a seriously scalable and relevant product: a course.

Courses are not just for educational businesses. You can teach people to do anything. If your fear alarm is ringing, "But if I teach them to do it, they won't need me!" then take a deep breath. People don't work like that. What we're offering is a solution. Courses can be much cheaper than hiring you, but people who do go through the course will want to hire you to help them.

Help them help themselves, then you help them. Show them how it's done, show them how to do it, and then do it for them. That's the scale, and the pay works up, too. Take your broad subject or result and use that as the course title. Similar to the book, we might want to focus on a benefit or a niche to give it specificity. Overall, though, this is your course. Be specific and narrow, too. Courses on "digital marketing" don't sell well. Remember the previous content and products we've created: e-books, webinars, blog content, and lead magnets. They all work because they're specific.

Whatever your business does, take another one of your products from the products/results/benefits list and look at the benefits that your product or service gives. Be very specific. If you're a digital marketing coach, maybe you have an analytics and reporting product. You teach how to measure conversions and optimize them for better results.

Now we need six broad topics that fit into that subject. You could take six individual blog posts you've already got, or map out the mini journey that you take. Look at the agenda you created for a stage in your delivery process or the process overall. What are the six topics that you can talk about on that subject to that audience? For analytics and reporting, we'd take these:

- What conversion is and how it's measured. What it means and how it helps your business.
- Installing an analytics tool.
- Setting goals.
- Measuring traffic.
- Measuring conversions.
- Optimizing conversions.

Break up each topic. Now we get to the meat of our course. Each broad topic needs to be broken down into six (or more) lessons. Teach your customers how to accomplish something. Think in small steps rather than whole processes. Each lesson should only be up to 10 minutes long. There is no need to go longer than that.

With six lessons, that's more than an hour of lesson content. For example, with our analytics and reporting course, the second lesson is installing an analytics tool. This would probably be broken down into the following topics:

- Creating an analytics account.
- Copying the tracking and embed code.
- Overview of the sections and panels.
- Testing.
- Creating a report.
- Support and troubleshooting.

We need to do this for each broad topic. Every lesson then teaches how to accomplish a small step. Ideally, each lesson also has a worksheet or template or something to use that supports the lesson. Again, think lead magnets and how they're used. Think of a useful piece of content that adds value. By this point, you'll have one course with six lessons and six topics in each lesson.

If your course is behind a paywall, you can charge people to access the course. You don't need complicated learning management software (LMS) yet. You can get away with a simple WordPress site. There are simple paywall plug-ins that protect pages so that users have to pay. There are tools available like Udemy and Thinkific, but they have control over pricing and promotion.

What we're trying to do is create a piece of valuable, teachable content that doesn't run out of stock. You could have 10,000 people buy your course tomorrow and each delivery would be exactly the same. It means you can focus on promoting products, too, because you don't have to build a course every time you sell it. Think about creating courses with one lesson and six topics, too, like a miniature version of a full course that you can use as a bonus lead magnet, or even a splinter product.

Using a worksheet. A massive value add-on for a worksheet or template is to teach people how to use it. For example, if we have a lead magnet that is a worksheet, it might not be enough to talk people through it in a blog post. When our new subscribers are looking at the worksheet, they might like someone to go through it with them in real time. Often, new users like examples and a little hand-holding through the process. If you can provide a video walkthrough of you or someone filling out the worksheet, that's a huge bonus to new subscribers. It works best as a bonus, not something that's promoted with the lead magnet. We're trying to overdeliver on their expectations. Also, video walkthroughs are a fantastic time to promote splinter products and other services.

For example, you're a book publishing consultant who teaches authors how to promote their books. Let's say you have a series of worksheets on creating a social media presence, self-promotion, and finding publishers. For each of those worksheets, fill out the worksheet in real time and record the screen while you are doing it. There is no need to go overboard: A screen capture recording (Camtasia or Screenflow work great) and a voice-over are enough to fill in a worksheet. If you want to use an example customer, go for it, but don't think you need to do this. What we're doing is giving a demonstration of how to fill in the worksheet.

Teach someone else. When it comes to paying for walkthroughs, going through a worksheet with someone one on one can be charged for. However, it's time consuming and harder to scale. What we want to do is teach someone else to consult your customers. If you have a series of worksheets, think about the structure of a course and teach someone to go through all the worksheets. That's something you can absolutely charge for.

Offer a series of walkthroughs, examples, and tutorials, all focused around all the worksheets. Charge something low barrier, like $9 or $19, to access all the video walkthroughs. Position it as a complete consulting course or workshop series. Give customers access to worksheets and walk through each worksheet like you did with the single worksheet for free. However, you're also going to teach them how to work through the sheets with someone else. Add this as bonus content to the course. They buy access to the whole series for themselves.

What you are trying to do again is overdeliver on customer expectations. A short bonus video and document for each worksheet, explaining how to consult someone else on these worksheets, is bound to be valuable. Teaching someone else to use your worksheets is simpler than you probably think. When we're going through the sheet with them, we outline the whole worksheet, then go through each step with examples. Then we explain why each stage is useful and at the end sum up what they've completed.

When we teach someone else to teach, we give them quick notes on those same points, so they can explain in their own words why each section and sheet is important, what each sheet does, and what they're going to do. In the past we have tried to sell this as a consulting course, so they can consult other businesses, but neither way has explicitly achieved better results. Again, you might wonder, "But if I teach them, won't my customers leave me for them?" Probably not. What you're doing is teaching your customers to find you more customers. We're going to talk about how to monetize this in the next section. You're empowering your customers to reach out and find new sources of revenue. The truth is that most people are honest enough not to rip off your content. If people are doing that, take it as a sign you're doing something right.

External consultants. Here's where we can start getting clever. People who do buy the worksheet walkthrough series have essentially been taught how to complete a worksheet. Offer to pay them to teach others how to complete the worksheets. An easy, scalable, and profitable product is to work through a series of worksheets on Skype with a customer. You can charge $100 or so for the hour and offer $60 to those who have already done it to teach it.

These numbers are purely for demonstration purposes. Our coaching, for example, costs $497 for the hour and we pass $350 to the coaches. This means is that you're not taking the time to consult, but you are delivering results to a customer. Package up the hour as a coaching or consulting session. Ask your current worksheet customers if they're interested in coaching a little on the side. All your leads and customers that haven't bought the walkthrough series can be offered this consulting hour. All the bookings go through you and you take the payment, giving your part-time coaches $40.

You might have to negotiate on the rate, but there is a balance that most people understand. Besides, you're not forcing anyone to do anything. You're spending time and money promoting the product, it's your system, and you built the worksheets. Your coaches don't worry about lead generation or customer payments, they just take their time to deliver the consultation session.

Sell your transcripts. Remember those raw transcripts we spoke about earlier? If you've done 10 workshop or coaching sessions, maybe a few webinars, there's no reason you can't package those up. I like transcript selling because there's something really authentic about them. There's something quite gritty and real about a Word document with eight transcripts inside it, raw, unedited, and easy to produce. The best way to position this is just as I've said: raw, unedited, and open use.

If it's a particularly specific series, position it as the insiders' content, like expert transcripts with tons of information. We have seen people offer transcripts with PLR, which means the customer can use them however they want:

Sell them or use them as content. Do whatever. It becomes a commodity sale, as your customers could add value and charge far more. Honestly? That's probably fine.

Use webinar recordings. If you have webinar recordings in a video format, they're probably teaching people how to do a certain task. Make a list of the short steps that you teach in the whole webinar. Think like the course topic lessons we mentioned earlier. Can your webinar be cut up into several (or more) topic lessons and sold as video tutorials?

Take a look at the typical presentation format for a webinar:

- Introduction and promises
- Problem
- Myths and changing
- Knife twist
- About us
- Solution
- –Three to seven points

The first section, up to the solution, is a free video tutorial talking through a subject. The next three to seven demo points are cut up and charged for. If you have a worksheet per lesson or point, too, that's even better. For example, we're a web site designer. Let's say we have a webinar on writing great search-engine-based content designed to help you climb Google's rankings.

The first section becomes the free video tutorial. We talk about the environment, Google, content, and what does and doesn't work. When we look at the main points, we can charge for access to all of them. Again, use a simple paywall and store your videos on Vimeo (great protection).

Offer a subscription. Moving past your core product, is there a way to make products after your core offering? Is there hidden profit past what most of your customers end up buying? Most customers want support when something goes wrong. We're not really buying just a web site; we're buying the support and updates to make sure it doesn't break.

Support, maintenance, and protection services are available for almost all products and services. Creating a subscription program or recurring payment product is going to become a core component of almost all businesses in the future. If you're building web sites, or even if you're a social consultant or SEO coach, you can offer plug-in updates and security sweeps, backups, reports, and small bug fixes. These are all things that you can provide to your customers that are recurring revenue opportunities for you in all businesses.

It's a relatively simple concept: What do your customers want every month? What is it that they need every week, or every four weeks, to keep their business running? Coaching and consulting over Skype is the fastest method of setting this up. Coaching calls can be fast, with relatively little setup, and you can record them for future customers. Scaling up, weekly group coaching, and webinars are great ways to reach multiple people. The cost can be lowered for all members and you reach a wider audience. Again, there is no need to overcomplicate the delivery.

Finally, automated protection and reporting can be built for almost any service. Accountability calls and workshops all offer huge value to businesses and customers that need your help. Aim for more and more recurring payments into your business, focusing less on one-off projects. If you have a one-off project, think about what customers would need after that to keep those results. The easiest way to think about recurring revenue products and subscriptions is to think "How can I help someone get those same results faster and with more automation? How can I protect those customers and give them peace of mind? Do they want those results every month?"

All web sites require maintenance and updates. Doing it yourself for every customer at first might be okay, but eventually you'll need to document the process and outsource it to someone else. Updates, maintenance, and security are all very repeatable processes. Most of the time we can write down step by step what happens to every site:

- Make a database backup once a day.
- Make a site backup once a week.
- Save the backup somewhere safe (offsite and cloud).
- Check core updates.
- Check plug-in updates.
- Run spam comment sweep.
- Run malware sweep.
- Security check.
- Upload new content.

This is a very brief overview of what a web site maintenance plan looks like. You might have your own additions. There are also tons of examples of other items to add in maintenance plans. Some people include SEO, link checks, content updates, social posting, and more. Once you've executed a few maintenance plans, start recording what you do. Make a list of what you do, in order. Make a screen recording of what you do in the same order.

This checklist and video can now become a process that you outsource. Finding cheap virtual assistance from $5 can work really well when you have a checklist and video process. Charge your customers per month, and set up a subscription plan or direct debit from PayPal or your bank. Offer a "no-contract" service that lets customers cancel anytime, with no tie-ins.

This scheme is very simple to set up and it doesn't require a huge amount of effort. Maintenance and security plans are where your business will find traction with repeat income. You can have various levels of service, with a basic package and a few more inclusive services, too.

Hire coaches. If you're delivering regular webinars and coaching, your audience gets used to hearing what you have to say. Even one new webinar every month is 12 a year. Sooner rather than later, you'll become bored teaching the same things over and over. To combat presentation fatigue, it's fantastic to have other people coach and present for you. We've seen several coaching and course models hire other coaches to present and give talks.

Just two extra coaches, paid per webinar, will take hours off your workload. Split the webinars among the three of you. Hire people with experience and passions different from yours. An SEO coach and a social coach will do wonders for the variety of content. Your customers will thank you for the change in pace and difference in presentation styles. Again, a lot of this boils down to process: What's the process for your presentations and webinars?

Have a slide deck and a method and order of presenting. Your external coaches will thank you for having a structure around your presenting. Some coaches might prefer to have their own presentation method. It's important to be flexible when taking people on. If you start every presentation or webinar with a roll call slide, or a weather update, then make sure your coaches include that. Otherwise, they might want a more free structure. For example, our presentations always follow the same format:

- Roll call
- Webinar headline
- Housekeeping
- Promise
- Agenda
- Main problem
- Myth
- What's changing
- Main teaching points (–three to seven actions)

The main teaching points are where we let our coaches have free reign. Some coaches prefer slides, whereas some prefer screen grabs or shares.

Removing yourself. The goal is to remove yourself from all choke points. All activities that require your input are taking time away from growing the business. As a business owner, even of a small or microbusiness, it's your job to grow the systems and processes that allow the business to grow. If you've attracted an audience and you're growing your customer base, think about how you can build platforms that let others deliver work for you.

If you have a regular blog to attract traffic and grow your e-mail list, do you need to write the content each time? Do you need to produce the reports or coach customers? Can someone else repeat what you do? Often when we think about having other people deliver the work to our customers, we think that no one else can do it. This really means that you're not confident in the brief or process you've got. Someone else couldn't follow it and get the same results.

Provide further reading. A model that's becoming more and more popular, in the veins of Jeff Walker, Ryan Deiss, and Mike Michalowicz (although there are many many others), is to provide further reading and materials from the e-books and regular books. If you've written a book, electronic or physical, think about how you can make someone transition from reader to subscriber. The book content guides readers through a process or a new technique. It spends time to educate and help them. Really, books are longer blog posts, or collections of blog posts.

If you want to really help your readers, offer them worksheets and exercises exclusive to the book. They can get access to extra help, hidden chapters, and raw interview content, all just by going to a designated web site. Think in terms of lead magnets: What would really help someone get results faster after reading this chapter? What are the key takeaways? Maybe offer a checklist at the end of a chapter or section that readers can follow along with, or a simple quiz at the end of a chapter with the answers on the web site.

Think about a companion web site to the book. Let the readers know that they can download exercises and worksheets specifically for the book. The readers can then follow along with the book, complete the exercises, and smash through their goals with you. It's worth noting that you don't have to do this with your first book. If you've released a book or e-book already, don't panic. You can always go back and add more content later, creating a version 2 and version3 of the book. It's also not a great idea to hold off on publishing just because you want to put worksheets in. Getting content out there and published is exponentially more important than waiting for slightly more content.

What to do, how to do, and you do it for me. Publishing free content, lead magnets, splinter products, and core products all follow a basic funnel structure. When people read our posts and buy our products, they're following a relationship path. First, they're understanding what they need to do. They know they have a problem, such as low sales or back pain. They search for free content via blogs and posts.

Then, they sign up to a lead magnet, or buy a small course product, something that doesn't cost a huge amount, but lets them invest in themselves. They'll be taught how to do something. They learn how to properly execute the steps covered in the blog posts or free videos. Finally, when they're ready to accelerate their results (and not every customer will be ready for that), they can ask you to do it for them.

This relationship pathway is important to remember. It gives you an idea of what to create next. What's interesting is that the relationship of what, how, and for me, is cyclical. Blog posts and videos might show a reader what to do, what they need to think about, and what steps they'll need to take. There might be some how-to steps, and the blog posts might even be a how-to guide. To grow our e-mail list, though, we want to think in terms of the relationship of what to how. How can I help someone get those same results faster? Even if the initial post is literally a how-to guide, if I think about what I teach them, how can I get them those same results faster? Your lead magnet then acts as the how to the earlier what, showing how to get those same results but faster and easier.

A checklist, a cheat sheet, an e-book: What can you do to show them how to get those same results? Think of it like a walkthrough or a guide. To complete the relationship, let's look at doing it for them. After we show them how to do something, we can say again, "If you want those same results faster and with less work from yourself, let us do it for you."

At this stage we can offer them, the customer, automation. They've been reading how to get higher search rankings on Google. You've showed them exactly how to do it, and how you'd do it even. Now, though, we can look at doing it for them. It's a lot of work and effort for someone to execute a process themselves. We're providing them with the exact same goals we've got: automation for their business. As I mentioned, though, it's cyclical. When we're doing the work for them, think about the results they're getting. What are you helping them with? How can you get further results?

For example, let's say you've set up an SEO subscription for a customer. Every month they pay $300 to drive the rankings of their site up in Google. They're after more traffic, so would it be worth showing them what they can do to increase traffic? Could you show them what their options are with social, PPC, remarketing, and e-mail? Then you can start the cycle again. Start with what they're getting and what to do. Show them how to do it and end with you doing it for them.

Affiliate Marketing

Affiliate marketing and self-liquidating offers (SLOs) have had a bad rap recently, although I'm not sure why. Some people just like to steer clear of the whole situation. Don't let that put you off, though. Affiliate marketing is really just an extension of how natural marketing and sales works. People that trust you, within your network, want to promote your product to their audience. Affiliate marketing means you give other businesses and customers a cut for each sale they make. For example, if you have a course at $97, you can offer other businesses a cut of 30% or $10, or whatever, every time they sell your product.

SLOs work in a similar fashion, but they're better suited to lower cost products, as you give 100% of the sale to the seller. The idea is that if you make a sale to a customer—they buy a $10 e-book or splinter product, for example—you've now got a qualified customer. They're clearly interested in your area of expertise and you know they're willing to buy. If I just had those types of leads come in, I'd be a happy man. So, if I say to my customers who have bought that book, "I'll give you 100% of the sale for every sale you make," they'll see it as a great deal. I am acquiring customers for free.

I no longer have to pay for traffic or advertising, as my customer base is doing it for me. My list not only grows, but it's full of people who have bought my product. They're better qualified and they obviously like my content. It's much easier to sell them my future products, as they already know me and trust me. I've skipped an enormous part of customer acquisition and potentially acquired customers for free. There are plug-ins and web sites that easily allow you to create affiliate marketing and SLO sales. Warrior Forum is a great place to look, or WooCommerce Affiliates Pro.

Sell your old content. Finally, another product option is to take your current templates, blog posts, books, transcripts, and processes and "white-label" them. This means removing your branding, logo, and company name from the material and selling it as a blank slate. People love white-labeled content, as it means less work for them. Similar to what we talked about in Chapter 3, we can white-label our own content to sell, even putting it on marketplaces for other to see and use.

You can create marketplaces, plug-ins, apps, or just plain documents that sell your content, ready for others to use and promote, but it has nothing to do with you.

Summary

As you can see, there is a process to creating scalable products. You might have found yourself right at the start of the process, or somewhere in the middle. The key is to keep reminding yourself that you can always repurpose and reuse content.

- Work out what benefits and results your customers get first.
- Remove yourself from the process and create content that can reach more people.
- Record and document that content before changing the delivery platform.
- Increase the price the more results the customers get from the content or product.

CHAPTER 5

Creating Content for a Scalable Product

I truly hate the word *content*; it's dry and it doesn't have context. It's overused and most important, it's like creating a product. You can build as many widgets as you like, but if you're not promoting and sharing them, no one is going to buy. However, we have to create helpful, valuable content that attracts readers, converts leads, and makes sales.

Online, free content such as blog posts and videos are a core part of a content marketing strategy for online scaled businesses. The beauty is that you can write a handful of stellar pieces and they'll work in the background for you. Apply some heavy SEO and PPC to those posts and you've got an attraction strategy. How do we think of the topics and subjects that our customers want to read, though?

If we're writing free blog posts to give away, they should be good enough and of high enough quality that current customers would want to read them. The days of writing every day or every week, just to grow your SEO channel, are ending. To get attention and keep your readers' attention is harder than ever. Finally, all your blog content needs to capture e-mail addresses and data from traffic to grow your list.

© Michael Killen 2019
M. Killen, *From Single to Scale*, https://doi.org/10.1007/978-1-4842-3814-1_5

10 Topics

This content exercise is the fastest way to generate more than 100 content ideas. Incidentally, these ideas can be turned into products, services, posts, videos, presentations, lead magnets ... you name it. We start by looking at your before/after list and thinking about the 10 broad topics within your business that would help customers. If you'd like to use our worksheet for this exercise, just head to singletoscale.com/10.

Some of the topics might be focused on the before section, others on the after section, and a final selection on the gap between before and after. For example, if we're an e-commerce web site developer, our before list might include low revenue, low e-mail subscribers, and no promotion strategy. The after part would show regular repeat sales, a growing e-mail list, and a well-received promotion strategy.

So 10 broad topics could be the following:

- E-mail list growth
- E-mail marketing
- E-commerce store marketing
- Managing products
- E-commerce traffic
- Sales optimization
- Social marketing
- SEO traffic
- Content marketing
- Productivity and effectiveness

We call this exercise the 10 x 10. We're not going to use every idea, but it will give us the clarity and ideas needed to execute a promotion and content plan for us as freelancers, consultants, and single-person microbusinesses.

10 Subtopics

Once we've got our main topics, it's time to get specific. What we're writing down and listing now are subtopics that could become individual pieces of content. Don't worry about the delivery method or titles yet. We'll get to that. What we're listing now are the points that we can help people with.

It's important to know that the reason this works so well, as a planning process, is because it automatically creates funnels. If we have subtopic ideas for e-mail marketing, for example, we've got enough ideas for blog content, lead magnets, splinter products, and probably a core product, and maybe a repeat, membership, or subscription product, too. Start writing down the 10 subtopics under each topic. Be as specific as you like. Think in terms of steps and stages of that problem. We need 10 subtopics under each topic, giving us 100 content ideas and something to focus on. For example, taking the broad topic from earlier—e-mail marketing—the subtopic list might look like this:

- Subject lines
- E-mail design
- MailChimp
- CRM systems
- E-mail automation
- Sending to customers
- Sending to leads
- E-mail sales
- Mobile e-mail
- Traffic driving e-mails

At the moment these subtopics won't have much shape or form, but they will be useful to your audience. For each subtopic, ask yourself, "Would members of my audience need or want to know about this, if they want to look like the after list?" After you've written down all your ideas, it's also useful to give an audit of that content. For example, if you already have posts about your subtopics, mark that down as complete. This would include blog posts, videos, lead magnets, products, services, presentations, books, splinter products, or anything else that your audience or customers could consume. I find that people have a spread of subtopics, across a 10 x 10, but no real connection between the pieces. There might be five posts on e-mail marketing but no lead magnet, or a product under all topics, but no promotion above it. We want to see how your content grid or landscape looks, and how it's all connected.

After writing down our 10 subtopics, we're going to make the creation much easier than just writing 100 blog posts (no one wants to do that). Finally, don't think you're going to create every single one of these posts. What we need to do now is take the initial core or flagship product and focus on that. Maybe that product stretches across a few topics. Deciding on two subtopics for blog content and a third for a lead magnet and publishing is 100 times more effective than trying to write 10 posts at once. The key to growth as a single-person or microbusiness is connecting activities; not just doing one activity, but connecting the pathway between each action.

All 10 of the next exercises can be done for each subtopic, meaning that you could do it up to 10 times. Identify one subtopic under your main topics and mark it down as a blog post roundup.

Blog post roundup. A blog post roundup is itself a blog post that looks at –five to seven (or more) blog posts on other web sites and writes a short summary of that post. Let's take the subtopic of subject lines, for example. I just need to Google and search for around 10 blog posts on writing better subject lines: how to write high open rate subject lines, how they affect sales and clicks, different types of subject lines, and so on.

What we now do is write our post, with a short introduction. Our main copy, though, comes from copying and pasting a link, image, quote, or statistic and post title into our own post. Do this at least five times, but up to 10 is optimal. If we do any more, we risk looking like a link spam post, and people won't read them all anyway. What we're doing is taking expert posts on how subject lines affect e-commerce businessesand using the interesting parts of each to create an easy to consume and easy to write post.

We've got e-commerce stores as our customers, subject lines as our useful subtopic, and expert opinions as our hook. Maybe you've found posts on mistakes people make with e-mail subject lines. Maybe you've found information on how subject lines increase open rates. Write up a short summary per post, but have a quote from the post, too. Take an image from the post and insert that, use the title as a header, and remember to link back to that original post. If you find seven useful posts, use the following structure for your title:

> Seven experts tell you exactly how e-mail subject lines need to be written to increase your open rates.

or

> What seven e-mail experts tell e-commerce businesses to write as subject lines to increase sales.

As with any content, you just want proof to back up your statement. If you can find a quote from each post, supporting what to do for e-commerce sales, then you're golden.

YouTube roundup. This is similar to the blog post roundup. Choose a subtopic and find around 10 YouTube videos that talk about your subtopic. It's almost the same process as the blog post roundup: Write a short summary for each video, include the video title, and include a quote, but this time embed the video on your post. Video content does wonders for SEO, plus it's more likely readers will stay on your page if you've got the other content embedded on your site.

Use the same title structure for the post roundup. Include an introduction and promote it. Interestingly, if you reach out to the post or video creators, mention that they're on your post. They're at least likely to tweet you. By introducing ourselves properly, we've had authors send our post to their list.

Book review. This is similar to the post roundup, but take something a bit meatier and look at books. People love a good book review. Choosing a few books to talk about gives you some serious media to discuss. Book reviews are easiest when you're talking about them. Get in front of the camera and have a conversation.

Choose three books within a subtopic (or at least e-books) and read them. There is no need to go into great depth if you don't have the time. Speed read the chapters and highlight a few sections that really speak to you. As with the blog post roundup, we want a couple of quotes, a link, the book title, and images (if there are any). You'll find many books published now have companion blog post sites. This gives you access to images, written copy, links, and profiles. When reviewing a book, focus on five key areas:

- Was the book easy to read?
- The author's experience and context.
- Who else has read the book?
- Biggest takeaway.
- Personal opinion on the book.

Just talk through those points; there is no need for a heavy script. You can then top and tail the review of each book with a title, link, quote, and web site.

If you get the recording transcribed, that makes for an easy second piece of content. Again, if you mention or reach out to authors, they'll likely give you at least a short tweet in return.

How-to guide. This is the most common type of written blog post out there. How-to guides are incredibly useful and easy to create. The problem comes, however, from what we, as businesses, think our readers want to consume. Often, as experts, we think people are searching for process guides or how-to guides on actions; for example, how to optimize your blog post page for Google searches. It is true that some of your more experienced readers might be searching for specific action guides, but the title and implication for that post does not incite traffic clicks. If we think about our before/after list, what are the before and after that you can associate with a subtopic?

What is the process or steps that people need to take to get to that after status? What is one of the ways people can get to that after status? Structure your blog post title and format around helping people get to after, rather than a technical how-to guide on an action. "How E-Commerce Businesses Know

They've Had More Traffic, from Google, Every Month" is a far more interesting post title, than "How to Search Optimize Your Posts." It could be that some of the steps are from a how-to guide on optimizing your blog posts, but people want to read posts that help them do better, not expend time, energy, and money on an action. Make the post especially valuable with content upgrades, worksheets, and light-bulb moments (also called lead magnets).

Video process. A step above a how-to guide is a video process. It's like a user guide or walkthrough of a solution. You'll need some screen capture software such as Camtasia or Screen Flow to record a capture of what's happening on your screen, while you record a voice-over with a microphone. There are a couple of ways of doing video guides, and both ultimately get you the same results. We want a video that someone can watch, follow the voice-over instructions, and complete a task alongside.

Most people will watch a walkthrough video once then open it up again and follow along. You can record a video guide in a similar fashion. Video guides are wonderful demonstrators of knowledge and expertise. Even tasks that you believe are simple can be turned into short video guides. People need help with all sorts of activities.

This is also where video guides excel. Whereas how-to guides are great introductions to process, people usually want results- or benefits-focused guides. Video guides are perfect for people searching for action terms. Here are some examples:

- How to search optimize a blog post.
- How to publish an e-book.
- How to search and research your competitors' keywords.

Think of a subtopic and something for which you can do a walkthrough. Essentially, it's a training video. What would you do if you were talking someone through this, face to face? In what follows I present two ways of recording a video guide. However, before recording anything, it's a good idea to go through the process as a dry run. Be conscious of the steps you're taking. If necessary, take notes of the steps you're following. You'll need them when you're going through the video.

The first method is to set up the screen capture and microphone (you could use a webcam, too) to record all at the same time. Talk through the process you're performing in real time and explain what you're doing. The advantage of this method is that it's very fast. The disadvantage is that sometimes the quality is hard to keep up. You might find you trail off and don't explain things clearly.

The other method is to record the screen without the microphone recording. Just record the steps and keep that video. Then, record a voice- over of you going through the steps. Most professional video guides use this method.

It does take longer to create, but the results often sound much better. My advice would be to just start recording with your voice and screen at the same time. Get used to edit points, removing "ums" and "ahs" and publishing video content. If it's bad (and your first few will be), you can always rerecord it at a later date.

Interview. This is the easiest method on the planet of creating content. Take a subtopic and find someone to talk to about it. Interview them on the subject and record the conversation. If they're happy to have the audio or video published, then you just got yourself a sweet video interview. You can still transcribe the audio into a blog post as well. If you can interview people regularly, you just got yourself a podcast format.

Use the following e-mail template to secure an interview.

> Hey [name]
>
> I'm looking to interview an expert in [topic/subtopic] and I'd love the opportunity to ask you a few questions.
>
> I know you're a [prevalent blogger, industry expert, local hero] and my customers could really benefit from your experience.
>
> I know you must get loads of these requests, but it'd mean a lot if I could get 45 minutes of your time.
>
> [sign off]

The six basic questions to ask any interviewee are the following:

- What's your experience with this subtopic?
- What do people need to know to get started with this subtopic?
- Why should people be thinking about this now?
- What's the big problem you're solving or this topic can solve?
- What's the benefit from solving this problem?
- What's a common misconception about this topic?

Either get them on Skype or Zoom and record the conversation, or do it old school with a pen and paper. Send them the questions ahead of schedule and try to keep to a 45-minute length. Even a 20-minute video interview is long enough for people to watch.

Bust a myth. When it comes to very popular subtopics, your customers might have ideas about what works already. Every job and profession has myths and misconceptions about it. When we tell customers to take a certain action, such as stretching or pay-per-click advertising, they'll already have objections as to why that won't work for them. Usually these objections are founded on myths that come from previous bad experience or friends and family telling them something.

We have an excellent opportunity to overcome objections before our readers even convert to customers. It also gives us a wonderful post to send to people who are on the fence. Think about the big misconceptions around your subtopic. This can be cut up in a few ways (and there's no reason you have to stick with just one). How do people without experience try to solve this problem? What have you seen people do when they don't talk to you, that doesn't work? What's something that everyone takes for granted? Or assumes is true? For example, being on page one of Google results for a search term does not guarantee you more traffic. What's something that other professionals in your industry say or think is true? What do they teach their customers that isn't true? What did people usually do to solve the problem? Is there a better way? For instance, before Uber, you'd call a cab, wait in the cold or for a phone call, and then have no idea if they were taking you the right way. Now, you can see when the Uber will arrive, know how long it'll take, and pay by phone.

You could either create a list post (e.g., five things you thought you knew about SEO) or focus on one myth and explore why people think that, why it isn't true, and what the truth is. It helps if you can link to proof or link to other people saying the same thing. Opinions are fine, but when it comes to overcoming objections and myths, evidence is going to help even more.

Templates and examples. We talk about lead magnets, light-bulb moments, and content upgrades a lot. The idea is that if we help people with some valuable resources, they'll sign up or take an action that we want them to take. If you want to create a seriously useful blog post, take the subtopic you've got and provide templates or examples to readers for free. Think in the same terms as lead magnets: worksheets and templates, resources, or cheat sheets. Just give them away with no opt-ins or signups. It's more a show of good faith than anything, showing that all you want to do is help. If you create genuinely useful content, that gives value away to people, they'll appreciate it.

Businesses that know what they're doing give away the farm. Rather than protect it and horde information or resources like they're scarce, they share them with people. It doesn't have to be tons of stuff. In fact, research shows that too much content given away can overwhelm people. Choose two or three specific examples that you're happy for other people to download. You don't have to skip an opt-in or signup form completely, but free, no-opt-in resources go a long way toward building goodwill.

The free resources don't have to be worksheets or cheat sheets, either, or even be accessed via a link. You can just include the text for things like e-mails, training plans, questions for clients, and so on. A good example of giving away templates is the WP Elevation blog post available at wpelevation.com/2016/08/first-steps-email-marketing. It gives away e-mail templates, inside the blog post, with no opt-in. Alternatively, at the end, users can download a Google document with the e-mails via a link. Just copy and paste the text from the blog post and you're good to go.

Explorer Posts

Explorer posts are essentially the opening stages of a sales letter. The first half of the copy is designed to pique interest and grab the readers' attention. It's a good habit to get into, writing sales copy. We're not writing sleazy car advertisements or infomercial scripts. A sales letter is a series of steps, designed to bypass people's brain block against spending money. What's even better is that once you can write an explorer post, you can write a sales letter.

The headings are as follows:

- Promise.
- Problem.
- Myth.
- What's changing?
- What do most people do?
- What to do differently.
- Next steps.

Promise

Make a bold, clear, and specific promise to readers about this post: "I promise that …." For example, if you're going to help them lose weight without going to the gym more, promise that: "I promise I'm going to show you how to lose weight without going to the gym more." Obviously you can't promise that they will lose weight, but you can promise you'll show them how to do it. People are hesitant to make promises. They think it's like a guarantee or that customers will get mad if they don't deliver. If you're not comfortable making a promise about your business, or content, though, you probably shouldn't be in business. Don't promise the world, but promise on what you can deliver.

Problem

Outline the problem that this post is going to solve. Use problems and goal language, things that your customers want. What's the big roadblock facing their business or themselves? What are they trying to solve?

> *The problem is ... we need to drive more and more traffic to our web sites. But Google and social media don't seem to be delivering the results we need. Our web sites need more traffic and SEO and social media might not be the answer.*

People relate to problems. They see roadblocks and problems as where they are now. It's easier to identify with problems than with where they want to be.

Myth

What's a common misconception about this problem? What do most people get it wrong or assume? We covered this previously, but we're just providing a summary here.

> *Most people believe that ... growing your Twitter following means buying followers or following thousands of other people. In fact, most people believe that growing a social following is key to their business's growth, without thinking if that's really true.*

What's Changing?

Explain to the reader what's changing in your industry. They need to know what's changing because it tells them (1) what they need to be aware of and what's dangerous out there, and (2) what they can take advantage of in the future.

Focus on three areas: technological, economic, and sociological. What's changing, for better or worse, with the technology surrounding this problem or subtopic? What's changing with the economy, money, or spending habits with this topic? What's changing positively or negatively with people and society, with this topic?

> *SEO is changing. It's now no longer about keywords and ranking for all search terms. It's about creating quality content that people like to read.*
>
> *More and more people are spending money online, and if you're not providing easy access to your services from your web site, people will go elsewhere.*
>
> *Your customers expect you to be helpful earlier in the relationship now. If you can't match their expectations, they'll go somewhere else.*

What Do Most People Do?

Write a paragraph about what most people or businesses in your industry do to solve this problem. Highlight what might be making the problem worse. What were customers doing before they used you? What do most blogs and sites say to do, but you think isn't the best solution?

What to Do Differently

Explain to your readers what they need to do differently. What steps should they take if they really want to solve this problem? It doesn't have to be long; –three to seven points is plenty. You could even mix in some of the other post types with quotes, interviews, or embedded videos. Break down the steps into small, manageable pieces. Don't overwhelm people with content, because if it is too much for them, they'll drop off.

Next Steps

What do people need to do next? In a sales letter, this would be where we'd start putting Order and Buy buttons. For our post, though, a lead magnet should suffice. Tell people if they're serious about the problem or potential result, they should sign up and download your extra content. It's always important to try and move people onto the next piece of content or stage. Insert your booking details or a contact form, whatever gets people to start taking action.

Lead magnet. Rather than creating a post for the final subtopic, create a lead magnet that gives away some serious value. Remember, this is not just about providing tons of content. Creating a lead magnet that solves a problem fast, or with less effort, is more valuable. Think about saving people time, money, and energy. That's what lead magnets are really about.

The subtopic could be a mini-course, a series of worksheets, or a guide. What we're trying to do is create something valuable but still protect it, so people can sign up and take advantage of it. If you have a product or content that people usually pay for, say you're giving it away for free. Say it's an experiment and you're looking for feedback. Ask people to comment on what they thought of it.

Repurpose Written Content

When we talk about repurposing content, we mean taking something we've already written and recycling it for a new reason: a different medium, a different audience, adding something new to it, and so on. One of the easiest methods of repurposing content is to take a written blog post and use the text as a script. Record a video with slides and images and do a voice-over with the script.

You can publish videos to YouTube or Vimeo, but also remember to embed them in a blog post and share them again. Content that's timeless can be repurposed a few months later, providing an update to the older content.

Welcome e-mails. When visitors opt in to your e-mail list, you need to send them a welcome e-mail shortly after they sign up. One of the first e-mails you need to send, this welcome e-mail should include your contact details. There is no need to put several e-mail addresses, phone numbers, and a home address, but a contact e-mail, Twitter handle, and Facebook group mean you're opening the routes where people can contact you.

Why is this in the chapter on creating content for a scalable product? Creating automated e-mails like this is a huge part of sending valuable content to your audience. We're not thinking of more blog posts, we're thinking of where people are in their journey. They've just signed up to our list, so it's the perfect time to introduce ourselves and make it as easy as possible to reach out. If you want to scale content, think about all the content that you create, post, and promote: e-mails, blog posts, tweets, Facebook posts, and so on. It all needs to be able to scale. This means that people need to reach and view your content without you personally sending anything. Welcome e-mails are a great example of this.

Send old content to new leads. Once you've published a few posts and you've got a library of content, start putting older posts inside e-mails and e-mail automation. For example, let's say you have five posts on search engine marketing (SEM). If someone signs up to your latest SEM post, he or she needs to be added to a specific group or tag within your newsletter. If someone has signed up to your SEM posts, it's reasonable to assume that he or she wants to know more about SEM, so why not send that person your older SEM posts?

Automate your e-mail service to send your older blog content to people who have signed up to a lead magnet on the same subject. E-mail automation services have become extremely sophisticated in recent years. A little know-how can automate your e-mail to select posts from a certain topic or subject, and send those out on automation, ignoring the post that your opt-in signed up to.

Use Buzzsumo. Let's do a little research and see what people want to view. Head over to Buzzsumo.com and throw in a few subjects, topics, and keywords to see the most popular and shared posts on the Internet. You can export results, paying close attention to the three key parts of "viral" content: post title, post media (video, infographic, etc.) and the content itself.

Research the posts that are getting shared heavily within your industry, and look at these three features. Use the search tool to really understand what people are searching for and sharing. Are people actually that interested in your topic? The reality is that some topics are never going to get the shares that cat videos and celebrity wardrobe malfunctions are going to get. However, that doesn't mean it can't go viral within your own community or industry. First, though, we have to understand why things are shared.

How to Get More Shares

One of the key components to people sharing content, which means you are promoted without doing anything yourself, is the ease of sharing. This might sound obvious, but making it easy to share with widgets is key to getting shares. Don't spam visitors with hundreds of share widgets, but make it easy for people to post and share your content.

Next, posts are shared because they're easy to understand. People share things that they think their audience and network will enjoy and connect with. Use Buzzsumo to see why some posts are shared more than others. It's also important to know that people share things they think will give them recognition.

Promote three times a day. This is really a minimum standard. Any new content that you produce needs to be heavily promoted. What tends to happen is people write a new blog post, share it a little on social media, and then move on to the next piece. Your content is one of your products, and it needs to have more effort put into promotion than creating it. If you owned a shop that made widgets and every week you made a different widget and promoted it only a little, you'd be seen as crazy.

This is why it's important to focus on quality. You need to be confident that what you've produced is useful. Having one blog post that's exceptionally useful is far more important than loads of posts that are just there for the sake of it. You should spend 20 times the effort promoting content that you spend creating it. At an absolute minimum, you need to be posting and promoting it three times a day for a week, across different channels. Even then, if you're serious about growing your audience, you should invest in other audience traction methods, such as PPC, paid, social media, and so on.

Choose three different channels that you want to go after; for example, Reddit, Twitter, Facebook, SEO, e-mail, Google Ads, Pinterest. Choose whatever best suits your audience and post your content across three channels per day. After a week, promote it once a day for a month across one channel per day. There are tons of tools you can use to automate this. Postcron, Hootsuite, and Sprout social are all tools that you can use to schedule and automate your posting process. The key to this exercise is to get used to spending effort promoting rather than creating. Creating is extremely valuable, but it's only half the battle. You need to promote or you'll never gain any traction.

Update content. Post updates are a great way to keep a blog post timeless. For example, if you published a post last year about SEO and how to reach an audience with Google, a lot might have changed in 12 months. Or if you started and sent a campaign that was very successful, and a few months roll by, you might want to update readers as to the results of that campaign. You could publish a new post and call it a second edition, or just update the original post and draw attention to it being updated: Updated for 2017! For an idea on what that looks like, check out Digital Marketers post on Blog Post Ideas (http://www.digitalmarketer.com/blog-post-ideas/).

Collect Testimonials

Testimonials are important to businesses because they act as your social proof. It's feedback from clients asking for what they thought. You can use them as quotes, case studies, and videos. Collecting testimonials always seems like a bit of a roadblock. I've noticed that a lot of businesses are unsure of how to collect testimonials.

The easiest way is to ask questions. Asking people to give a testimonial will result in few actual testimonials because people don't know what to write. If you book a quick 10-minute call with them, tell them you're going to ask them about their experience, and record it, it'll be much easier. Book a call and ask these five questions:

- In a couple of sentences, what would you tell other [target customer] about what [product] has done for you?
- What was your biggest takeaway from [product]?
- What was your main concern that would have prevented you from buying this [type of product] and what put your fears to rest?
- What would you tell someone who was on the fence?
- What was your biggest problem that you tried to solve with [product name]?

Then ask if you can use the recording and their quote. They likely be more than happy to give permission.

Sales Letter Style Content

To write long-form, high-quality content, you need to think of selling the post. Think about writing a piece of such high quality that people would pay to read it. It sounds harder than it is. All you need to do is open the long-form blog post with a sales letter. Think of the problem you're solving and write a sales letter style introduction to solve that problem. A sales letter is similar to a presentation in terms of format:

- What's the headline?
- Make a promise.
- What's the problem you're solving?
- What's a myth about the problem or solution?
- What's changing in the world, for better or worse?
- Give a knife twist: "And to top it all off …." Give another roadblock or problem.
- Outline the solution, and tell them what you're going to do.
- Introduce yourself and why you're qualified to talk on this.
- Talk through the results and what they'll be able to do.
- Go into the solution in detail.

The idea is that people reading the post won't realize they're being sold to, and technically they're not. What we're doing is explaining to them things that they recognize and see. They connect with the introduction and are then rewarded with a long-form, high-quality blog post telling them how to solve the problem.

This could be a how-to guide, a series of video guides, explainers, or anything else. What we are doing is giving away a huge guide on how to complete something and solve a problem. You could include worksheets and PDFs that aren't protected (lead magnets without the opt-in), which sounds insane, but we're building huge levels of trust here. Absolutely include a lead magnet with an opt-in, but of course make it specific to the blog post.

Epic killer content. Go through some of your popular and older content, and look at creating a longer form blog post using several other pieces. If there is a subject that ties them all together, think about structuring an ultimate guide using all those pieces. What is the overall result that someone could achieve if they read all four of your posts on SEO? Maybe outrank their competitors? Multiply their web site traffic tenfold in six months?

An easy way to understand what people would get if they read all of the posts is to make a list of what people can do when they read individual posts:

- Post 1: Optimizing blog posts. Result: More traffic from Google to their blog.
- Post 2: Building links. Result: More referral traffic from other web site.
- Post 3: Choosing keywords. Result: Rank on page 1 for 10 long-tail, niche keywords.
- Post 4: Improving your page ranking. Result: Outranking your competitors.

Chapter 5 | Creating Content for a Scalable Product

Combined, we can teach people how to generate more traffic from Google to their blog. They'll get more free referral traffic and outrank their competitors. That's what the ultimate post is for. If you further narrow down and select a target customer, a problem, and a time scale, you've got yourself an epic, ultimate, killer post. For example:

> The ultimate SEO guide for accountants with three-year-old web sites who want to generate more traffic from Google for free and outrank their competition. All without spending a penny on PPC.

Is this a long title? Maybe. If that was presented to 1,000 accountant businesses, though, I promise you it would have a high click rate. You then break the larger post into chapters. Within each chapter, you have smaller blog posts. If you include worksheets and PDFs as downloads, too, you'll be amazed at how valuable the content is. Now promote that post constantly. Do nothing but drive traffic to that one post for months. This is your flagship piece, the killer piece that separates you from your competition.

Podcast roundup. A fast, easy, and great-looking blog post is a podcast roundup. Check out the podcasts in your market and industry and write up a short summary for each. Take –five to seven podcasts (or more if you want) and create a summary list of them all. Tell your audience why they should listen, why you like them, and which is the best episode. If you want an example, check out sellyourservice.co.uk/2016/08/6-best-business-based-podcasts-for-wordpress-businesses-to-listen-to/

The reason I love this type of post is because you can easily tag and contact the podcast owners about being on your list. Reach out to them and ask them to share the post. They'll usually be more than happy to.

Use GIFs. If you've got a webinar with a series of steps on completing a goal, make your "how-to guides" pop even more by cutting the video into small GIFs. Short 5- to 15-second GIF videos do wonders for explaining a step. It's like a how-to guide with motion steps. For each step that you explain and write out, illustrate that stage with an animated GIF. Similar to a screenshot or image, it adds motion to your post. It's very hard to ignore something that moves. Humans are drawn to motion and if your how-to guides and processes need illustrated content, why not add motion to them?

Round up your posts. A nice end-of-the-year post is to round up your most popular posts and create a list of them. Take a look at your analytics, or what you want to promote, and make a list of those posts. Include the title, publishing date, a link (obviously), and a summary of the post. You could also include an image, too, if there is one.

Send the content out to your current subscribers and to new people who sign up. There's great power in hand-holding new subscribers through your content. Explain that you have a lot of stuff to read, so it makes sense to show people your most popular material. Even better, if you're producing enough content, you can do top 10 posts per subject. Let's not get ahead of ourselves, though. Creating a top 5, 10, or 20 of your own posts is a very fast way to produce a post. It's easy to mail out and people like to see if their favorite is on there. It's not something that unknown people are really going to read. It's closer to something you could send after having a relationship with your subscribers or customers.

Product demos. One of our most popular posts ever was a series of three videos showing people what they got inside one of our products. I was always told that product demos and screen shares aren't that popular, and that people only want to see them if they're buying. According to my analytics, that's nonsense.

What we've found is that people want to understand what they get when they buy. A friend of mine explained that it's like the infomercial that sells fitness DVDs and equipment. They'll do a shot (very tacky in my opinion) of each DVD, the books, bonus content, equipment, and so on, adding new items each sentence. People can visualize what they'll actually be receiving. For service-based businesses, this might sound harder than it is. We've already got an overview of our process, so what are those items?

Sometimes a webinar-style demo or an overview of each thing they'll get is exactly what people want to see. We gave a demo of the resource page of an information product we sold. We just recorded the screen and highlighted each item, spending a few minutes explaining what it was and how users could benefit from it. We showed training videos, downloads, templates, documents, and the resource page. People loved it. We then gave away the first user guide video showing what people would literally be doing with that product.

For service-based industries, whatever process you go through is the demo video. Talk about the initial consultation, the traction coaching, the market research, the three-hour workshops, the web site design, the development, the testing, and so on. Sometimes people like something tangible and it's a bit like a sneak peek. People like a "behind the scenes" view of something.

Transcribe the videos. Now we can take those videos, head on over to Rev.com, and get them transcribed. You just created the features and benefits section of a sales letter. You'll be surprised at how much you're offering when it's listed for you.

Again, this makes a great "Okay, what's actually in the box?" post, or a sales page if you're sending people those. Take the list of what people get and include that in any future sales letters. Take the benefits and your explanation of why that feature is useful, and that's your benefits section.

Tool roundup. Tool and resource list posts are very powerful. They're easy to create and people love to devour them. "The 15 most essential tools that accountants need if they want more traffic to their web site," for example, is easily understood, has a clear audience, and is easy to produce.

Make a list of 10 to 20 tools and resources that you'd recommend to your market and audience. You might want to scour forums and groups to see what they use. Ask people what they use, too. E-mail your list and ask them to refer their favorite tools.

Cloud software, apps, software as a service, and downloads all make for compelling reasons to read. People like to buy shiny objects and you're making a definitive list as to what they should get. Include the name of the tool and the company that makes it, along with a link, a logo, and a short summary of what it is.

You might even want to break the tools list into different sections for keyword research, analytics, conversions, and so on. Break the whole list into smaller chunks. Don't say you've used a tool if you haven't. Be honest and talk about why it comes recommended. If you have used a tool, talk about it. If it's a tool that you couldn't live without, let people know why. Again, this is a fantastic outreach method, as you can reach out, tag, and contact companies that make your list. They'll happily share your content with their audience if you're specific about who it helps and why it's on the list.

Networking Lunch

One of the easiest methods of discovering and creating content is a live event. What's even better is that it doesn't have to be a huge deal. If you can get four people to a small lunch and offer to talk them through a subject, they'll happily spend some time with you. If you want to go larger (which isn't tough), reach out to networking events and coworking spaces to give a talk for free. It only needs to be 20 minutes and you can have time at the end for Q&A.

The questions that people ask are perfect for new customers and subscribers. Record their questions and your answers. Get the whole thing transcribed and publish the post. Even better, a video recording of that would make a great lead magnet: "See behind the scenes at the whole event and watch the presentation." Finding 20 or so people to attend a lunch is not hard. It's just boring. Do some Googling and search for people who it makes sense to give this talk to. The goal is not necessarily to sell to these 20 people. The goal is to present to them and use the presentation and recording as content.

Find 20 people, get their e-mail, and reach out. Don't use a mass mailer; use your e-mail and explain what you want to do. Make it authentic. Say you're not pitching, it's a free event, you are providing some free food (or drink), and you just want to meet some people. Give a date, a time, and the subject. You'll be surprised how many people attend.

FAQ and SAQ. Following on from a Q&A session, two great pieces of content are frequently asked questions (FAQs) and should as questions (SAQs). Pick a subject and make a list of the questions people always ask about this subject. When you introduce yourself and talk to new customers, they'll often have the same questions that come up again and again. Check your e-mails from people looking for advice and see what they ask. Often you'll have more frequent questions than you realize.

Also, think about what people usually think to themselves, but maybe don't ask: How much does it cost? How easy is it? Scour forums and groups, searching for common questions and advice that people are asking for. Then, make a list of those questions and answer them.

Finally, make sure to create an SAQs post, too, which includes 15 questions you should ask if you want more traffic to your web site. Often, this is more insightful to your customers because they don't know what they don't know. Make a list of 10 things you wish people knew before working with you. Make a list of another 10 questions that you ask your customer on a new project. Those 20 questions are probably part of your process. By simply asking them and answering them, you've got a beautiful worksheet for customers who sign up. It also makes great blog content.

Summary

Hopefully you can begin to see a pattern here. It all starts with a core message or result. We're just trying to help people achieve something or solve a problem. The trick is to then translate that content into other formats for people to consume.

- Create a 10 x 10 topic and subtopic matrix and use it to create your own content.
- Interview others, record talks, and transcribe videos for future written blog content.
- Share and promote your content with others.
- Continue to reuse and repurpose older content into new formats.

CHAPTER 6

Building a Larger Audience

In this chapter we're going to create an audience that listens to us, knows who we are, and most important, trusts us. Although content might help someone who already knows who we are, we must build out that audience of people who want to continue hearing from us. At its core, we'll be building an e-mail list and remarketing lists. We'll also be capturing e-mail addresses and contact information to communicate with our audience later.

We're Building Two Lists

We need to build a larger audience to scale our business. One of the problems micro- and single-person businesses face is that their potential audience is much larger than they're allowing. Typically, we promote our posts and some curated content via Twitter and Facebook, maybe other social channels, and we grow a few followers. Actively scaling our audience is a different process, though. It's not happenstance, it's strategic work designed to build two outcomes.

Those two outcomes are the two different lists we're building. These are not two lists in one system, but two totally different lists on two totally different platforms. Both are vital to the growth and scale of a business. Both also require a similar strategy to grow them. It's how they grow and what we get from each list that's so different. The two lists we're building are an e-mail list and a remarketing list.

Chapter 6 | Building a Larger Audience

We used to just grow our e-mail list. Then remarketing and social advertisements meant that we started to build a remarketing list. Now we need to actively grow our remarketing list because how we send traffic to our site differs from how we have sent traffic in the past. E-mail lists and remarketing lists are both fantastic for launches, promotions, and product sales.

E-mail lead database list. Our e-mail list is categorically important to our business. It's our data, and we can use it how we need. At absolute worst, we can download a `.csv` file and e-mail people manually. E-mail lists are fantastic for building trust and automating a campaign. If someone signs up, we can talk to them, follow them through a process, and talk to them about how we can help. We're in control of how our e-mails are sent, where they're sent, and how often people will see us. I can see names, phone numbers, addresses, how often they've bought, and more. Your e-mail list is imperative to the growth of your business.

However, it's also hard to build an e-mail list because of the barrier to entry. People need to have trust in you before they hand over their e-mail address. Sure, you'll offer them a lead magnet, but is everyone going to sign up right away? Here's what's interesting about people taking action—signing up, buying, or whatever. Even if they're 90% ready to take that action, they still won't. That final 10% is a barrier that they need time to get over. That 10% does not mean they'll never sign up or never buy; it just means they're not going to do it right now.

If they saw your sign-up box or offer a few more times, would they sign up? Probably. This is why your e-mail list is so important. It's a list of people who trust you and want to hear from you, but it's only able to grow when people want to sign up. People who need some more persuasion need another tactic.

Remarketing list. This is when someone visits your web site from Google, a social link, or an advertisement, or they got there some other way. We tag their browser and know that they visited our site. We then show advertisements to those users on web sites and social sites, promoting another piece of our content.

What we're doing is being top of mind for those customers. If they've visited our site we can advertise something to them that we know they've shown interest in. We're told it takes —six to eight interactions to generate a sales lead[1] and remarketing can account for some of those interactions. Rather than advertise to a wide audience, we advertise to people that we know have visited the site.

We have a remarketing list because we build a list of people who have visited our site. However, we don't get to see the data or export the names. The list is ours and specific to our settings, but we can't manually view each person that

---

[1] See https://www.salesforce.com/blog/2015/04/takes-6-8-touches-generate-viable-sales-lead-heres-why-gp.html

goes through it. The reason remarketing is important is because it's a much lower barrier to entry than someone clicking a link and visiting a web site. Rather than asking for a name and e-mail address, we're just asking them to look. We can position further content in front of them, draw them back to the site, and potentially get them to sign up at a later time. This is the solution to people who are 90% ready to buy or sign up. That final 10% that needs more time and trust can be dealt with via remarketing.

Would You Honestly Read That?

So, if we're producing content and writing blog posts, we need to make sure that content does everything it can to increase the trust and authority people see in us. Here's the hardest question you'll have to answer with creating content:

Would you honestly read that?

Does the title make you want to click? What about the image? Does the summary mean you understand what you'd get? More important than would you read that, of course, is whether your audience would read that. In truth, there is no secret formula to creating content that people want to click on and read. There are a few areas we know we can focus on, but compelling titles and advertisements are tough to get right all the time.

You'll need to test your headlines and titles. Mix different images and see what gets higher click rates or lower costs per click. Some easy areas to look at are subject, results, and language. Is the subject something that your customers actually want to read? If you're a web site designer, do they want to read about responsive web site design, or do they want to read about attracting more traffic to their web site by not ignoring 50% of their market (mobile readers)?

Is it clear what someone would get if they read your content? Are you just promoting a buzzword? Really think hard about what someone can gain if they click on that link. Finally, does the language resonate with your audience? You might know what SEM and landing page column break point are, but will your audience? Use terms and language that they use and recognize.

Would You Really Share That?

Now when they're on the post or content, ask yourself if you would really share that. First, have you made it easy for people to share? Don't spam them with hundreds of share buttons and widgets, but make it easy for people to click and share your content. Second, would someone want to share that with their audience? Do their colleagues and friends want to read that? Does the reader gain something from sharing your content?

People share content that they wish they'd written themselves. If it's funny, informative, or gives a mind-blowing secret away, sharing your posts and pages is a demonstration of excitement from you. That also means you might have to ask for shares. Don't be afraid to talk to your readers and ask them to help you out. Ask yourself this when you read your post: Would my audience really share that?

Provide free webinars to an audience. When we talk about tactics to grow your lists, both e-mail and remarketing, we need three things:

- Advertising copy
- Content that attracts people to your site
- A CTA (call to action)

Webinars create perfect opportunities for all three elements. If you create a webinar for your audience, use paid traffic to drive traffic back to a webinar signup page. You could give a real live date, a cutoff point, and say you're only doing it once. Talk about how it's totally genuine content, not prerecorded or a webinar pitch. Drive people to that signup page. When people sign up, they're added to your e-mail list.

People who don't sign up are perfect candidates for remarketing. Create remarketing advertising copy to ask them to come back and complete their signup. You could even get smarter and pay cold traffic to come to blog posts on the same subject as your webinar. Again, ask people to sign up for a webinar at the end of the post, but use the blog posts for cold traffic.

Remarket the webinar to people who have already viewed the blog post. You've shown them you know what you're talking about, and you're not hiding any content or expecting anything in return. If they're interested in a subject, though, it stands to reason that they'd be interested in a webinar, deep diving that same topic.

Make sure the webinar is recorded and you save the video file somewhere. Once people are signed up, follow up with an e-mail campaign moving them onto another product. Send some e-mails talking about the free handouts or key points from the webinar. Offer them the recording on another landing page, then start to position your products to people.

Promote recorded webinar to paid traffic. Now that you've done a live webinar, make sure you've got the recording and upload it to a site like Vimeo or YouTube. What we can now do is run what's called an *evergreen campaign*. This means we can create a campaign, including landing pages, e-mails, redirects, and upsells, that runs constantly in the background.

Here's an overview of how it works:

- **We run paid traffic campaigns** to direct traffic to a landing page. The page has a signup for a webinar and some free handouts.
- **Some businesses like to run campaigns in blocks,** meaning they say the webinar is live or opens in an hour or in 30 minutes, for example.
- **They might have four webinars running a day,** all recorded, but they're blocked off in time blocks. Even more complex, perhaps, every new signup is told the webinar doesn't start for another 30 minutes and they have to wait.

Personally, I prefer to be totally transparent and let people know the webinar is a recording and they get access as soon as they sign up. I understand why businesses use exclusivity and scarcity with their webinars. It means people don't see them as something they can just sign up for whenever they want. Personally, though, it's more important for me to be authentic and give away information that's useful, rather than get more people to sign up.

After customers have signed up, you can send them the exact same e-mail campaigns you sent to your live webinar attendees. As long as the automation chain isn't broken, you can continue to just drive traffic to a webinar landing page and watch as the e-mail list is followed up with. This is also a perfect opportunity for remarketing. People who are driven to the page are great candidates to be drawn back to the same landing page.

Cut the webinar up. Once you've been running a webinar for a few months, it makes a perfect base for creating a video series. If you've followed a template similar to our explorer blog post formula in Chapter 5, you'll have your content already in neat little sections. Split the introduction, promise, myth, and so on, into the first video. Then cut each learning point into another video. If you have five learning points in your webinar, you'll have six videos (including the introduction).

This makes great YouTube video content. It's easily consumable as a series and you can send people to each video via an e-mail sequence. Make sure to include links and good descriptions in the description box, making sure you're ranking for YouTube search terms. Finally, if the video series proves popular (even if you get just a handful of people saying they liked it), it's probably a good candidate for a mini-course that you can charge for.

Speak at a university. Saying you've spoken at a college or university on a subject is an instant authority boost. However, the reality is that most universities and colleges don't ask local business people to talk for no reason. Here's how you can talk at a university and tell people you have, without the luck of being asked to. Universities and colleges have loads of speaking places, as in literal auditoriums and rooms for people to talk in. Call up a local institution and ask to use one of their facilities for a talk. Some might charge, but others might offer the room for a very low rate if you play the entrepreneur card.

Say you're not charging for the event, it's purely to gain experience with your talk, and there won't be hundreds of people there. Say that students are more than welcome to attend, should they want to. Once you have a booking, promote your event (you'll need about six weeks lead time) to your list and audience. E-mail current contacts and networks and ask them to join you there to talk about a subject. Say it's free, there will be refreshments, and it's absolutely not a pitch. You just want to share what you know about a subject for 20 minutes and you want the experience.

My most popular attended event was on a Friday evening in late November. I e-mailed 50 local web site, graphic, and digital businesses and asked them if they wanted to network and listen to a quick talk, not a pitch, so I could get some experience. My hook? Free beer. That was it. I talked to the pub and told them I would have around 30 people (who had responded) in this evening. I asked for some pitchers of beer and the pub discounted them, as they knew the 30 people turning up would be worth it.

Once you've given the talk, facilitate a bit of networking and thank everyone for coming. It doesn't have to be that many people at all. Ten people is enough to talk in front of and it's a great way to get a university down as somewhere you've spoken at. In future, it'll be easier to get speaking gigs as you've done a talk at a university. For bonus points: Record the talk, even just on your smartphone, and turn that into more video content.

E-mail a lead list. Speedlancer.com offers a range of freelancing services at very affordable prices. One of my favorite methods is to use their lead generation service. They'll generate a list of names and contact information from a source of your choosing. Now these leads are not suitable for mass e-mailing, but they are perfect for the networking and speaking type events just mentioned. I sent the below message to start my networking with people I'd never met before.

> Hey Frank,
>
> We haven't met properly, but I run Devon Digital Design.
>
> I basically just wanted to reach out and invite you to drinks on 28th October in Exeter (on me).
>
> I haven't arranged a location yet, but I'm really keen to meet some of the other web site, digital, and marketing businesses in Devon.
>
> I'm a massive believer that Devon has some great digital creative talent out there and I want to have a pint with them (:

No marketing, no sales pitches, nothing cringe like that. Just a drink (did I mention I'm buying?) and a chat with a few digital nerds.

Let me know if you're in (:

Good to meet you.

Mike

I sent—or rather my virtual assistant sent—these e-mails, one by one to the list of leads that Speedlancer got for me. It was way more successful than I thought it would be. I got to meet some cool people and started to see I could grow audiences from anywhere.

Add lead magnets to blog posts. To continually and passively grow your e-mail list, you need to be converting visitors into e-mail subscribers. The easiest and most effective way to do this is by offering lead magnets on your blog posts. Most web sites already offer opt-in forms with lead magnets. They're usually light boxes or site bars that offer a lead magnet across the whole web site. Although useful, they often don't convert as highly as they can, due to how people use the web site and what they're currently browsing. We've covered this already, so here's just a quick reminder: A lead magnet is a specific chunk of value that seems worth handing over an e-mail address for. The key to continual e-mail list growth is offering lead magnets after and during blog content, free, useful content that people can read and consume. This should be followed by an awesome, specific, helpful piece that users can get in exchange for an e-mail address.

In an ideal world, we'd have a specific lead magnet for every single blog post. In reality, though, that's probably not going to happen. Instead, we want to focus on *content silos*. The 10 x 10 that we created in Chapter 5 went over creating nine different blog posts and pieces of content and a lead magnet. We know that posts and content within each broad topic are connected. That's our content silo, a series of posts within a subject.

We support that content silo underneath with a lead magnet from within the same subject, completing our content silo. Lead magnets connected to a blog post topic have a higher conversion rate. This is because of *congruency*, which means there is a clear link between what someone is reading now and what they could read, similar to a sequel book or a two-part newspaper article. If your customer is reading blog content about SEO and Google rankings, a lead magnet on keyword research and long-tail keywords will do better than a lead magnet on Facebook posting.

The trap people fall into is creating one lead magnet and offering it to every visitor. A five-step guide to increasing e-commerce purchases might be a great resource, but if they're interested in mobile e-mail marketing it's probably not going to convert as well. Keep your lead magnets specific to the content people are reading. If this means scaling back your content creation, then so be it.

There are a few routes to creating lead magnet and blog post congruency. Some businesses will choose one silo and create the lead magnet, then populate the whole silo with blog posts. This gives them nine or so posts and a lead magnet. Others will create one new post and a new lead magnet for the first 10 topics, then go back and fill up each silo per week. There isn't a right or a wrong way, but it might be wise to start creating content that you think will get you the most traction.

Content upgrades. Content upgrades are similar to lead magnets. They're almost always PDFs or worksheets. Templates, cheat sheets, and reference lists make good content upgrades. What differentiates them from lead magnets is that they not are a barrier to entry, or accessing them is much easier. Sometimes it's just a share button (e.g., "Click here to tweet and share this post and you'll get access to our cheat sheet"). Sometimes there are no barriers at all; it's just a PDF via a link in the text. Content upgrades need to be seen in the light of adding huge value to a piece. Don't always believe the content you create needs to be protected. When people first started blogging, the concept of giving away all your ideas and secrets seemed insane. A similar thing is happening to lead magnets, and now people believe they have to protect any kind of download.

If there are a few exercises, like brainstorming or listing ideas, these make fantastic content upgrades. Content upgrades are usually offered during the blog post, inside the actual copy, almost as part of the text. In my opinion the best example of a content upgrade inside a blog post is WP Elevation's Definitive Guide to Winning WordPress Clients.[2] The main lead magnet at the moment is a course. However, the content upgrades (e.g., worksheets that are included in the post for free) don't require an opt-in. They also provide enormous value to the reader. As you can see, they're worksheets and brainstorm sheets designed to help readers get clarity. They aren't huge exercises or long e-books. They're designed to help someone get a result while reading the post.

Killer Blog Post with Lead Magnet

More and more, businesses are creating a flagship blog post and targeting all their traffic efforts toward that post. A long-form, epic, killer blog post is like a self-contained funnel. It starts with a sales letter style introduction, ramping up and explaining the problems and barriers the reader faces. Rather than actually selling the solution, the blog post provides the solution for free. A how-to guide goes through the points and explains how the reader can achieve a solution.

---

[2]Seehttp://www.wpelevation.com/2016/07/definitive-guide-winning-wordpress-clients/

At the end, a very specific lead magnet is positioned to the reader. Rather than our content silo lead magnets, which are just related to the topic, our new long-form blog post lead magnet is specific to just that post. Your thinking for a lead magnet, delivered in this way, needs to be slightly different. The process of creating an opt-in form and sending the new subscriber an e-mail with the lead magnet is exactly the same.

However, to create the lead magnet you need to think very specifically, "How can someone who is reading this get the results I talk about in the blog post faster and with more automation?" How can a reader take your blog post and do something about it today? Rather than just reading the blog post and trying to implement it themselves, what would help the readers and assist them in executing the steps in the blog post?

The type of lead magnet can be exactly the same as other lead magnets: cheat sheets, checklists, worksheets, and so on. All the steps need to be related to the original blog post, however. Use a phrase like, "If you're serious about [blog topic], you need to download our [resource/cheat sheet, etc.]." An example of a blog post with a specific lead magnet is Sell Your Service's Content Funnel Post, at `https://sellyourservice.co.uk/2017/01/how-any-wordpress-businesses-can-create-an-entire-killer-content-marketing-funnel-in-as-little-as-1-hour-and-of-course-teach-to-your-customers/`. It talks through an entire content funnel creation process, and at the end offers a handbook to teach people how to run through the exercise with customers.

Install Sumo. Sumo (see `https://sumo.com`) is one of our favorite, easy tools to start collecting e-mail leads. There is a free version that works on almost all web sites and can be targeted to specific pages and posts. With the upgraded version, you can target down to the level of individual posts, read content analytics, and create heat maps. Sumo.com is where you can go to set up an account.

Retargeting with PPC. Pay per click (PPC) means targeting web sites, forums, and other areas with an advertisement for your content. There are advertising networks, among which Google Display Network and Outbrain are two of the largest. Hundreds of network options are available for displaying your content on other web sites.

PPC means that you only pay for the advertising when people click on your ad. For example, if I'm on a web site with a Google Display ad space, advertisements for different companies will be displayed. It all depends on my demographics, sites I've visited previously, and a few other selectors. If I'm a 25-year-old male who's heavily into working out and nutrition, chances are I'll be visiting web sites relevant to those interests. It also means that fitness and nutrition companies will advertise to me on other web sites because they know I'm interested in that area.

A few years ago companies would use PPC to drive people back to landing pages. At first this was pretty successful, but now click rates and conversion rates are much lower for going straight to a landing page. Before that, PPC ads would drive people back to a product that had an even lower conversion rate. Now, smart businesses drive targeted PPC traffic to blog posts, interesting and free content that readers know won't require a payment or e-mail address.

After clicking and visiting the web site, the user's browser is tagged with a pixel. This tells Google, or whichever PPC network is used, that this user has visited your web site. This is building your retargeting list, a list of people who have visited your web site. Now is the right time to start positioning landing pages to your display network, only to people who have visited your web site and seen your business already.

Retargeting from SEO. SEO is such an enormous topic that it can't possibly be covered in an entire book, let alone one chapter. However, the purpose of an SEO strategy is to drive more traffic from search engines. Google, as the largest search engine in the world, acts as a librarian. It scours the Internet and indexes all the web sites and pages it finds. It then makes a "best judgment" selection of keywords to that page depending on a variety of factors. It's a process similar to going to a library and saying to a librarian, "I'm looking for books on French cooking." The librarian doesn't know the content for every single book in the library, but he or she does know the most likely books that will contain the relevant information.

If there are three books called *Cooking the French Way, French Cuisine,* and *French Gastronomy,* the librarian is probably going to recommend those books. Google works in exactly the same way. The more obvious it is that your web site, business, and content talk about French cooking, the more likely you'll appear for those search terms. This is your content, copy, and blog posts on your web site, words and media that humans can read and interpret as related to your chosen subject and therefore, keywords.

In our imaginary library there might also be a book called *Chicken and Wine*. The title doesn't scream obviously about French cooking. However, our librarian has been recommended this book by and friend and a library regular. The friend says it's the best French cooking book he's read. Even though the title might not suggest it's suitable for our search, the librarian now knows he or she can select this book and present it to readers. This is how link building works with Google. If you're talking about French cooking, all your content talks about it, and you're regularly updating your copy talking about French cooking, you can bet your chances for appearing in a search for French cooking are pretty high.

However, if other web sites start linking back to your web site, acting as a recommendation, you can bet Google will rank your site better for your chosen keywords. If you want to climb Google's rankings, check out Moz's beginner's guide to SEO at `https://moz.com/beginners-guide-to-seo`.

The idea is that we can attract traffic from search engines, then we tag their browser and can remarket further content to them via remarketing. The idea is to drive traffic back to our web site from a variety of sources, search engines being one of them. When visitors land on your web site, you can start remarketing to them at other locations. A remarketing strategy that starts with SEO traffic is more likely to benefit from long-tail keywords rather than more broad "fat-head" search terms.

Long-tail keywords are keywords that are more specific but have lower search volumes. They often have less competition but are easier to rank for. Fat-head keywords are more broad and might look impressive when you rank for them, but they are very hard to rank for. On the other hand, they'll drive lot of traffic, but might not indicate what someone is looking for. For example, "running shoes" is a pretty fat-headed search term. It might drive millions of views a month if you rank for that term. Why are people searching for just running shoes, though? Do they want to read reviews? Are they looking to research and buy them? Is it for marathon running, trail running, or the gym? Are they male or female?

On the other hand, "women's size 8 marathon extra wide running shoes Brooks" is a pretty clear indicator of what they're looking for. This is a long-tail keyword. If you can rank for long-tail keywords, it's also clearer on what you need to remarket with. People searching for that term who land on your web site would be better served with women's Brooks marathon running shoe remarketing ads. Drive targeted traffic back to your web site from SEO and tag people for remarketing. Not only will you increase visitors from cold traffic via the search engine, but you'll increase the remarketing list of potential warm traffic, too.

Retargeting from social media. Social promoted posts are similar to PPC ads in that you pay a network or web site to display your posts to an audience. Facebook, LinkedIn, Pinterest, and Instagram all offer paid options to reach a wider audience. You can create an audience demographic that you want to target and position your posts and blog content to them.

Again, paid social is such a huge topic that we couldn't cover everything, but there are a few basics:

- **First, choose your social platform wisely.** It's better to focus on one platform at a time until you have a formula that works.
- **Also, understand that different platforms have different audiences.** LinkedIn probably isn't suitable for cushions shaped like emojis, but it's perfect for financial consultation.

- **I'd like to point out a huge misconception at this point.** Whereas platforms like LinkedIn have traditionally been seen as purely business-to-business (B2B) and Facebook is more business-to-consumer (B2C), the reality is that nearly every human is on Facebook.
- **Businesses might be on LinkedIn, but the people who work there are on Facebook.** Don't write Facebook off just because of what ill-informed social media experts tell you. Unbounce has a great guide to paid social media at http://unbounce.com/social-media/measure-your-first-paid-social-campaign/.

What most businesses do is attract new readers with paid social posts. They'll attract visitors to their web site via a social platform, to blog posts and free, easy content. Then they'll use remarketing via web sites and display networks to get that same traffic back. It's worth mentioning at this point that as a rule, remarketing traffic is cheaper than cold traffic, at the moment anyway. Spending big bucks on cold traffic isn't sustainable. You need to drive current readers back to your web site via remarketing. To grow that remarketing list, though, you need to invest in cold traffic.

Retargeting from AdWords. AdWords are search results inside Google's search results that are paid to be displayed above the organic search results. Searching for women's running shoes has displayed 22 million results. Right at the top are sponsored links through Google's AdWords product.

The very first results are Google Shopping paid results. Underneath that, are two ads for women's running shoes. These are all via AdWords. You can bid for search results and keywords, bearing in mind that fat-head keywords and popular keywords can run into tens of dollars per click. "Loans," "mortgage," and "insurance" run about $50 per click. It is still PPC, but if your customers aren't converting, that's some expensive traffic. However, it's worth investigating long-tail keywords for AdWords, as it can be a great source of cold traffic and building up your remarketing list. Check out WordStream's guide to PPC at http://www.wordstream.com/articles/most-expensive-keywords.

Send Remarketing Traffic to Squeeze Pages

The key to remarketing traffic is understanding the difference between warm and cold traffic. Cold traffic is just how it sounds, like a cold lead. It's a visitor who has never heard of you or visited you before. Like any relationship, it take a while to warm people up enough for them to reach out and visit you by themselves. Warm traffic is made up of visitors who have seen your brand and web site before. They've read your content and either return to you by choice or are encouraged to come back again.

A few years ago, we used to drive traffic to landing or squeeze pages. The idea was to drive a ton of traffic to a squeeze page, collect a load of e-mail opt-ins, and e-mail market to them later. Now, however, people are wise to the squeeze page. The headlines "Get more traffic" or "Increase your Twitter followers" attract people who are looking for free blog content. Driving cold traffic to landing pages doesn't work as well as it used to. What we can do now is drive a load of traffic to our blog content and free, no-opt-in material, then remarket landing and squeeze pages to our traffic later on.

In truth, abandoning PPC or cold traffic to landing and squeeze pages completely isn't wise. It's about a balance and testing what works. We know some businesses (Frank Kern, Neil Patel) that drive cold traffic from YouTube PPC ads straight to landing and even sales pages. However, they have massive levels of authority and don't need to ramp up the relationship.

On the other hand, we do know of smaller businesses that drive cold traffic to landing and squeeze pages for specific items, too, including e-books, reports, free trials, and so on. The power of remarketing comes from content silo specific pages. For example, if you're driving a load of cold traffic to blog posts on SEO and keywords, your remarketing needs to bump up that value and show people SEO tools, resources, and lead magnets.

Frank Kern once told me (and 1 million other people), "If you help people and get the real results, they'll want you to help them again." It's such a simple model, but that's what you need to bear in mind with traffic. Help people by offering them useful and valuable information and insight. That's your cold traffic. If you're delivering on their expectations, help them again with even more insight, but ask them for an e-mail address in return.

Write to podcasts that your audience listen to. Podcasts are the massive lead, traffic, and authority generators of the 2010s. Everyone has a podcast and there are an infinite number of podcasts for any subject. I guarantee that if you search a keyword and "podcast," you'll find dozens or even hundreds of podcasts on the same subject. Sure, *Entrepreneur on Fire* and *Freakonomics* don't just get anyone on, but the medium podcasts do need guests and content.

At its core, this is old-school PR, which is good PR. It's not about press releases and advertising; it's about reaching out to people who have an audience and a medium who need content. Your job is to get comfortable being uncomfortable. If this is way outside your comfort zone, you have to decide if you want comfort more than reaching a larger audience. Reaching out and asking to be on people's podcasts and shows will yield more positive results than you think. Those who don't want you on their show simply won't respond to you. No one is going to call you pompous or arrogant for offering to be on their show. You always have to offer something in return, and most of the time, that's going to be your time and knowledge. It doesn't hurt to have a list and mention how many people you'll promote the show to as well.

Search for podcasts that reach similar audiences to you. Also, search for podcasts that you'd listen to. There's enormous authority in being the person who talks to your peers. For example, let's say you build e-commerce web sites. Your customers might listen to e-commerce podcasts, marketing podcasts, and business entrepreneur podcasts. If you can offer a very specific insight, maybe how e-commerce businesses can double the average sale that they make to one customer, you'll have more chance of being on. E-mail and reach out with a specific story and hook, an angle that makes it obvious you should be on their show.

Start a podcast. What if you can't find shows to be on? What if you want to be the host? Start a podcast then. Starting a podcast has nothing to do with complicated technology or being a radio personality. A podcast is a show where you provide entertainment or insight. Some shows rely on interviewing guests, and some have regular hosts who always do the show together. Some podcasts have only one host who talks through a specific topic each week.

There are three keys to a podcast is:

- Consistent publishing.
- Being easy to listen to.
- Being entertaining or informative.

If you're not willing to do all three of these things, week in week out, you're probably not ready for a podcast. The easiest way to test if you want to try a podcast is to create a 10-part series. Do a one-off series with 10 episodes. Plan out the content, invite the guests, and record the content.

You don't have to record video, and it doesn't have to be in the same room. The hardest part is getting guests to commit and sign up to your show. Having said that, I've landed some huge interview guests for our shows, and even just video interviews. Again, you might need to reach out a lot to a lot of people to get the show off the ground. Record the audio and share it on your blog; it's as simple as that. Getting your podcast on iTunes and listed on podcast players is easier than ever, too. WordPress even has podcast functionality built in.

Previous versions of this book talked about uploading RSS feeds and submission guidelines, but instead I'd like to update this section by talking about Anchor and Podbean. Both Anchor and Podbean make podcasts 100 times easier and simpler than before. With both platforms, available as apps on iOS and Android and online, you can record straight to your smartphone. You can also upload previously recorded content and it does everything for you. At the time of writing, both platforms offer a free version. There is literally no reason not to start a podcast.

Use e-books to capture e-mail leads. "Mike, you literally said that e-books are boring?" Good point. However, our e-books are not going to be the free type that are given away. We're going to create an e-book that makes people want to buy. We're really writing and publishing a book that we feel would be good enough to sell.

Rob Cubbon probably has the best guides for publishing e-books on YouTube. It's free to get your book in the Amazon Kindle store. When it comes to writing an e-book, or any book, I've talked about how you can take your current content and repurpose it into a book relatively quickly. It's not hard, it just takes time and some structure. Even though we all read books, the structure of writing a book escapes a lot of us.

If you want to write something from scratch, there is never such a thing as writer's block. Writer's block is an excuse for not having or using a framework. Song lyrics, musical scores, fantasy novels, short stories, blog posts, and news reports all use structure. If you're yelling at this book now, shouting that I obviously don't know what I'm talking about because creative writing and artistic output require complete freedom and no structure, or maybe that a structure is restrictive or suffocating, talk to any consistently creative person who produces great work and they'll tell you they use a structure.

For a book, the overview is pretty simple. We open with a problem, explain the world as it is now, and then lead to how it can change. That's pretty much the beginning, middle, and end of most books, both fiction and nonfiction.

If you want to structure your writing, think about dedicating one hour per day. First thing in the morning, write your content. I found it particularly helpful to know what I'm writing each day, too. I broke this book into 12 chapters outlining the broad steps someone needed to get from point A to point B. Then each chapter was broken down into 10 to 30 sections. Some of those sections would be entire pages, whereas others would be just a paragraph. Each section had a prompt or a title that would give me a handle on what to work with when I sat down to write. I wrote for two hours per day, no matter what. Usually, I completed six sections a time, including research, links, or quotes. It took about 60 days to write this book, around two-and-a-half months in total.

You'd be staggered at how much you can write with a structure and a plan and just one hour a day. I'd recommend starting smaller and maybe having six chapters and 10 sections per chapter. It's not about how many pages you have; it's about making sure your book is useful. Now we can sell the book online. You can publish via Kindle or another e-book distributor, or just provide the PDF download or even a mobi (e-book) file for a one-time purchase. Gumroad.com is a fantastic place to start if you want to make selling an online product very easy.

Tag or mention people in your content. One of the content types I mentioned earlier is a list post. Listing podcasts, experts, books, and so on is a very fast and powerful way to both produce content and get on people's radars. The power from this post comes from reaching out to those featured on the list. The options are endless: e-mail, Twitter tagging, Facebook, and more. Keep your lists simple. The areas you can focus on range from podcasts, books, experts, quotes, web sites, and predictions, to their blog content, and Facebook groups. Just search "top 10" on YouTube and you'll see how easy it is to create list posts.

Start a Facebook group. One of the most powerful ways to grow an audience is to attract people to an already populated network. Facebook offers everyone the ability to set up a group and manage users. One of the ways we gained traction within our audience was to offer our marketing advice group to anyone who signed up to our list. New subscribers were told about the Facebook group via e-mail automation. This meant that our list subscribers would join our Facebook group.

It meant we had another channel to reach people and talk to them. The advantage of a Facebook (or LinkedIn) group was that we could position richer media to our audience, including live video, polls, and images. What we did to start our coaching program was to offer free webinars to our group. We used their feedback and attendance to gain attention and create very fast and easy content. We recorded the webinars and positioned them again to the group as a freebie or paid content. The beauty was that we had real people attending the calls, which made it feel more authentic.

Use Facebook groups for people who both are and aren't customers to reach out and talk to more people. Fair warning, though: Managing a Facebook group can be hard work. It is worth managing a community if you're serious about scaling, though.

Create a closed group. Growing a community of customers is fast becoming a critical part of any scaled business model. Most businesses and entrepreneurs pitch the closed and private group as an included benefit of being a customer. You get unlimited access to the group, you can ask questions that only other customers can see, and you're part of an exclusive and private members area.

As a business owner, this cuts down on people e-mailing you for advice. Often if one person is asking a question, several others will want to see the answers, too. It's a fantastic place to pitch larger ticket items as well, such as live events and mastermind sessions. Also, your customers will be very vocal about what they want to see, what they want help with, or what they want to achieve.

A word on private Facebook groups is in order. Facebook has caught on that businesses are doing this. In their policies, you can't specifically sell access to a group. However, access to a private group included with a purchase of another product is fine. Despite this, Facebook is now looking to advertise to and within groups. Your competition and other businesses will be able to target members of other groups. With Facebook groups, you're using Facebook's platform. The rules could change at any time. Check out the post from The Membership Guys at https://www.themembershipguys.com/should-you-use-a-forum-or-facebook-group-for-your-community/ to understand the pros and cons of a Facebook group versus your own online forum.

Your own online forum can easily be added to your membership web site, but it isn't easy work. The advantage is that the posts last a long time, as opposed to Facebook, which can move on very fast. On the other hand, if people don't get value from your forum, they'll stop logging in and it's very hard to get them back. The key is to create a community that focuses on helping your customers and using your product. That's all you should be focusing on.

Comment Marketing

Comment marketing is a fast growing method of obtaining back-links and traffic. The idea is to find a series of posts, forum threads, and articles that suit your audience. Then scroll down to the comments section and respond to the post. You can also include a link back to your own web site or blog post, hoping the comment readers will also see your link and click there.

Full disclosure: I do run comment marketing sessions for my own content. However, I have a small virtual assistance team that does it for me. We target the blogs and posts we want to comment on, craft a nonspammy and intuitive response, and then the team physically posts the comments.

Comment marketing is not a method of fast traction, however. As it's very easy and just takes time to copy and paste, other marketers might tell you to start doing it. It also helps back-links to your web site. In reality, blog commenting as a marketing, traffic, and back-link strategy takes a lot of time. It requires regularly posting in the same forums, blog Web sites, and threads. It's not just posting a link once and moving on.

Comment marketing is the result, not act of, building a relationship with bloggers. You'd be in much better shape if you spent that time reaching out to bloggers in your industry via Twitter and e-mail, and talking to them. Develop a relationship with them and go from there. Don't spam comments with links just for the sake of it. If there's no relationship behind your actions, they're not sustainable.

Host a networking event, breakfast, or lunch. One of the easiest methods of growing a real authentic following is to host small live events. Our alarm bells start ringing when we think about this: What if no one comes? I hate being the center of attention! I don't know how to organize an event!

First and foremost, if you're not willing to organize a small eight-person lunch, how are you going to scale and build more relationships? We have to move far out of our comfort zones to start getting the results we want.

Organizing a networking lunch or event is no different than organizing a dinner with friends. You just need a time, a date, and a place. There doesn't have to be a speaker, and there isn't a pitch or team-building exercise, just a group of people talking around a table. Find or research 20 people or businesses who you'd like to talk to in your local area. They don't have to be total prospective customers, just people who you think it would be interesting or wise to talk to. Keep it informal and casual.

E-mail current customers. If you're serious about growth and traction within your marketplace, the most powerful resource you have at the moment is your current customer list. Actually, it's more than that: your current network, including your customers. When it comes to more work, back-links, blog opportunities, and interviews, use your current network and reach out to them.

Send an e-mail asking if they know any businesses looking to benefit like they did. Don't ask people if they know someone who's looking for a web site or for social media consulting. Ask them if they're looking for more traffic, more customers, or increased revenue, or whatever the benefits are that you offer. Here is an example:

> Hey John,
>
> Do you know any businesses in your network that are also looking for more traffic?
>
> I'm asking because we recently took on a new team member and we've got some capacity. I just want to share the benefits that you got with someone else that you know.
>
> It'd be great for your reputation, too, if your network benefited from your introduction.
>
> Let me know.
>
> Mike
>
> P.S. We have a 20% referral bonus for the referrer for any businesses that sign on.

This goes for guest blog posts, back-links, and interviews, anything that requires you to talk to other people. Your current network and customers are the best source of new contacts you have. This is why it's so important to develop those relationships properly. Keep them growing and keep them strong because you're going to need them when you grow.

Affiliate lead magnets. This probably isn't the right term, but I couldn't think of a smarter phrase. In short, the lead magnets you've created could benefit massively from other people sharing them. There are plug-ins like Vyper that help you grow an e-mail list with a competition. What's so smart about them is that they have built-in sharing capabilities. At the moment, I use a web site called Maitre.com to gather leads and create referral campaigns.

Opt-ins who enter the competition are encouraged to share the competition to get more entries. It's a fantastic model for growth. Be careful about the types of prizes you offer. They need to be strictly related to your audience, otherwise you'll have really poor quality links. For example, a $1,000 cash prize will attract anyone, but a $1,000 bundle of plug-ins and themes for life will only attract web site and WordPress businesses.

Another route to opt-in growth is offering your current list and customers the opportunity to win a prize or get a reward if they generate opt-ins for your list. Using an affiliate link plug-in, you can create unique links for each customer or opt-in. That unique link sends people to a squeeze page and if someone opts in, he or she is tagged with the unique link, meaning you can tell how many people signed up per link.

Systems like this can be complicated to set up. They're also not really suitable for smaller lists and people starting out. You need at least 1,000 people on your list before you'll see any growth from methods like this. In terms of growth and traction, though, competitions work well to start with, and affiliate lead growth is a great way to continue that growth.

Self-liquidating offers. Finally, we have the opportunity to generate customers from our current customers. Imagine being able to generate leads at no cost—I mean 100% no cost, not seemingly cheap methods like content marketing or social marketing, but genuine leads at no cost.

How much does it take to convert a lead to a customer? If you have a $19 splinter product, maybe it doesn't cost a lot, but it still takes time and money to convert 1 in 10 people into a splinter product customer. What if we could generate customers at no cost? What is every new opt-in to your list was not only a no-cost opt-in, but they were also a qualified customer?

We can do this with SLOs. An SLO is where we use current customers to sell our products. As a method, SLOs are designed to work with splinter products best. The idea is that we want to acquire customers at a break-even point. If you have a $19 course or e-book, or another splinter product, the $19 is designed to pay for the cost of acquisition; not to make a profit, but to pay for the traffic and marketing it's taken to get 10 opt-ins.

We can accelerate this by offering our current splinter product customers 100% of the sale if they get new customers to sign up. For every new customer that we get through our SLO customer, we'll give them 100% of the sale. This might sound insane to you. Giving away 100% of a customer sale? How does that work?

Let's say you spend $100 on traffic and get 50 e-mail opt-ins from that. At $2 per opt-in, each lead is now −$2 in value. They haven't bought anything, they've just cost you money. We know already that a splinter product not only increases the chances that someone will buy again in the future, but it also means we can pay off that $100 of traffic acquisition. If 1 in 10 people buy a splinter product at $19, that's five new customers at $19 each, meaning a total of $95. So now we've made back $95 and the 50 new opt-ins are essentially free.

If we wanted to skip all that, we could offer our current splinter product customers the opportunity to sell our splinter product. We tell them they'll get 100% of the sale for every new customer they sign up. Now whenever someone new is on your list, you know they're a customer. They haven't cost you anything and your current customer is making a little cash on the side. If you can get this model to work, it's incredibly powerful.

Summary

If we want to continue a conversation with someone, we have to offer them something valuable. To capture as many leads as possible, we need to scale our lead capture efforts.

- We can scale our e-mail list capture by offering lead magnets and opt-ins across our site.
- We can remarket those same lead magnets via a squeeze page to visitors who have been to a specific blog post.
- We're more likely to capture e-mail addresses and leads if we ask for them.
- We must build an e-mail list on our own "turf" as well as our social platforms.

CHAPTER 7

Connecting More of That Audience to a Scalable Product

Connecting more of your audience to a scalable product means showing your audience, traffic and e-mail subscribers a product without needing you to be there for the sale. Smaller, low-cost products up to about $50 are suitable for splinter products. Splinter products work to pay for the cost of traffic and lead acquisition. They also make great scalable products to sell on automation.

If you want to connect more of your audience to a scalable product, remember your content silos. Your content silos are your free blog content at the top, a lead magnet, and then a splinter product, all within the same subject or topic. You're more likely to see higher conversion rates and increased signups and sales if you remember your content silos. The key is to build the automation within the silo first, then focus on populating the top of the silo with blog content.

© Michael Killen 2019
M. Killen, *From Single to Scale*, https://doi.org/10.1007/978-1-4842-3814-1_7

Chapter 7 | Connecting More of That Audience to a Scalable Product

This chapter is a step-by-step guide on how to build that automation funnel within the silo. We'll also cover how to create a splinter product later. We start with a diagram shown in Figure 7-1. This is an overview of our web site, the blog content and lead magnets within it, and the products for sale. You can use a WordPress web site and a page builder for this. I recommend Beaver Funnels and Beaver Builder, but there are other options.

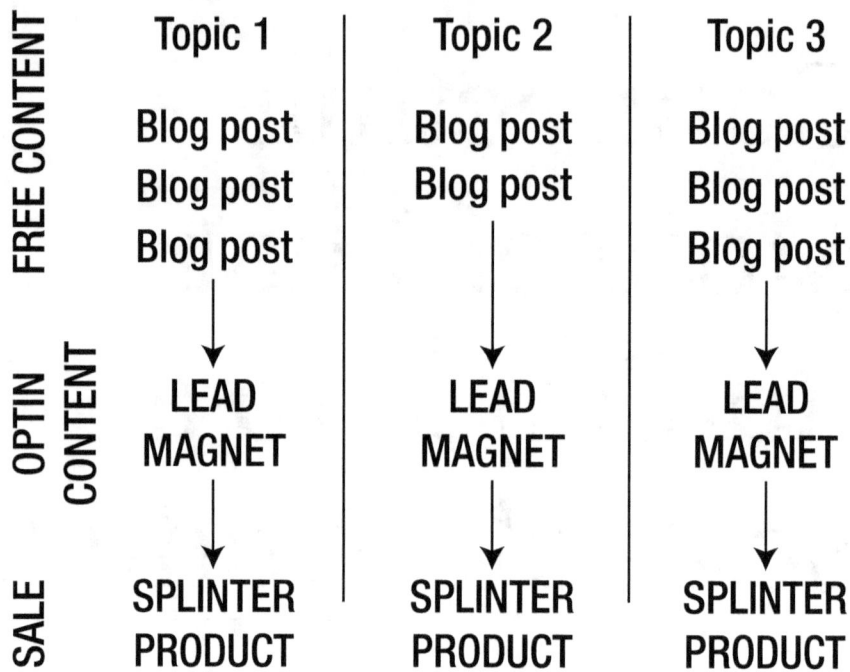

Figure 7-1. Web site content silo

You don't have to have three or even one blog post yet per silo. We recommend building out each silo one at a time. Focus on the splinter product and lead magnet, makw sure the automation works for each stage, then populate the blog content at the top of the silo.

Content Silos

Your blog content needs to feed into your lead magnets. We used to just slap up a landing page, but now we need to give people a lot of value first before they'll sign up. Again, focusing on content silos, offer a lead magnet via an opt-in form at the end or during your blog post.

How you capture e-mail subscribers is entirely up to you. Almost all e-mail and CRM systems will include an e-mail form embed code, something you can easily paste into a WordPress site. Other options include OptinMonster (http://optinmonster.com), which is a specific plug-in and tools just for capturing e-mail leads. OptinMonster is what we use at Sell Your Service.

There's also Sumo.com, another option that works similar to OptinMonster. If you're using a WordPress web site, you could use Gravity Forms as a plug-in and just embed a form at the end of a blog post. Also, most page builders such as Beaver Builder and Divi have e-mail subscriber forms baked into their builders. Your blog readers need to be encouraged to sign up. Content silos help, keeping the topic relevant, but also you need to look at the language and messaging that you apply to the copy.

For example, a SEO post "Sign up to our SEO newsletter" will have a very low opt-in rate. It's related to the content topic, sure, but it doesn't give anything specifically valuable away. Conversely, a lead magnet that says "If you're serious about SEO and growing your traffic from Google, then you need our SEO checklist. Make sure every blog post you publish is an SEO goldmine" is far more likely to connect and convert. That's pretty much the key to creating lead magnet messaging. All we're trying to do is connect with people, businesses, and customers who have desires, hopes, fears, goals, and objections.

They're looking for guidance and you can offer that to them. All we're trying to do is help them get more guidance and value from the blog post. Think to yourself, what would really help someone get more results from this post?

What to do, how to do it, I'll do it for you. The easiest way to start thinking in terms of scale, automation, and growth is with this little funnel mantra:

- What to do.
- How to do it.
- I'll do it for you.

Remember Chapter 3, when we covered what to do, how to do it, and I'll do it for you? That's the mantra to your silo and automation funnel. Blog posts and lead magnets are what to do. Sometimes the lead magnet is a little "how to do the thing." When people are learning what to do, they still might not know how to actually complete the action.

It's worth noting that even though a lot of our posts are titled "How to ..." (e.g., "How to search optimize your blog posts" or "How to get more free traffic from Facebook"), you're really only telling people what to do. A lead magnet should then expand on that with checklists and cheat sheets. It might also show a physical walkthrough of how to really do the thing.

The blog post might give an overview, but your lead magnets can go into more detail, or your splinter products can show someone how to do something: a course, a piece of software, and so on. We'll get into splinter products later. Finally, your highest ticket product should be "I'll do it for you." You or your team will do the actual thing. You'll build the blog posts or execute the work.

Many businesses believe that if you tell people what to do and how to do for free or a low cost, they won't want you to do it for them. This might be true of a small percentage of people, but most customers will enjoy the learning introduction. However, they'll return to you asking for you to complete the work. It's a well-known trope that the more consultants and coaches give away, the more they're asked to complete work. I even know of one consultant who got so tired of building WordPress web sites that he set up a course just to help other businesses take on his excess business. Ironically, he is now inundated with higher paying work. He has to turn down almost all his new leads.

Faster and easier. Another messaging hook to remember, for lead magnets and sales, is to ask "Do you want these same results, but faster and with more automation?" Which is to ask, "The blog post you've just read, do you want the same results that the blog post talks about (more Google traffic, higher rankings, better fitting trousers, etc.) but faster than doing it by yourself? Do you want those same results with less work from you and more automation? Then sign up for our checklist below." Or "The mini-course you've just watched on building the perfect marathon training plan, do you want to run that marathon and get fitter, faster? What if there was less work from yourself and the plan was more automated? Then you need our training plan builder. It's a one-off cost of $19."

We ask this question to get people thinking in the future and asking for more commitment from them. Some people won't be ready yet, which is fine. Others, however, will want to start seeing those same results faster and with less work from themselves. It's an incredibly powerful proposition to place in front of someone.

Splinter Product Creation

A lot of people complicate splinter products and how to build them. Most of the time we see people work on from a lead magnet and think "What would be the most logical step here to sell to someone, after this lead magnet?" They'll think in terms of delivery, whether it's a course or an e-book or some software. We have a different approach, though. The problem with thinking what makes sense to sell after a lead magnet means it might not connect with your final product. A splinter product is designed to help people move toward your final product. If your final product is a web site or a social media course, you need to offer something that allows a logical step into your final sale.

Sometimes, when we create a splinter product after a lead magnet, it doesn't seem obvious that the final sale is the next step. So instead we ask, "What does someone get for $25,000?" That might be too low for your final product, in which case just add a zero. Even if your final product doesn't cost nearly that amount, play along. Humor me. List everything that someone would get if they deposited $25,000 into your bank account today. You don't have a choice; they're putting that money in there and you better deliver. If you'd like a worksheet to help with this exercise, head over to singletoscale.com/25k.

List out everything you'd deliver: the results you'd get, how much time you'd spend with them, what they'd get at the end of it all, and how long the project would last. Inside that list are your splinter products. They're hidden, but they're there. This exercise, by the way, is called a reverse funnel. We're starting with the end, final, high-ticket product in mind.

Once we've listed out what people get for our high-ticket item, let's see what someone gets for $10,000. Let's say your next customer loves what you did for $25,000, but only has $10,000 to spend. What do they get? What do you have to remove from the $25,000 package that someone could get for $10,000?

List out again what they'd get and add anything or reduce anything if you feel it's necessary. For example, the $25,000 package includes the following:

- A weeklong retreat to focus on the exercises.
- One-on-one coaching on their business.
- Building a funnel for their business.
- 12 months mentorship at one call a month.

For $10,000 they'd get just the funnel and six months mentorship.

Once you've got a list for the $10,000 and $25,000 products, make a list for the following price points:

- $25,000
- $10,000
- $5,000
- $2,000
- $100 per month
- One-off $97
- One-off $47
- One-off $19
- One-off $9

- Lead magnet free
- Blog content

Once you get to about $1,000 the list might just have one or two items. Hopefully you can see now how your splinter products filter into your core offer. It's not about upscaling your lead magnet, it's about cutting back from your core offer. Maybe your core offer doesn't immediately lend itself to a small one-off sale. I encourage you to think hard about splinter products because someone who has bought a small product is more likely to buy a larger product.

It might be that your splinter products are different delivery methods from your core offer. If you offer one-on-one coaching, your splinter product could be recordings of your bestselling coaching. Think creatively about getting customers the same results, moving them from that same before status to an after status. It's not the delivery that matters, it's the results and benefits they get. It's moving them from one place to another.

The Thank You Page

When someone opts in via a subscribe form, if they're signing up to a lead magnet, common sense would dictate sending them straight to the content they've asked for. Common sense is wrong on this one, I'm afraid. All your new signups should be sent straight to a thank you page. It prevents spam signups, increases download and conversion rates, and gives you a great platform to sell. After someone signs up there is an element of risk and fear that you won't deliver the goods. Nothing is more frustrating than signing up for a cheat sheet or checklist, never to receive an e-mail with the resource. People might try again to sign up, but what they need is literal confirmation that you've got their e-mail and their resource is on the way.

A thank you page solves all these problems. Sometimes, people will use spam or fake e-mail addresses to fill out the form. They're not keen on being marketed to, which is fine, but it means our e-mail list gets filled with fake e-mail addresses. We combat this not with double opt-ins (although your country might require a double opt-in by law) but by delivering the resource via e-mail to the address supplied, rather than redirecting them to the resource.

When users are redirected to a thank you page, we give four very clear messages:

- We've received your e-mail and your resource is on the way (it might take a few minutes).
- We'll send your resource to your e-mail with the subject line "example" and from the address "name@email.com".

- Check your spam folder and mark us as a safe sender.
- This is how we got those results even faster.

First, we confirm that their action has been acknowledged. There is a risk in filling out an e-mail signup form, but we're telling people they've done the right thing. We thank them, tell them what's going to happen next, and what they can expect.

Second, we tell them what e-mail address we'll be sending from and what the subject line is. We make it really clear that we're sending the resource to the e-mail address that we were given. This way, if they gave us a fake e-mail address, they need to enter a real one to get the resource.

Third, we remind them to check their spam folder and mark us as a safe sender. Finally, we position a sale in front of them (more on that later). Thank you pages are easy to set up. They needn't be complicated or have too much on them, just acknowledge the customer's actions and tell them what's going to happen next.

Track conversions. Thank you pages also allow us to measure the success of our campaigns. Facebook, Google, and even LinkedIn now allow you to measure a conversion via a pixel. Very basically, we leave a small piece of code on a thank you page to measure where people have converted from. If you have three traffic campaigns running—LinkedIn ads, Outbrain, and Google organic SEO—you put a pixel from each supplier (Google also can use goals within Google Analytics) on your thank you page. When users sign up, depending on their traffic source, you'll get accurate data on where the conversions are coming from.

Thank you pages are powerful because we can now see how many conversions $500 from each traffic source gets us. It might be that $500 got you 1,000 clicks from Outbrain, but only 10 signups, for a conversion rate of 1%. Each signup cost you $50! However, LinkedIn might send you 250 clicks for $500, and 25 people signed up, which is a 10% conversion rate and a signup cost of $20 per lead. Thank you pages can give you enormous insight into your marketing activities. The great part is that they keep working and measuring 24 hours a day.

Upsell on thank you pages. Finally, we can use the thank you page as an area to upsell to a splinter product. If you've got a small $9 or $19 splinter product, maybe a course or an e-book, your thank you page is the perfect time to upsell from a lead magnet to that splinter product. You know viewers are interested in the subject, and this is the perfect time to propose, "If you're serious about [results] then you should see how we got [results] even faster."

On your thank you page, use video sales letter (VSL) to talk through your splinter product. A VSL isn't complicated or hard, it just requires a little time and writing. If you want an example, check out https://sellyourservice.

co.uk/ty/100-in-30-days-thank-you/. All a VSL has to be is a sales letter written out. Then each line is a new slide. You do a voice-over of the slides talking through the text. There are software packages such as EasyVSL that make sales videos very quickly, but all you really need is PowerPoint and some screen capture software.

When it comes to writing a sales letter, there are entire books written on the topic. However, at a high level, we can follow the same principles for our webinars and blog posts.

- **Headline and promise**. Create a headline that makes people want to read on and listen to the rest of the video.
- **Make a promise**. Use the simplest concept that your audience can understand. What are they going to walk away with?
- **The main problem**. Let's outline the main problem that your audience faces. Typically, it's that they don't generate enough cash, but why don't they generate enough cash? For example, most businesses don't generate any leads through their web site. If you don't have leads, you don't grow your business.
- **Typical myth with solutions**. What's the current solution that people buy and why does it not work? For example, on the web site lead generation front, most people will have a web site built for them and then have a lot of SEO work done. SEO does not generate leads for businesses through web sites as fast as other methods.

Scarcity and Changes

What's changing in the market, financially, technologically, sociologically, and competitively? Make customers understand that they need to be ahead of the curve. The world is changing, and you can help with that. Another cool idea is talking about how your solution won't be around forever. Maybe there's limited stock, a time limit, or you only have space for two more customers. For example, with web sites, 78% of Internet browsing traffic is now done on smartphones and tablets. If your business doesn't show people what they want via their mobile device, they don't care what you have to say.

Knife Twist

This sounds gory, and it's supposed to. What makes the problem worse or what is the main thing that drives the problem? For example, with selling a web site, the customer's main problem could be that they don't trust that the web site will make money, let alone pay for itself. "Most web sites are sold cheaply but are then expensive to run. How can we make sure that your web site is an investment, not a cost?"

Solution. Give a very short solution presentation. Don't give the cost, just present the name and maybe a product shot.

Results. Talk about one big result that you've gotten with your previous customers. Don't mention three or four, just one big one: return on investment on any previous projects, customer testimonials, screenshots, or income value.

Benefits

Often, if there's a brief, copy and paste what they want. Talk about why working with you makes their life better: more time with family, their company makes more profit. The more obvious this is, the better.

CTA 1: Act Now

Finally! A call to action. What's the next step they need to take—e-mail address, phone number, talk to you, URL, buy now. Make it very obvious that they need to do it now, as time is running out and things are changing.

Our Background

Talk about yourself and your business. Tell a story. Start with banging your head against a wall, then say how you created this product, and why people love it. Mention one big result that your business has achieved.

Guarantee

If you're not willing to guarantee your product, you need to seriously think about why you don't trust your own product. Go overboard, go nuts: dollars per hour wasted, a 200% refund, 30-day/60-day no nonsense. If you're not willing to make a promise about your own products and make a guarantee, you shouldn't be selling it.

CTA 2: Safety and Results

Explain how they have the guarantee and they could have these results. There is no reason not to buy: "Look, we've laid out that we will refund you if you're not happy. You could be seeing the results that we got for your own business. Go ahead and buy now."

Pricing

Talk about the pricing model. Offer a low version that doesn't have any results, the version that you want them to buy, and something far beyond their budget but with even more results. For one-time products, talk about one price but upsell and compare it to other products on the market. Don't ever say you're cheaper. Is it the price of a meal out or a cup of coffee? Use that.

Fear: Ego

No one likes to miss out and everyone has an ego. Use something that incites fear of not dealing with change: "The world needs hard workers too, who don't make money." Ask them why they want their business to keep doing what it's doing.

CTA: Next Steps

This is the final CTA, big and obvious. Ask if people know what to do next.

Dos and Don'ts

Finish with a list of dos and don'ts. It's a really nice finish to make sure that people see you delivering value over asking for money. Keep a URL/CTA at the bottom.

Withhold the lead magnet. If you can, set your autoresponder software to send the lead magnet, via an e-mail, after the VSL has finished. All you need to do is tell MailChimp or Active Campaign, or whatever system you use, to send the e-mail a predetermined number of minutes after they sign up. However long the VSL is, send the content after that length of time.

If someone signs up to your lead magnet and buys immediately, you don't want to send them follow-up e-mails selling them the splinter product. You want to put them into a new autoresponder sequence that treats them differently. As long as you always tell people that it'll take a few minutes to send their content to their e-mail, they'll be fine if they don't buy.

If they buy, redirect them to the product delivery page. "Always have an upsell." I've heard this over and over, but when we're starting out, the easiest thing to do when someone buys is redirect them to the splinter product page. It could be a download page, access page, and so on. Whatever it is, make sure you can take people straight there.

If you can include the original lead magnet, too, that's even better. Why don't we use a thank you page for splinter products? The truth is, you can. Treat it more as an upsell page and get people to purchase the next product. We have their contact information now, though. We'll have their name, e-mail address and maybe even their real address. There's no need to protect your list now, as now they're also a customer. They're not a lead; they've bought from you, so you can exceed their expectations and develop that relationship further.

Stop the lead magnet. As we mentioned, if they signed up and bought, you don't need to send the lead magnet via e-mail. You can send it, combined with their purchase, in another e-mail or send it again later after they've purchased. The main thing, though, is to stop the upsell e-mail automation sequence.

Send a welcome e-mail. If your lead hasn't bought a splinter product, don't call them up and demand to know why not. If they haven't bought after the lead magnet is delivered, send a welcome e-mail. Welcome them to your list, your community, and your business. Tell them a little about who you are, provide a bit of background, and let them know how they can reach out to you.

This is a good time to tell them about your private Facebook group or ask them to follow you on Twitter. It might sound stupid, but welcome e-mails are really important. It's recognizing that your new lead isn't just an e-mail address. You're saying hello and letting them know you want to help them.

Send three valuable e-mails. The fastest way to grow your trust and authority with your new lead is to send them free, valuable content. One day after the other (that's right, three e-mails over three days), send them content within the subject or topic of the lead magnet they signed up for. "Won't they see that as spam?" you might ask. Well, are you planning on sending spam?

Here's the deal with e-mail marketing, spam, and content. If you received an e-mail every day from a company, and it deposited $1 into your bank account, would you open those e-mails? Of course you would open those e-mails every day! On the other hand, if I sent you one e-mail a month, every month, but it was just a sales letter telling you to buy from me, that would probably get pretty annoying.

Spam has nothing to do with the amount of messages you send. It's about not providing value to your list. If you aren't comfortable with sending your content out every day, if it's not valuable every day, you probably shouldn't send it at all. Can you say that your content is worth at least $1? Are your e-mails helping people? Are people going to enjoy reading them? They should, because otherwise you have a problem with the quality of your content, and not sending it isn't going to make it any better.

After someone signs up, place them in an autoresponder sequence within that topic that sends them more content. Send them useful information based on what you know about them. Show them that you've got plenty of helpful materials related to what they want to know.

Send three sales e-mails. After sending your value stack e-mails, give it a bit of a break and over the next week or two, start sending up to three sales e-mails for your splinter products. You can use the same copy from your VSL and written sales letters. You can even direct them to sales pages with the same written content or VSL on your thank you page. The easiest method for writing sales e-mails is to write with emotion.

Purchasing and buying are emotional decisions. Talk about how their life will be after they buy or how they'll feel if they use your product. You can even use a story-type arch of the first e-mail introducing the product, the second e-mail asking if they are crazy because they're ignoring you, and the final e-mail telling them you won't contact them again about this product. If you have offers, limited stock, or other scarcity factors, be sure to use them, too.

Offer lead magnets from other silos. After your sales e-mails, if your e-mail subscriber hasn't bought your splinter product, the easiest thing to do is move them into another content silo. Let's say we have two content silos: an SEO silo and a social media silo. We have a blog post on creating SEO blog content, designed to get you more traffic. The lead magnet is a blog post SEO checklist. After our visitor has signed up for our SEO checklist, we position a blog post course and SEO template in front of them for $19. They don't buy, which is absolutely fine, but we still want to keep them engaged. At the end of the sales e-mails for the splinter product, we start a value stack series for our social media silo.

Rather than try to get them to sign up again, we send a few e-mails showing them our social media lead magnet. We'll probably need to look at the messaging behind why someone would be interested in social content. The link between one content silo and the next needs to be clear enough so that people are interested.

> Hey [name],
>
> We know you were interested in driving more traffic from Google.
>
> If you liked that idea, you'll love our social media cheat sheet.
>
> It talks about the five fastest ways to generate free traffic from social media.
>
> As you're on my list already, you don't need to sign up.
>
> Just click here and get the cheat sheet now.
>
> Mike

Most e-mail automation programs will allow you to easily automate when someone clicks on a link or views a page. If your e-mail subscriber clicks on the new lead magnet link, start sending them the value stack and sales series for that content silo.

Send another three value stack e-mails. Once someone clicks a new lead magnet link, make sure to put them into the next content silo. You don't have to do anything particularly special, just start sending them the value stack series for the next content silo. It might be that they just need more relationship building with you, or need to see more options from you. Again, have three e-mails over three days with free blog posts or content related to the lead magnet. Then go ahead and start sending sales e-mails for the splinter product in this content silo.

Another option is to offer all the splinter products and lead magnets as a suite. Either you can offer this option to subscribers after they've bought one splinter product, as an upsell, or offer it to people who haven't bought individual splinter products. You could discount the price a little because they're buying all the splinter products, but an even better approach is to include all your lead magnets, too, as a toolbox. This way your customer gets loads more value rather than just the splinter products.

Retarget lead magnet users. When you have your e-mail subscribers, after you've built a decent list, those who haven't bought splinter products are perfect candidates for remarketing. MailChimp even has a built-in Facebook advertising platform that allows you to select a list and segment (i.e., lead magnet subscribers who haven't bought) and position advertising in front of them. ActiveCampaign also has a wonderfully easy "add to remarketing list" function in its automation suite.

There are other platforms, of course, and doing it manually like this isn't true automatic remarketing, but it's a great start. Remarketing means we take people who are already aware of us and position content and products in front of them. Often after people have signed up, if they haven't bought right away, it just means they need some more time for consideration. We can remind them we're here to help and get advertising in front of them to remain in their mind.

"Behind the scenes" webinar. Webinars are fantastic ways to really connect with your leads, giving —one or two hours of unbroken time to demonstrate your expertise and knowledge. The key to a great webinar is to give away tons of value. Really work hard at being the most valuable resource you can for your leads. A great way to connect with your subscribers, rather than just any webinar topic is to do a "behind the scenes" webinar.

Behind the scenes follows the same basic format as any other webinar. However, this time you take a topic and do a live case study. For example, if you're a social media traffic expert, just do a live screen share of how you work with customers and get them results. Again, put the fear monster to bed. Just because you show people what to do and how you do it does not mean they won't need you to do it for them.

It doesn't have to be a real customer; you could keep it anonymous or just use a dummy example. Bringing your list a behind the scenes webinar is a real trust boost, though. Everyone loves exclusive and secret access. Explain that it's usually just for customers, but for one webinar only, you're blowing the doors open on your social media traffic techniques. You can easily invite people from outside your list to join a call like this, but it's important that there is something for your list that rewards them for subscribing to you. I've found that behind the scenes webinars work best.

Include splinter products in your newsletters. When you send weekly newsletter e-mails out (which you should), make sure to include a link or section somewhere that sells a splinter product. You wouldn't believe how many customers we've reeled in by reminding them of our products in our newsletter e-mails.

Get on the Phone!

A very powerful way to connect with customers—in other words, people who have bought splinter products—is to book a one-on-one call with that customer. It doesn't have to be long, maybe 30 minutes. Offer it as a one-on-one Q&A session, letting them ask anything they need about the product.

It might not sound scalable, but it doesn't have to be you after a while. If you do enough of them, you'll notice the same questions come up time and again. You could even get previous long-term customers to take calls. You are adding massive value to their purchase. It's also the perfect opportunity to get to know your customers. If you're seen as the face of the business, or people can interact with real people after they buy, you'll have a customer for life.

What do they want help with next? This could be on a call, in a webinar, via e-mail, or through any kind of communication where people can easily respond to you and reply. When you want to start upselling or cross-selling (x-selling), the logical thing to ask would be "What do you want help with next?" I've found this question to be a little counterproductive. Customers might not really know what they want next, or they might feel embarrassed that they just want the same results again (which, of course, is absolutely fine).

What we want to ask, is "What results have you got so far?" then lead into asking if they want more, faster results or with more automation:

"Hey Brian, I'm glad you enjoyed the course. What was the big result or takeaway?"

"Well, I loved seeing how I can better manage my time. Using time blocks and priorities has really helped my productivity."

"That's great! When it comes to ticking items off your list, achieving your goals, would you like to explore how we can do that faster?"

"Yeah, that sounds good. But I'm not sure how we'd do it!"

"Let's explore how we can leverage your time better. Make you even more productive. What if we help you be more productive, but with less effort too? Automating some of the process? Would you like help with that?"

"Sure! What do we need to do?"

This is then where you lead into your upsell, x-sell, or core offer. The splinter products and other products and services you offer are designed to lead into a sale through which you get serious results for your customers. You're going to do a lot more of the legwork for them, though: You're going to get the results they want faster and with more automation. People buy change. They want to buy a better version of what they have now. If you can make that better version, which is in the future, appear faster, you've got a perfect sales process.

Main product sales letter. We now need to position a sales letter to our audience. We've already explored how we write a VSL. You're going to use the exact same formula to write a written sales letter, too.

How long should the sales letter be? Honestly? I've seen 20,000-word sales letters that make $100,000 sales. I've seen short 600-word sales letters that consistently sell 10 x $150 products a day. The key to writing a sales letter is to write from your heart. That might sound trite, but sales are emotional transactions, not logical ones. If you write with emotional language you'll connect with the other human beings who are reading it. A good rule of thumb is to read over what you've written and try to halve it. Try to remove 50% of the copy. It's hard work, but it'll force you to keep only the good stuff. You need to try and remove 50% of the copy before you publish it.

Create a sales page. We need to move that sales letter onto a sales page. This needs to be on your web site or in your sales funnel. You might want to pay a designer to make the sales page look great. Having said that, don't stress too much about making the design look incredible. Publishing a sales letter and sending it to people is much more effective than a well-designed page that's never published.

Good sales letter writing comes from emotion. Be emotional and use emotive language to write your sales letter. Use your before/after list and product/results/benefits sheet to understand the language, goals, and journeys that your customers are going to go on. Writing a personal letter explaining the benefits and change they'll see, combined with emotive language, will act as a wonderfully strong and compelling reason for people to buy. Your sales pages don't need to be fancy. When you have time and budget, go for complicated and fancy products pages. Until then, though, writing copy will still make the sales.

E-mail sales campaign. The beauty of a sales letter format, such as the one I've given you, is that it can be repurposed into multiple other formats. When we want to start driving people back to those sales pages, we need to connect with them and compel them to click. The easiest way to do this is to use the individual sections from your sales letter and cut them up into shorter e-mails.

For example, the promise, problem, myth, and changing sections are perfect for a "problem intrigue" type e-mail. Send that with a link and a CTA to understand how to solve the problem, and you just got yourself a sales e-mail. You could also try the problem, myth, knife twist format and introduce the solution for an "agitate solve" type e-mail. These are really good to launch your product with.

Play around with different types. You could even take some of the sections that you've cut from your first sales letter draft (remember when we cut the copy by 50%) and use those to drive traffic to the page. Finally, make sure that you try writing new sales e-mails. Again, write from the heart. Write emotionally and appeal to the human beings who are reading it.

Automate your past campaigns. Now it's time to start building your automation process. You can now take the e-mails you've written and use them in e-mail follow-ups. Once subscribers buy a splinter product, start sending them (after a week or two) the sales e-mails to your main product. Drive them back to that sales page with the same e-mails you sent your first round of customers.

Create a "problem" webinar. Your sales letter also makes a perfect webinar format. Webinars are fast becoming one of the most profitable outreach methods on the Internet, and potentially in marketing overall. When it comes to creating webinars it's important to give value and again, give away stuff that makes you feel a little queasy (am I giving away too much?). I'm talking about value and content; don't give actual products or services out for free.

The first type of webinar we're going to create is a "problem agitate" webinar. This is designed to break down a problem in your marketplace, demonstrate that you know what you're talking about, and work the audience into a frenzy about the problem. It can be very dangerous to try and explain why something is a problem. For example, construction companies are renowned for making millions of dollars, but hesitating on spending over $1,000 on a web site. If you try to spend time convincing people that they have a problem or spend energy on why they're wrong, you'll go insane battering against stubborn egos. Flip that instead and look at problems that they recognize they have. It's really important that people connect with the problem right at the start. For some businesses it is keeping costs low, or it might be getting new customers in, or creating recurring income.

Whatever the problem is that you can solve, your audience needs to understand and connect with it. Construction companies don't have the problem of needing a web site; they have the problem of competing with other construction companies.

The layout for a "problem agitate" webinar relies on similar principles to the sales letter. Make a big promise about what you're going to explore. Outline the main problem the customer faces. If you can introduce statistics and case studies about this problem, that's even better. You're going to expose the problem and attack it from multiple angles. Next, explore the myth, or more specifically, what people are doing wrong. This is where you can introduce what they're doing now as incorrect. You need to explain what happens when they keep doing it this way.

Go over the consequences of keeping up that activity; for example, spending $1,000 on a web site. You know why that's a bad idea: It doesn't ever generate you leads and you'll regret paying $1,000. The consequences of spending $1,000 on a web site mean you'll never make a return on that investment, so you're wasting $1,000. Explore how that dominoes down the line. You'll think all Internet marketing is a waste of time. You start to see online and digital marketing as an expensive waste of time.

Really hammer home the consequences of both the problem and the current way of thinking. Finally, end with a knife twist: "To top it all off ...." This is a final angle, probably from your before/after list, which affects their status. Explain how they're just seen as "another business" and nothing exciting. Knife twists work really well if you show them their status now. After you've whipped people up into a frenzy with the problem, they'll be begging for a solution.

Now we can introduce you and what you're about, the big result (solving this problem), and the experience you bring to the table. We can now explore a case study and the results you've seen solving this problem. It doesn't have to be a real case study, but talk the audience through a journey and the changes that businesses see working with you. This particular webinar doesn't go over the specific tactics or solutions, even at a high level, but we do explore the journey through to change that your audience wants to see.

They'll pick up bits and pieces, but this is more an exercise in demonstrating results and value. Your expertise and knowledge need to be seen as valuable. Finally, mention to them that there is another webinar in which you demonstrate how you solve that problem, every day.

Create a solution webinar. Take the problem from the previous webinar and create a webinar that solves the same problem. Again, our internal "shortage" brain sees knowledge and information as something that should be hoarded, not shared for free. If you're serious about growing and scaling your business, though, you need to help as many people as possible. Here's what really happens when you give information away for free: 100% of people who watch the webinar are interested in solving that problem.

About 80% are going to think you know your stuff. They'll always believe that you know what you're talking about. About 50% aren't going to buy anyway. They're just looking or not ready to commit yet. You're not selling anything on this webinar yet, but we'll get to that. About 30% are going to try doing the work themselves. However, the very nature of a webinar is like information overload. There will be too much for them to process. In fact, it suits you even more to support people who do want to do it themselves. You can continue to provide free content to them and shift them over to a sale later.

About 10% are probably already customers, looking to see what you can help with further. Another 10% are going to buy from you at some point. Give away a serious level of value in your webinars. Really help people solve their problem and show them the steps to take. Show them tools, worksheets, and screen shares. Show them how to accomplish their goals and what they need to do to solve the problem.

The goal is to become an invaluable resource. Make the viewers think, "Holy cow, Mike just solved that problem that has been bugging me for years, in 45 minutes." The objection people feel to this, and the fear they feel is because deep down they don't think they can solve another problem. If they give this one away for free, what will they have to sell? There are two ways to look at this. Very few serious problems, roadblocks, and issues for businesses can truly be solved in a one- or two-hour webinar. It's highly unlikely that 120 minutes on a call will solve anything massive. You'll still need to help them with the deeper aspects of what they're suffering from.

Second, if you've only got one trick up your sleeve, what are you expecting people to buy next anyway? If you were going to charge for that information in the first place, what would you have done if someone said, "Okay, what's next?" If that's how you feel, I can't help you at all. You need to go out and learn more solutions to problems. Get some expertise and experience. Don't live in fear of sharing knowledge, because it stunts your growth as a business. Remember our before/after list. The goal is not to provide a want or even a feel; it's to change people's average day and raise their status. That's what they're buying. Run a webinar that solves a big problem for a customer, and cement yourself as their trusted source of information.

Create a sales webinar. Finally, run and record a webinar that talks about the product and solution you're selling. This webinar is pitched and advertised as, "We're going to give you a high-level overview of everything we do and give you." This is the most terrifying content of all. You're going to give a 30,000-foot view of your entire product or solution. Your entire offering is going to be exposed and shown to every person on the call.

Why do we do this? This is the webinar where you open the gates and get people to buy. Your audience members still have problems in their life or business. Your product or service should solve more than one problem. It should help elevate their status and change their average day. So now we go over everything that you're going to give them to change their lives.

It's a high-level overview of the plan or process that you use. Remember the process we mapped out earlier? Every stage in that has a purpose, a result, and a benefit, just like our list. We talk about the other problems and roadblocks they face, the future of their lives, and what their average day looks like. Then we focus on what their lives and businesses could look like: what 12 or 6 months (or even 30 days) looks like into the future, what they'll be able to do, and what they want to do and feel. We talk about what their status will be in the future and how their customers, friends, colleagues, and competition will think of them.

Go over what they get as part of the process. Go over each stage, not in detail, but how it helps them. Include results, testimonials, benefits, and what it does to your current status. For example, let's use one stage of our process, a web site content and copy session.

> Next up is our web site content and copy session. It's part of our process and is one of the consultation sessions we run when we start a project.
>
> Before a content session, businesses are expected to know exactly what they need to write for a web site. This means they either produce poor quality content, none at all, or it takes ages and slows the process down.
>
> That's fine, because you're not expected to know how to write content and copy. However we're not experts in your field, so we can't write specifically to it. We do, however, know how to write fantastic, compelling copy and use your expertise to fill in the gaps.
>
> Imagine having everything you know clearly demonstrated to your customer. The home page, product pages, and landing pages all read well and give enough away for people to call. What if writing for your web site was easy, not a chore? Wouldn't that make life easier? Well that's why we have our web site content and copy session.

You then just rinse and repeat for each stage in the process. Go over what this would cost individually sometimes, for coaching and consulting, per product too. When you show a list of everything they get, tell them the price, and sometimes when the offer closes.

We'll usually run a few "closes" such as objection closes, fear of missing out, or money replenish closes. Then, after we list everything and offer a buy now link, we go over the list again. This time, though, we start adding bonus material. Bonus content is not 100% necessary to a sale, but it can help. There are three levels of products: The first is your main delivery, the thing you're selling. Second is a few bonus products or services, and third are bonuses that you don't tell them about. This gives you something else to overdeliver with.

The key is to make sure that whatever your core offer is, it's clearly worth the value. The bonus material is just icing on the cake. If you're struggling to think of bonus products, reports are a fantastic and easy way to add value; for example, keyword reports, competitor SEO insight, and social media follower reports. These things are easy to automate. Add to the bonuses in the exact same way you did with your regular products. Give an overview, why it's useful, and how it helps. Give a price individually if necessary and add to the list of deliverables. Finally, close with a strong CTA and buy now link or button. Give people time to purchase, but let them know it'll run out. This is your product sales webinar.

Three-page microfunnel. Once you've run and recorded those webinars, you can create a microfunnel. Something like this only needs three pages. It's essentially a take on Jeff Walker's Product Launch Formula (PLF). What we're doing is splitting a sales letter over three individual webinars. The first webinar is perfect for driving traffic. You can sign people up and use the webinar recording to demonstrate the problem facing them. People will want information on that problem and they want to learn how to solve it.

Here's where we get clever. Everyone who signs up gets access to the first video, but the second webinar recording is released the day after. There are platforms and software that can release a recording to a subscriber, meaning that the second and third pages are blocked from view until they watch the first and sign up. You release the second video and e-mail them with a reminder. The second video is where you solve one of the problems facing them. They'll be blown away by how much value you're giving away. You'll solve a problem for them, walk through the solution, and keep telling them that tomorrow you're going to give even more away.

Finally, just like before, you can release the next video to subscribers. This time, show them everything about your product and service for total transparency and a high-level overview of everything that customers get. This final video is where you place the buy now button and get people to sign up. Again, most businesses that run three-page funnels like this release their products in stages, meaning that they only allow people to sign up and buy two or three times a year. Scalable businesses work like this because it allows them to focus on getting core customers and running them through a process. If you'd rather run these funnels "greenfield" (meaning you keep running them on and on), go ahead. It's your business and only you know what works.

Make payment as easy as possible. This is imperative to the success of your new scaled business. Make your payment system and method as easy as possible. I can't stress this enough. Test and test and test. When I first started, I used PayPal (which is simple to use, but not so great at integrating with other systems). I lost count of how many sales I missed out on because my payment system wasn't easy.

If people decide to buy, they're making an emotional commitment, not a logical one. It's like asking someone out on a date. They say yes, but if you're late, or even worse you don't turn up, they'll never come back. I use Stripe now for online payments with subscriptions. PayPal is fantastic to get started with, but requires a little more manual work.

Make sure your button to buy works and everything is automated. Reward the risk that customers take, clicking that button, with a smooth payment process and put their fears to rest. Test your payment methods and don't leave it to others to tell you something is wrong.

Summary

Connecting your audience to a scalable product is about scaling out your voice across multiple platforms. Remember, your list and audience have already trusted that you can help them. You have a duty to continue helping them as far as you can.

- If someone is interested in a certain topic, it's reasonable to assume that they'll buy something related to that topic, too.
- You can prove your products are useful and helpful by actually helping people during the buying process!
- Use live events and then record them to automate a sales process.
- Never underestimate the power of a live conversation; it could massively increase your conversions.

CHAPTER 8

Why Process Is the Key to Scale

Process, systems, and protocols sound like very boring concepts. You got into business to be creative, solve problems, and help people! No one likes the idea of setting up processes or workflows. Even less, you especially hate the work of bookkeeping, answering e-mails, sending your newsletter, and social media posting. There are loads of activities that our businesses have to do that are in fact very dull. Frankly, they're not high value either.

Posting to social media and e-mailing customers can definitely be outsourced to other people. The key to getting great results is writing up that process. You can either (1) continue to do the boring work week in week out, or (2) spend some time writing up a boring and time-consuming process, and then never have to do that job again. In this chapter, we're going to create a series of processes that allow us to do more, with less.

Processes Are an Investment

When my customers start to write up processes, they often complain about how much time it takes. "It'd be faster to do it myself at this rate!" or "It'll take forever to train someone to do it just how I do it." Writing up processes is like any other habit. It takes time to get it right. You have to learn to create and write and do something new. We're going to go over how to create those processes and start to allow you more time back from your business.

Spend your time better. There are critical and noncritical aspects of any business. Ask any successful entrepreneur and he or she will tell you that there are high-thought, high-value tasks and low-thought, low-value tasks. Grant Cardone, Timothy Ferriss, Al Ramada, Cal Newport, Daniel Priestly, Brian Moran, and many others have written books on prioritizing your time and getting goals done. Most people treat their e-mail inbox like a to-do list. This is toxic. You're letting other people dictate your workflow.

If you have objectives and goals, you need to decide what to do. Ignore everything else (seriously). Your time is not best spent tweeting or assigning account codes to expenses. Your time is best spent talking to customers, creating products, and helping people. All the other low-value tasks (which we'll go over next) can be written up, outsourced, and taken off your plate.

Get more of what you've got. The important thing to know about automation and creating processes is that they work both ways. If you have a system that is efficient, cost-effective, and time-productive, writing up and automating that process will scale the positive effects exponentially.

For example, it used to take me two hours a week to produce the weekly social media content. I'd write it up, schedule it, create images, link it to posts, and select the platforms. So I decided to write the process up, train someone, and have them do all that. Now I just write new blog posts and press Publish. Somehow, it's given me more than two hours back a week. The best part is that my social media consultant gets faster at it each time, so her time back increases, too. On the other hand, a process that doesn't work well also scales. If something is badly run or poorly managed, once it scales it'll just take up of your time, not less.

Another example is a telecommunications company I used to consult for. They ran an internal newsletter with all the press and mentions across the Internet, magazines, and other media so the various marketing departments could keep an eye on what was happening. It sounded pretty smart, but as new people came on board, they all started to contribute to the newsletter. Social media teams, PR departments, and marketing teams all started to give more and more content to this newsletter. Eventually, a committee had to be set up to deal with the amount of content being sent to them.

They had meetings on what to send people, how to lay out the e-mail, and what else they could send in the newsletter. This in turn required another newsletter to inform the committee about what the committee was going to inform the teams about. Needless to say, I just moved the newsletter into my junk. All of that could have been solved with an RSS feed and Google alerts. Processes that don't work, "don't work more" (sorry Mr. Malone, my old English teacher) when they scale. Make sure your process works first.

Great Interviews

When hiring staff, outsourcing, or using freelancers, having a process makes a fantastic interview. When I was looking for VA staff, I had a process for editing some videos for YouTube. I also had a process for uploading and publishing the content, creating thumbnails, and scheduling the videos. As I had been doing the work for a few weeks, I had a very good idea of what worked and what didn't. However, I am not a videographer or editor. I just did what I thought was right. I recorded my steps and wrote out the process. I use Process.st for almost everything in my business.

I then used the Process.st document as the interview and brief. People could read the guides and tell me if they thought they could do it. VA teams, video freelancers, and other people applied and I chose to interview four or five. The editor who was chosen got the job because not only did he follow the process to the letter, but he also gave me his professional feedback on how I could improve it. He talked about changing the screen ratio, better sound quality, and other editing techniques.

Because the process was written up, I could rely on the results being the same. With expert advice, though, the results were better than I expected. Outsourcing usually fails because expectations aren't set and met. I had a manager at an old company who was constantly arguing with suppliers and consultants when she didn't get what she was expecting. To be fair to her, the companies should have set her expectations, but it was also up to her to be clear on what she wanted. You're only going to be disappointed if you're not clear on what you want. Written up documentation is a fantastic and easy way to create a brief for scalable, outsourced work.

Process = Scale

Here's another point, which we sort of covered earlier: If you can write up your processes, you can scale. Whether its product creation, delivery, support, marketing, or reporting, if you can write up a series of steps to get someone else to do the work, your business can and will scale. If you're serious about scaling, get serious about processes. It's hard at first, and boring even, but the results are well worth it.

Use one-off staff or freelancers to start. When you first start to scale, use outsourcing. Don't jump into full-time staff straight away. You need to get used to managing people and providing work for them. My advice would be to start with freelancing marketplaces first. Upwork.com, Freelancer.com, 99designs.com, and Speedlancer.com are all great options for exploring hiring staff. Anything you can think of, from logo design to copywriting, is available.

Chapter 8 | Why Process Is the Key to Scale

The key to hiring staff is following a process (there's that word again). First, make sure you're not overwhelmed by the available options: "Start small and sacrifice." This means choose a job that you're going to do anyway. There's nothing worse than hiring someone to do a big, vital job, only to see them do a poor job. You should be hiring people to take care of work you're already doing. I provide loads of examples later, but think of the jobs that you do that aren't maximum impact work. It could be client work or your own work. Jobs that come in might need contracts sent out or proposals written. Maybe there is some logo design or color palette work. Whatever needs to be done can easily be achieved by other people. When you post your first brief, you want to be as clear as possible. I often use a written process as the brief. I want people to execute a task rather than do creative work from scratch. I've found in the past that when it comes to creative work, you get what you pay for. Just because someone says they can design a page for $50 or write a sales letter for $100 doesn't mean it's worth it.

Hiring staff, for me, started with executing tasks that I needed done and work that I didn't want to do anymore. I do have a developer and I do have a designer, as well as a social media coordinator and an operations manager. I have an accountant, mentor, and business development manager. All of them came from months of interviews, testing, and relationship building. Your initial hires for short-term, one-off work might well turn into longer term working relationships. That's absolutely fine. My video editor started with a one-off job, then we began working more and more together. The beauty of the Internet means we can hire when we need it. Scalable, elastic workforces mean as long as we have our systems written up, we can outsource almost everything.

Start a "done work" diary. Not sure where to start? What do you outsource first? Well the easiest way I know of is to keep a "done work" diary. This is simply a diary of the work you've completed today. Just write a few notes down at the end of each day and watch for any recurring work. Small things like "posted to Twitter" or "posted to Instagram" are great work notes. As they happen pretty regularly, you'll soon want someone else to do this for you. After a couple of weeks, look over your done work items and look for repeat tasks. Those are the ones you should start outsourcing.

Record a regular task. Take a look at your tasks and work done and pick out something that happens every week or every month. It doesn't have to be a huge item. Even a small, 20-minute job is a good place to start. What we're going to do is create our first process. First, get yourself some screen capture software. Camtasia for PC, for me, is the best on the market. For Mac you have Screenflow, which is also very good.

All you're going to do is record the screen, recording your actions for your regular task. You might want a dry run, doing the actions without recording, just to familiarize yourself with the steps. You'd be surprised how many extra steps there are, even in a small task, that you aren't consciously aware of. Next, simply record the screen and capture the steps you take. You can do a voice-over while you do the steps, or you can do a separate voice-over, whichever is more comfortable for you. Produce the screen capture as a video and upload it to YouTube, Vimeo, or another platform. This will be the main resource for your outsourcing staff. It'll allow them to see exactly what you do and gives you a great template to write up a written version of the documentation.

Write up that process. I use Process.st to write up checklists and documentation. You can use absolutely anything you want to document and store processes. However, the reason I use Process.st is because it acts as a series of checklists and can hold lots of different media. As opposed to writing in Google Docs, Process.st lets us create checklist templates. Then, whenever a new task needs to be done, we use a checklist template and our team follows those steps.

Process.st lets users click a Completed and Next Step button, which means it measures their progress and I can see how far through a process they are. Anyway, the key to writing up a process properly is to use your video as the steps and guides. A written process also needs to include links to resources, images, written steps, and a small brief. If you'd like an example, go to https://www.process.st/checklist/process-for-uploading-tweets-to-post-cron/ to see our process for social media posting.

We include a brief at the start, links to all the resources and the video, then we break the video down into steps. A good rule of thumb is any step that needs you to change programs is a new step. Also, a change in result is a new step, too. For example, using this process, "editing the tweets" is a step because at the end of it, they'll have edited tweets. The next step is "downloading as a .csv" because at the end of that, they'll have a .csv file. Write up your video process and provide as much detail as you can. Include resources, links, and images and you'll have fewer questions from your staff. I'm going to give you examples of processes and their steps next.

Social media posting. Like the earlier example on social media posting, this is the most common and easiest task to outsource. At the very least, you just need your main social accounts and some content to share. Don't fall into the trap of "brand recognition" or follower growth. It's nonsense. Lots of social media freelancers will try to convince you to tweet quotes and other people's content, but it needs to be your own content.

All you really need is a steady stream of your own content and a process to take copy and quotes from your own posts. Use that as the social content to publish and share. There's no need to write tweets from scratch; the easiest thing to do is copy lines and quotes from your own post and use them. Don't overcomplicate it. We get our social media coordinator to copy quotes and headers from our blog content.

Paste those into a `.csv` file and make a few copies. Recently, we've also started using Canva.com, a free graphics tool to create images to accompany the text content. Then we upload all of that to Postcron.com, our preferred social media tool, and schedule three tweets per day and one Facebook post per day.

Customer e-mails and enquiries. Most customer e-mails and enquiries are support tasks that are frequent: How do I reset my password? How do I add a user? What's this on my billing? Outsourcing customer services is a fantastic way to really start to scale. Using a tool like Zendesk or Teamwork (my favorite) you can allow users to e-mail a central help center rather than e-mail you.

Dealing with customer services and enquiries requires two things: training and freedom. We make sure our team knows exactly all our policies. We have a strong refund policy and they know where all our resources are. It's honestly easier than you might think. Make a list of all the resources you offer, with any notes or policies that might come with that service or product. Create a video (or a few) of where those resources are, from PDFs to calendar booking apps. If a customer wants to get in touch with you, what would he or she usually ask for?

Also, it's important that your staff know they have freedom to handle customers. We had a rule that if it cost $100 or less to satisfy a customer, just do it. There was no need to run the cost through us; just get it done. Refunds are almost always handled, no matter what (the four that we've given last year), and, most important, the customer queries are documented so future staff can see what the solution was. Your job is to delight the customer. Really, when it boils down to it, that's it. Focus your customer service on delighting customers. Be natural, friendly, and personal. Most successful businesses now consider customer service a marketing expense. Spending time with customers is the fastest way to grow trust and increase their likelihood of telling others about you. A good product might do it, but great customer service will trump good products every time.

Booking networking events. These suit outsourcing so well because they can be created from nothing. If you want to kick off a regular networking event, you need three things: people, a location, and a date and time. Most VAs and staff will know the basics of organizing an event. It's up to you to give specifics.

First, choose where you want to hold the event. You'll need a rough location (i.e., a city) and you'll need some specifics for the location. For example, if you want to have 20 people there, with drinks and something to eat, these will all need to be features that your VA needs to know. The more specific you are with your wants and requests, the better the outcome will be. VAs aren't psychic. You need to tell them everything you want. Next, you'll need to set a date and a time and use that in your invite. Don't fall into the trap of trying to please everyone. Finally, you can send e-mail or contact information to your VA to get them to invite the attendees. In the past, because we haven't had an e-mail list, we've even asked our VA to find businesses within a certain geographic location. We've collected their e-mails and e-mailed them individually (no mass marketing). Use the e-mail template from Chapter 6 on holding a networking lunch as the template to send.

Booking time to speak to clients. Realistically, you should be talking to your customers at least once a month. Most of our more regular customers are on weekly or biweekly calls anyway. Have a rolling calendar appointment to remind your VA to book a call with all current customers. It's a fantastically easy way to start writing processes and getting regular results. After some time, if your VA is comfortable, he or she might even be able to take the call.

If you give a structured approach to a catch-up call, your customers will tell you what's on their mind, what they're working on next, and what they're struggling with. Get the call in regularly and they'll wonder how they lived without you.

Bookkeeping and accounting. A slightly more complex, but vital outsourcing task, is accounting and bookkeeping. Depending on your business, you might only require a bookkeeper. Personally, I've found an accountant invaluable. They've helped me arrange my finances and I get a lot of help from them. You probably require a specialist, at least in the area of accounting. Bookkeeping is slightly less complex, but no less vital to a business's financial health.

Essentially, what you want is a method of tackling expenses and income. I use Xero, but Quickbooks is also a fantastic option. Programs like these allow you to connect your income and expenses as well as "rectify" what the cost or income was from. Combined with someone looking over your finances, this will save you hours of work in the future. It's well worth the cost and something I'd get from day one if I was scaling my business. Even if you can do it yourself, the key isn't to continue working for your business. There are hundreds of things you can do for your business, but it's not as productive as getting someone else to do it.

Weekly newsletter. One of the first tasks I started to outsource was blog post promotion. Aside from social media, our other outreach method was via our newsletter. The big problem I had was that I wanted my new blog posts to be sent out on Friday after they were published on Thursday.

I would write up the e-mail and send it. Although this only took me an hour or so to do, I felt I could easily train someone else to do it. This was also my first experience with getting outsourcing wrong. I assumed that a VA would be able to write a newsletter blog post e-mail. It wasn't necessarily his fault, as he wasn't a native English speaker, but the e-mail copy didn't read well at all. It would have been obvious I hadn't written it. I also tried copywriters to create the copy, but it all felt and looked a little bland and generic. I take total responsibility for not being clear enough with my e-mail copywriting techniques, and it's something I need to look at again. Instead, now is I'll write the e-mail copy, sticking to a format that means my VA can see what text goes where, and I send that to them to upload to MailChimp. I don't really use images in my e-mails and most of the time I'm only sending one item at a time.

Uploading and editing YouTube videos. On the opposite side of the complexity spectrum, I was editing and uploading my own YouTube videos, which was taking me hours. Anyone who has edited videos knows how long and tedious the process is. I wrote up and screen-captured what I was doing before writing the process up.

I used that document as the brief and asked applicants to tell me if they could perform such a process. Eventually, I hired a video editor who not only edited the videos the way I needed, but also had professional experience and insight on making my videos better. He talked about changing my recording setup, how to set up cuts, and other extremely useful ideas. Before long, my videos were being created faster than I could upload them.

This was also my first experience creating and managing a longer chain process. After the videos were edited, they sat in Google Drive. I wrote up the titles, YouTube descriptions, tags, and links for each video in a spreadsheet. I then sent the videos and spreadsheet to my VA, who created thumbnails in Canva, uploaded the videos, and added all the metadata. Eventually, I had an automation program, Zapier, tell my VA when a new video was available on Google Drive and fire off a checklist for her to follow. Honestly, this is my perfect example of how processes can run.

Researching and compiling list posts. Some types of content need real attention to detail. It's no good heading to Fiverr and getting a $20 blog post, because it will read like a $20 blog post. Most of the time it's copied and pasted from Wikipedia and other blog posts. However, compiling and researching list posts is a fantastic way to outsource content. We've explored list posts already, but as a reminder, they're essentially "Top 5 tools for …" or "Best 10 web sites that …."

List posts can be outsourced easily, as all you need to ask for is a checklist:

- Please research 10 tools for WordPress businesses that allow you to edit images (e.g., Gimp, Canva, etc.).
- Mark down their price or if they're free.
- Write down the tool's name.
- Write down the tool's web site.
- Copy a short paragraph explaining what the tool does.
- Save an image of their logo.

- Find one testimonial or quote from a user and copy and paste it.
- Please feel free to use other list posts as research, but do not copy and paste directly from other blog posts.

You literally don't have to write anything Except perhaps a short introduction. Other than that, you're good to go.

Maintenance and reporting. Web site maintenance will become an integral part of any web site or digital business. The basic concept is that web sites, plug-ins, code, themes, and hosting need updating, maintaining, and securing. The steps taken to update a site are pretty simple. They're repeated every day and there are loads of plug-in and software options to automate a lot of it.

Updating plug-ins, code, and themes takes a little more care, as you need to update a site and then test it before going live. Maintenance is a great process to outsource because it starts with a fundamental set of steps. Once people become comfortable with the basics, you can look at more complex operations such as adding new plug-ins, customization, and child themes.

Reporting, as well, is a very tedious but repeatable task. Your analytics and reporting software probably has some great automation tools to send reports. However, the customizing and sending of reports might need a human touch. With tasks like maintenance and reporting, price your products with a 30% margin on top of what it would cost you. Websites like Gowp.com offer outstanding maintenance, backups, updates, and unlimited tasks (content uploading, etc.) and you can white-label the solution. If they charge $29 per month, charge your customers $45 per month.

Bearing in mind what your customers are paying for are solutions and trust, they don't want to go to the supplier themselves; they want you to sort it. Be fair with your pricing for yourself more than anyone. The same is true with reporting. If it takes about an hour to process and send a report, find out how much it would cost for a VA to do it and charge 30% more.

Writing up and publishing processes. Let's get a bit meta, writing processes of process. Let's say you have a task that you know will become a weekly or monthly fixture. In fact, here is a pro tip: When you do anything for a customer, do yourself a favor and record the steps. Screen capture the process and send that video to a VA to write up.

Help them use Process.st or Kissflow.com to take your video screen capture and turn it into a written document. I've found I've needed a native English speaker to write up processes like this. I adore my VA team, but the work of translating back and forth, despite their level of English being impeccable, means some of my habits and phrases are lost on them.

Ultimately, what we're creating is a machine that means you can take tasks, run them once, and capture the steps with screen captures. Then, by sending that video to a process writer, you can outsource the entire system to another team. This allows you to grow and scale faster and faster.

Automate the Start

Something worth looking at early on is automating the start of your processes. We call these triggers. For example, every Monday at 9 a.m. might be a trigger. Other options could be a new blog post being posted, a new video posted to YouTube, or a new meeting request on your calendar.

I use Zapier to connect tons of tools to each other. They help tie together the project management sides of the start and end of a process. For example, when someone books a new meeting in Calendly, a new meeting is created in Zoom, and e-mailed to both me and the other people in the meeting. Also, we have a zap in Zapier, which means if a new WordPress blog post is posted with a certain category, we'll populate a Google Sheet with a load of tweets. When that's populated, an e-mail with a new Process.st checklist is e-mailed to our social coordinator.

Once she's filled out all the social content and posted it, another e-mail is fired to me saying the process is complete. Fair warning: Some of these automation machines can get complicated. If one breaks, it can break a system or process. Stick with it, though. Like all skills, it takes time to learn how to troubleshoot a problem. Most of the time, Zapier and IFTTT (another automation app) have epic support and can guide you through a problem like this.

Pay for quality but buffer with detail. I know of VA teams who work out to cost $5 an hour. If they're just doing data entry or very specific repeat tasks, you're going to be fine, but they need very specific instructions. The mistake people make when hiring VA staff is covering cost per hour. What happens is they'll go for a cheap VA team and wonder why the results are subpar. If you hire a $5 an hour team and expect them to do complex writing or research, they're bound to get it wrong. You get what you pay for.

Accounting for the time you spend rectifying the problem and fixing what's been done, it'll cost you more than $5 per hour. Pay for what you can afford. Get 10 hours at $15 per hour per month, rather than 30 hours at $5 per hour, just because you want more hours. You're better off paying for quality. The key to making any VA work go well is providing details. Be specific about the time scale, results, examples, sources, and cost of a task.

For example, when asking your VA staff to research a topic, tell them not to spend more than two hours on it. Show them examples and give them all the steps they need. The more freedom they have, the further they'll likely stray from your initial expectations.

Referral, FAQ, and wiki pages or sites. A more complex task, but certainly one that is a symptom of a business that is scaling, is to create a wiki or FAQ. A wiki (think Wikipedia) is a microsite or series of pages on specific topics. For example, new customers might have a load of questions on the new product or service. They can access the wiki and get self-help and guidance on all the topics they need.

We've found the easiest way to create a wiki is to take e-mails and messages from customers with the questions. Then we take our responses and paste them all (without names) into a wiki. We use Quip as a way of keeping documents in a wiki format for people to access. It means we can edit and amend the details when we're learning new things. On the other hand, creating a wiki for your staff is useful, too. Responses to questions or customer issues can be stored. Processes can be linked for larger systems. Quip has a great guide on creating a wiki at https://quip.com/solutions/company-wiki.

Outsource Without Process

You can outsource work without process. It depends on your expectations, trust, and the task. For example, I trust my accountant 100% to do all my financial stuff how he sees fit. It's ludicrous of me to assume I could do it better and he should follow me.

Similarly, my graphic designer is outstanding. I can get her to do whatever I need. She knows me, knows the brand, and is good at her job. She's not cheap, but I never have to ask for redesigns. On the other hand, if I asked a cheap VA from Fiverr to design a landing page for $50, without any guidance, it's very likely he or she would produce something totally different from what I had in mind. Be realistic about your expectations and don't outsource too much, too fast.

Process Is Communication

Creating machines that automate work and systems that take work off your shoulders is all about communication. Process is the practice of repeatedly carrying out tasks that generate predictable outcomes. We cannot create sustainable processes without communication. The reason projects and tasks fall through is because of a lack of communication. Have you ever had a manager or customer get upset when something doesn't go their way? We all have. Every time it happens, if we're honest, it's because we weren't clear about expectations and results.

If you're finding that you are unhappy with work or results from others, it's usually because you weren't clear enough on what you needed them to do. If you give people too much leeway, they'll start to stray from your vision.

Your job is to skipper the boat and direct where it's headed. If your team aren't getting the same results you get, it's because your process isn't clear enough.

You need to provide every detail and every angle when writing up your processes and systems. They need to become habit when people execute them. Leaving out steps, or taking for granted that someone knows how to do something, is poison to workflows. It's worth noting that detail during a process isn't the same as micromanagement. Peering over the shoulders of your team while they work is demoralizing and no one likes it.

The reason that people micromanage is because they're not confident in the process and instructions they've given. It's as simple as that. Micromanagement isn't a reflection on the person being managed; it's a reflection on the manager who can't put together a process. The worst type of micromanager is someone who refuses to create detailed goals, processes, and outcomes, but then expects you to read his or her mind and do everything without being told. Micromanagers make up excuses all the time: "I can't trust anyone else to do it properly," "They need guidance," or "I don't have time to write down everything you need to do." That last one, by the way, is like saying you don't have time to tell someone what to do.

If you're happy for people to go off and do what they want, which as I explained I often do with a few members of my team, you'll get results, but they might not be exactly what you expected. Maybe that isn't a bad thing. Maybe you need some perspective on what else someone can do. However, if you want people to execute tasks that you need done in a specific way, you have to provide that specificity. Be specific about your instructions and steps, and don't take anything for granted.

Customers are happier with process (they just don't know it). A lot of creative businesses believe that their customers don't want a process, and that they want free-form creativity and unbridled access to their creative centers. Most creative businesses believe that a process will put off customers. That is just not true. Customers are like any other human beings: They need guidance and structure. People love boundaries. Children, teenagers, and toddlers are all happier with boundaries and routine. When in a new environment, which your customers will be, they are looking for structure and guidance or they become overwhelmed. If you've ever joined an online course or a new learning environment, it can be terrifying. The new people, the resources, and the locations can be overwhelming to people, so they look for structure.

If you're talking to a new customer, don't take for granted how much you know. Your customer has probably never gone through this before. Perhaps they have never had coaching, a web site, or a consultation. They need to know what's going to happen.

If you write up a six-step infographic, explaining the high-level steps you're going to take, they'll love that there's a map, a process, or a guide to what's going to happen. Professional businesses that understand their customers have a process. Process gets a bad rap because banks have processes that seem to block progress for no reason, like a "Computer says no" mentality, or a restaurant that won't cook something another way because "it's always been done this way."

Listen to your customers and they'll tell you the changes you need to make in your process. It's about balance, being flexible but not a walkover. Customers might not say they love process, but they do. Even if they don't realize they're in one, they are much happier when they're doing it.

Does it take your time? If so, you can probably outsource it. The only thing we have access to every day, but that runs out over a long period, is time. Time is the single most important resource you have. It's truly a commodity, because it runs out and you can't ever get it back. Tomorrow, though, you'll be credited with another 24 hours. What are you going to do with them? Waste them on trivial tasks that take time, or invest them into real work and get other people to execute those tasks?

Above all else, if a task uses up time, you can and probably should outsource it. Spending eight hours in one day to write up a process that takes you one hour a week means that in eight weeks, or two months, you're earning a return on your investment. People treat time investment like any other investment. Most people believe that investment is about a small input and getting a large win, like winning the lottery. This isn't true; it's a myth.

True investment and realizing a return is about making small inputs, regularly and repeatedly, until they start to work for themselves. Putting in that eight hours to write a process isn't going to pay for itself in Week 1, or 2, or even 7. After Weeks 9, 10, and so on, though, you'll be making time back on your initial investment. You don't want to make the input because it seems like hard work, but it's preferable break one rock in a day and complete the task, instead of spending an hour every week breaking lots of new smaller rocks.

If it takes your time, even if it takes a few days to get the process written down, you can outsource it. Try it for one repeatable task in your diary and see the results. It becomes addictive, getting other people to worry about your time and work.

You're not that special. Someone else can do it. Here's some advice for all the special snowflakes out there.

Chapter 8 | Why Process Is the Key to Scale

> *What I do is unique, no one else can replicate it. I do it a certain way and it's the best way. I've been doing it like this for years, I think I know a few things about it.*

Those are all excuses. It's a reason to not invest your time into writing up and outsourcing processes. Sculpture, art, design, music, development, money, cooking, writing: They all fall under the guise of "unique." This book is called *From Single to Scale*. Hopefully you remember in previous chapters we've talked about how if your product isn't repeatable, outsourceable, and scalable, it's not profitable.

- Do I have to do the work or can I outsource it to someone else?
- Can I receive 1,000 orders tomorrow and handle it?
- Is the process or delivery repeatable so anyone can do it?

Your artwork, music, or design might be the most incredible work ever seen by humans, but if no one can repeat it and outsource it, or you can't deliver 1,000 orders tomorrow, then are you going to sell that many? Besides, every creative endeavor is supported by structure, routine, and process. Do you think the canvas you paint on is handmade every time? What about the recording equipment or process for recording music?

There is process in every stage of our lives and unless we want to wait for the big score, our products will never be profitable unless we can scale them. I say this with love: You're not that special. Almost every task you do can be done by someone else. You're right that no one can be you. No one has your purpose, your drive, your personality, or your vision. Everything you do to accomplish those things, though, can other people do them? Probably. Take comfort in that. Give yourself more time to focus on what matters and have other people work on the time-consuming stuff.

Manage the Process

Finally, a word on managing the processes. It's too easy to chuck it all and quit when your first exploration into process doesn't go well. Maybe it took longer than you expected or the results weren't quite what you were hoping for. Look at what you have done, though. You've taken your first steps into scaling and growing a business, not charging more per product, or finding more customers. You're giving yourself room to grow past and beyond what you were capable of.

We all say, "If only there were two of me," or "If only there were eight more hours in the day." Well there can be! There can be 2 or 20 or 200 of you. There can be eight more hours in the day. Other people's days can give you the time back that you want. When providing feedback, make sure you're always positive. It's too easy to moan, "Oh, that's not what I wanted." Remember, if people aren't delivering on the process that you wrote, it probably means it wasn't clear enough.

I'll be honest: Sometimes people just don't get it. My first foray into logo design for a sports company was a total disaster. The designer I hired could not understand, no matter how clear I was about the colors we needed. I provided hex codes, RGB codes, words, and screenshots. No matter what, he just wouldn't do it. Rather than scream and shout and ask for refunds, I told him what I thought he did well. I then explained that his approach to our color scheme wasn't productive and we decided to move on.

Some you win and some you lose. Be positive about what you're doing, what other people are doing, and make sure you're always there to help them execute. Don't be one of those managers who just says, "Get it done" when someone asks for help. No one wants to work with that person. If you feel someone is just stalling, or maybe not confident in what you've asked them to do, ask them what they're afraid of. Tell them to go through the process as best they can. If they mess it up, it's not the end of the world.

Summary

Process and scale go hand in hand, but process is often seen as restrictive or suffocating. Nothing could be further from the truth. The more structure you give to your time and systems, the freer you'll become.

- Time is the only resource you can never get back, so work on systems that give you time back.
- Everything can be outsourced; if it can't, then examine if you need to continue it.
- To truly become free with your time, you must invest in systems and process.
- Commit to the system and be content to take a smaller cut of revenue if it delivers you more time.

# CHAPTER 9

Outsourcing the Scalable Process

In this chapter we're going to learn how to outsource our processes to other people. Outsourcing has become much easier, but with that it has made people sloppy about their hiring process. If you want to keep standards high, your outsourcing needs to follow its own process.

Take the Day Off

What should have been done? That's your first process. As an exercise, take a day off from work. Just go and do something else that isn't delivering projects, replying to e-mails, or doing usual work stuff. One day isn't going to make or break the business. What you're doing is seeing what activities need completing on that day. At the end of the day, go over what should have been done. Those items are the processes that you should write up.

Writing blog content, e-mailing customers, handling social posts, and replying to customers: All the items that needed to get done today are what you should focus on writing up the process for. Everything can be systematized. There are other people who can take work from you. If literally no one else can do it, it's not scalable. If you can't teach other people to do it, it's not scalable. What would have had the biggest impact on your day if you didn't have to do it? Interviewing guests for a podcast? Writing to sponsors or suppliers?

© Michael Killen 2019
M. Killen, *From Single to Scale*, https://doi.org/10.1007/978-1-4842-3814-1_9

If you think you can't afford to pay other people, that's where you need to look at scalable products first, products that allow you to scale and reach more people. We need to deliver more results to more people, with less effort. We're going to go over the steps needed to hire VA staff and outsource more of your work.

Brickwork India is high quality. High quality comes at a price. We use brickworkindia.com (http://www.brickworkindia.com) for our VA services. They're based in India and are one of the more premium VA services out there. I've found they're worth every penny. They do have a cheaper $5 per hour service, but, as we've explored already, it's better to leave that level to pure process tasks such as data entry.

Some of the VA team at Brickwork have master's degrees; they're polite, fast workers and I rarely have to correct their work. They have a research team, SEO team, and some very affordable packages. On average, I'm paying $15 per hour for my VA. Although this might seem expensive, it's as we talked about earlier: If you have to correct someone's work all the time, how much is that really costing you?

Other Options

There are plenty of other options for VA and outsourced work.

Fiverr.com (http://lp.fiverr.co.uk/)

Fiverr is on the lower end of the scale when it comes to cost. Blog posts might be advertised at $20, but you get what you pay for. Having said that, it's a perfect place to test your outsourcing process. For data entry and copying text over, we've used Fiverr to start with, hiring a cheap VA to see if they can do the job and how much instruction we have to give.

Upwork.com (https://www.upwork.com/)

Upwork can provide workers for almost any task: development, VA, design, content, and so on. Like any marketplace, you get what you pay for. We've found Upwork's system easy to use and we've found some great long-term partners through it.

Freelancer.com (https://www.freelancer.com/)

Freelancer.com is another marketplace for freelance work. We've used them to find designers. They provide good customer service, one-off hires, and a nice system for managing projects.

Studio Envato (https://studio.envato.com/)

Studio Envato is Envato's freelancer marketplace, which is the company behind Themeforest. We often use Studio Envato for WordPress and theme-specific work. However, we've found the marketplace flooded with copy profiles recently.

99 Designs (https://99designs.co.uk/)

99 Designs is an interesting change to the process because you submit a brief and whittle down the winners each round, offering feedback and design changes as you go through. They have various price levels and have some pretty good designers. However, be careful to notice that the submissions are public. We found we had a lot of copies and similar designs. We also found people to plagiarize other logos unless you paid on the higher end of the spectrum.

OnlineJobs.ph (https://www.onlinejobs.ph/)

I've never used OnlineJobs.ph, but I've heard great things about them. They are similar to other marketplaces, but they specialize in Philippine VAs and workers.

Google (https://www.google.com)

You might have heard of Google. It's a search engine. You can search for anything on the Internet. Try using Google to find VA services in your local area. You'll be surprised at how affordable and efficient local VA teams can be.

Interview with a basic task. When hiring people for outsourcing work, if you're planning on adding a permanent member to your team, don't hand the job over to one person straight away. It might sound like a hassle, but you have to interview a few people. It will save you hours in the long run. First, it's worth mentioning that we pay for all our interview candidates. The task should take two hours at most and will cost you a few bucks. You're only interviewing –two or three candidates so it shouldn't cost a lot. They don't even have to know they're being interviewed.

Interview candidates with a basic task, something you've written up and doesn't require a huge investment. Try to choose a task that can go wrong, too, but it wouldn't be the end of the world if you had to ignore or correct them. Ask them to carry out the task and report back to you when they're done. Ask them how long it took them, if they were comfortable with the task, and if they have any questions. You're absolutely interviewing people. It's

Chapter 9 | Outsourcing the Scalable Process

imperative that you hire once and hire right. If this is a long-term arrangement, you'll want to run an interview as few times as possible.

Ask candidates what their working hours are, how they communicate, and then check this with their interview task. A few years back, I was interviewing for a VA position on my team. It boiled down to someone in the United Kingdom and someone in India. The candidate from India was a lot cheaper, but I was concerned that her English might not be so good. The UK candidate had all the right checks and talked about daily updates and shorter time scales. With the task (uploading YouTube videos, adding metadata, and creating social content to promote it), the Indian candidate not only followed my instructions perfectly, but e-mailed me after the first upload to check she had done it properly. She also e-mailed me when the task was complete, gave an estimated completion time, and offered some feedback on the process. The UK VA was nowhere to be seen until that Friday when she sent an e-mail saying the task had been completed, but there was nothing else: no updates throughout the week, and very little communication. We went with our Indian VA and haven't looked back.

Don't accept the first candidate. Ask to see a few. If you're using a VA agency, ask for a few candidates and read over their profiles. Ask to interview them all with a simple task. Some VAs in other countries won't want to talk on Skype. They also might be unsure of their English skills (most of the time they're fluent). If they want to call you Mr. or Mrs. Surname, don't tell them to call you by your first name, as they're more comfortable calling you by your surname.

Ask them how they'll do it. Asking someone to repeat back a task and asking them how they'll complete a task can prove to be very insightful. It sounds like a stupid question, but it shows you their level of experience and if they've done similar tasks before. Even if you've got a written-up process, ask them to repeat back the task and ask for steps of what they'll do.

If they're competent they'll give an overview of your steps. They'll also include when they'll contact you and if there is anything that isn't covered by your process. They should also mention whether they'll contact you if they need help. The problem is that most people don't ask for help straight away. Encourage them to check in every day for the first task to give an update on where they are and if they're struggling with anything.

Ask for a list of tools they can and will use It's important to understand two things:

1. If they're pulling the wool over your eyes.
2. How experienced they are.

We've all embellished our resumes a little, but I've lost count of how many people have told me they're proficient with HTML and PHP or graphic design software, only for me to give them a simple task at which they utterly fail. It's important to me that I know what their capabilities are. In a weird way, I'd rather have someone admit to me that they have no idea how to use Photoshop, but that they're keen and willing to learn.

On the other hand, I find more experienced VA and external staff are more specific about the tools they use. My operations manager and project manager both have very similar skill sets and tool sets: Asana, Trello, Quip, Workflowy, Zapier, Process.st, Kissflow, and so on. At no point do they mention Photoshop, Sublime Text, WordPress, or something that isn't pertinent to their requirements.

They might be the greatest PSD wizard in the world, but that's not what I'm hiring them for. Lots of VAs will tell you they're good with Excel, Word, Outlook, WordPress, and the other standard packages, but if you're looking for a specific person to fill a specific role, it's better to see some tools that they're going use. On the other hand, make a list of the tools you use and would expect them to get comfortable with. Our social media coordinator hadn't ever used Google Docs or Postcron before, but she was very willing to learn. Combined with my written process on uploading, editing, and scheduling social content, she came to grips with it very fast.

Check their English. Ask them to repeat back their understanding of a task. When you work with nonnative English speakers, it can be tough to make sure they understand the task. The simplest way to lower this risk is to ask them to repeat back, in their own words, the task. It might sound laborious, even patronizing to both you and them, but it's imperative to see if you can leave them with the task.

Over time you'll ask for this less and less. My VA has been working with me so well, for so long, that she can even interpret what I mean with certain instructions. For example, let's say you're asking a VA to upload two Google Docs to WordPress for blog posts. You'd like them to keep the formatting of the headers and run a spell check through Grammerly. You'd also like them to find two suitable images from Unsplash, Pexlar, Picxel, or another stock image source and then set those as featured images with suitable alt tags and descriptions.

Finally, you'd like them to use SEO, social, and search engines as categories for both posts, but one of them needs the laptop and software categories, too. You'd expect the task to be completed in less than two hours and to check in with you when they've uploaded the first one. You'd like it completed by Thursday at 5 p.m. and for them to contact you at Thursday at 9 a.m. by the latest if it will take longer.

This is the level of detail most of your tasks will require. Combine them with a written process and video screenshot and you won't go far wrong.

Ask them to repeat the task back to you, in their own words. This will show their interpretation skills and language skills, and they'll have to ask you what a certain section means if they don't understand it. It's actually an important process to ask even native English speakers to do this. When people repeat back tasks to you, it cements in their mind what they're going to do. They'll start to visualize their task. Finally, the reason we use slightly more costly services like Brickwork is because I have never had a problem with their English. In fact, some of it is better than mine!

Give detailed e-mails and instructions. Take the time to write them. As I mentioned previously, the more detailed your e-mails and communications, the better the result. Take the time to write the right amount. Don't dump everything in the e-mail. This is a time investment. Spend 20 minutes writing the perfect task e-mail and prevent hours of chasing later.

Feel free to use the following template.

- **Intro**. Quick hello and ask how they are.
- **Task and results**. I need you to upload five videos to YouTube and create five new WordPress blog posts per video. This means we'll be publishing five videos over five weeks and a new blog post each week. Each video needs to be scheduled from the 24th at seven-day intervals, with the 31st being the next. The posts are to be scheduled for the day after each video goes live.
- **How to**. Here is where we'd usually include a screencast or Process.st of what we want them to do. This might seem like a lot of work, but trust me when I say the more you invest up front, the less work you need to do later on. I've included a Process.st of the steps here, as well as a video. You'll find the videos in the Google Drive folder. Each video is labeled 1 to 5. This spreadsheet here shows what each title, blog title, categories, and tags are required per video.
- **Time limit**. This task should take no longer than four hours.
- **Deadline**. I need this task completed by Thursday at 5 p.m. at the latest. Please confirm that this is fine. If you're unable to do the task by that time, can you please let me know by Thursday 9 a.m. at the latest.
- **Repeat back**. Can you repeat back to me the task, in your own words Outsourcing:e-mails and instructions, just to make sure I've given you clear enough direction?
- Thanks! Mike

Give a time limit. Time limits are critical to managing VA and outsource staff. I once asked a VA to carry out keyword research, some high-level, Google keyword planner stuff. It wouldn't have taken longer than two hours. When I checked in, after not hearing from him for a few days, he sent me a report that had taken him eight hours to complete. He was researching depths that I didn't need and spent a lot of time trying new techniques. I'm lucky that my current VA always completes things faster than I expect anyway. However, the first time was entirely my fault for not giving a time limit. Time limits mean three things:

1. Your VA will know they have a limit to how much they can invest in the work. They'll know how important the task is. If it's a 10-hour project including research, that gives them the space. Smaller one- and two-hour tasks can be process oriented.

2. If a task is going to go over "time budget," they'll have to contact you. It might be there were unforeseen problems and you failed to take other things into consideration. As a rule, something usually takes four times longer than you think. However, don't give too much time allowance, as some VAs might take advantage. If they come back to you and tell you it's too short a time, tell them to get done what they can and you'll assess their results when they contact you.

3. Time limits begin to tell you how skillful your hire is. Someone who knows what he or she is doing will exceed your (reasonable) expectations on task completion. They'll ideally be better than you, but this comes at a price.

Give deadlines for 48 hours (maybe 72 hours).

Deadlines, on the other hand, are important to tasks because they prevent Parkinson's Law: Work expands so as to fill the time available for its completion. If you don't give a deadline, don't expect your VA to see it as important. There's nothing wrong with asking for a deadline. It's critical to task prioritization. If your hire thinks that next Friday isn't going to happen, you need to know. Similarly, if you need the task by tomorrow, it might not happen. If you don't give a deadline, it won't happen fast. It'll keep getting pushed back.

Offer examples of results. Results examples are a great way to show what's expected of a task. Sometimes people need a visual goal to work toward, like an example of a task that's previously been completed. For example, if you do a screencast of performing the same task, include a link or image of what the final result looks like. If you're asking them to execute process or data entry tasks, fill out the first row, post, or paragraph for them.

Make sure there is no way to misinterpret a sentence. Clear instructions are an important part of running any business, but it's surprising how easy it is for people to misinterpret what you say. Even to other English speakers it can seem like there is a disconnect between what we want, what we say, and what other people hear. This is why clarity of instruction is so important. The misinterpretation and disconnect can be magnified when speaking with nonnative English speakers.

Don't leave anything to chance. Use 5 p.m. instead of 5. Give dates, days, months, and years when you have a deadline. Don't say "head to sellyourservice.co.uk for the blog post on landing pages"; instead say "go to https://sellyourservice.co.uk/2016/06/the-definitive-guide-for-creating-outstanding-landing-pages-in-wordpress-with-copy-and-content-that-generates-more-email-sign-ups/" and include a link.

Levels of Outsourcing

I've briefly mentioned that there are different levels of outsourcing, depending on where you are within your business, the model and structure you use, and what needs to be done. Different levels of outsourcing suit different tasks. It's important to match outsourcing levels with two things: your budget and the task.

Anyone can find VA staff for $5 per hour, but if you have that VA handle a content creation task, you'll get what you pay for. On the other hand, more valuable VAs at $15 an hour are perfect for research tasks, customer communications, and more complex processes. Finally, some tasks, like logo design for a customer, for example, only need one-off hires. Even hiring a great UK designer could cost as little as £600 and it's something you don't have to do. One-off data entry from handwritten bookkeeping to an Excel spreadsheet might just need to be done once.

Small, repetitive process-driven tasks that don't require skill. Tasks like social media bulk post uploading, copying content from Google Docs to a WordPress blog, or entering customer e-mail addresses manually from forms into MailChimp are all repetitive tasks. These kinds of smaller, process-driven tasks don't require a huge amount of skill and are perfect for lower end VA staff:

- Social post uploads
- Data entry
- Data transfer
- Copying text and posting
- Scheduling blog posts
- Sending prewritten e-mails

- Scheduling e-mail campaigns
- Following processes and instructions

Lots of VAs at this level either aren't skilled enough, starting out, or they don't want to do more complex tasks. Some hires are genuinely happy just performing low-skill tasks. They're usually polite, timely, and get jobs done quickly.

Medium-level tasks that are frequent or require education and experience. Some tasks (e.g., video editing) require a little more skill and practice and are better suited to VAs who can execute complex tasks with fewer instructions. I created a template for editing and uploading videos in Camtasia. My VA was not only able to follow those instructions, but also took content from another spreadsheet and included it in the video.

Finally, if I gave examples of where we should cut things or make small edits, he was able to easily take that example and apply it to other videos. When the videos were uploaded to YouTube, another VA was able to create thumbnails, YouTube captions and end screens, tags, and descriptions. She was also able to schedule the videos to go out and create a series of tweets and Facebook posts for each video and schedule those. We did have written and video processes for all those tasks, but they were more complex, as they required some creativity and initiative. Combined with instructions, the tasks were carried out perfectly. Other examples include the following:

- Booking meetings
- Booking networking events
- Customer services
- Simple image and content creation
- Scheduling complex content
- Report creation
- Maintenance and security

One-off tasks that only need to be done once for a specific result. Sometimes there is a task that needs doing that you don't want to do or don't need to do yourself. Here are some examples:

- Logo design
- Landing page design
- One-off graphics or images
- Data entry
- Research
- Security upgrades and installs to web sites

One-off tasks are great for freelancer marketplaces. Stick to the same rules as hiring regular VAs and you won't go far wrong. Give specific instructions, have a process, and give timings, deadlines, and example results (even from other businesses). Don't hire the first person who bids. Ask candidates how they'd complete the task and what tools they will and can use. Never fall into the trap of "Well, I'll just do it myself, it'll be quicker." The first few times, this might be true. What you're trying to do, though, is learn how to push more work to other people.

Personal tasks that aren't part of the business. The final tasks that you can start to outsource are personal tasks: booking restaurants, ordering gifts, and booking flights and travel accommodations. There is so much potential in getting other people to do low-value, low-intensity work. Think about how you can grow your time if other people are organizing travel and leisure activities.

I don't book flights anymore, hire cars, or book hotels. My VA does it all. I'll give her very explicit instructions, such as "My partner and I need to be in Phoenix by March 6, 2017. Please book me a flight from London Heathrow using the company card. I have a budget of around £2,000 in total. Please find the cheapest flight possible, flying with BA, AA, or Virgin. I want a direct flight to arrive in Phoenix, Arizona, before 9 p.m. on March 6."

Often she'll come back with car hire, hotels, and activities, too, which we sometimes book also. The point is that I could spend hours searching the Web for deals and an extra $100 off here and there, but that $100 is not really worth all the notes and saved tabs. Spending thrifty is not the way to grow your business. In the time it takes my VA to book all my travel arrangements, I'll have done an entire day's work.

Pay per result, not per hour. Overall, what we're trying to do with outsourcing is pay for results. It's important to focus on that when we're looking at costs. The idea of paying per result, not per hour, helps us with two aspects of the process.

First, when we're comparing prices for individual hires or VA staff, it's tempting to look on the cheaper side. How much can the difference be between $5 and $10 per hour? What we want to avoid, though, is paying $5 per hour for six hours' work on a task that should take two hours. Believe me, it happens. Seemingly simple tasks can balloon in scale. Before you know it, that two-hour task has cost you $30. In addition, the $10 per hour VA might have completed it in two hours, meaning you're overpaying by $10.

Second, a task that requires you to fix it or make changes costs you time and money. For example let's say the $5 per hour VA completes a keyword research task in two hours. $10 is pretty good! However, they've only included 30 keywords when you asked for 100. They've forgotten the target market and location. There are no estimated monthly traffic statistics in it either. You now have to complete part of the task, provide feedback to the VA, and manage the task yourself going forward. If it takes you another two hours to complete it, that's $200 or $600 or $2,000 that's been wasted.

Note that I'm absolutely not saying that $5 per hour VAs aren't worth looking at. You need to be clear, however, about what their role, capabilities, and expectations are.

On the other hand, a $15 an hour VA gets the job done in the same time, two hours. $30 is still pretty brilliant, I think. You check over the results and sure enough, everything is there. They even have a few suggestions about some other tools and other keyword topics for future research. When you have trouble with outsourcing work, it can feel cheaper to just do it yourself. You're partly right, in the short term. In the long run, though, you're using up your most precious asset—time—to complete tasks that can be taken care of by someone else. It's tempting to go back and do it yourself after a bad experience, but work out what's going wrong and allow yourself to push past that.

Use Process.st to manage repeated tasks. Process.st and Kissflow are two great tools for managing repeat tasks. For example, our social media process for taking posts from our blog and sharing them via Twitter is repeated every week. It was a perfect thing to outsource, because we knew it happened every Thursday and it would give me back two hours a week, every week. You can use Word, Google Docs, Google Sheets, or Quip, of course, but I've found Process.st to integrate wonderfully with many other applications.

Automate the start of tasks with Zapier; go and investigate Zapier (https://zapier.com) to see how you can start automating all sorts of tasks. Zapier is a cloud-based automation program. It connects applications together that don't usually connect. For example, whenever I publish a new blog post, I've built a zap in Zapier that sends Facebook posts out as tweets. It also creates Twitter content for my social process.

I have another zap that every seven days sends out a curated RSS feed of important articles for me to read over, combining all my blog reading into one session. One final example is that my Calendly app (a calendar booking application at https://calendly.com), whenever someone books a certain meeting, will create a meeting room in Zoom (or webinar software) and send both me and the guest a link. It also reminds them a day before and an hour before the call. All this is automated from Zapier for about $20 a month. Start playing around with Zapier and see which of your tasks can be taken care of by a cloud application.

Always offer to guide and help, but people rarely ask. A note on assisting your new hires: I've found that no matter how often I offer to help or check that they're okay, they won't ask me for help, sometimes until it's too late. Always offer help and assistance or guidance, but don't be surprised when no one (not just your VA staff) takes you up on it.

The key is to ask questions, rather than just ask "How are you doing?" Ask how a specific task or stage is going. You might have to rotate each stage you're asking about, otherwise you'll seem like you're interrogating them. I'm lucky that my VA will clearly state when something is unclear or when it's not working. However, we have had hires try to figure out the solution and spend hours working on the problem, rather than working on the task.

Be clear and sure about tasks. If you're asking someone to do something, make it crystal clear you want it done and be clear about the results. We've covered being clear about getting the work done, but you'd be staggered at how many people outsource tasks, or ask for a process to be run, that they themselves are unsure what to do with. I had a customer, the manager of a telco team, ask us to create a content marketing plan. It was pretty in depth and the entire team got involved with customer personas, content funnels, and remarketing—the works.

After we presented it and handed the guide over, the customer wasn't really sure what to do with it. "So what do we do now? How do we use this?" Despite literally having two content members on the team, the manager refused to implement the strategy because he wasn't really clear on what he'd do with it. Sure, part of that is down to us maybe not being clear enough on how to start the content marketing, but why would you ask for a task to be completed, costing time and money, when you have no idea what you'd do with it?

Unfortunately, this "dog chasing a car" characteristic of running a business is all too common. Sometimes, people have no idea what to do with results when they get them. Make sure that's not you.

Don't let people up the price after you accept their bid. This has only happened once to me, but it sent me into a near homicidal rage when it happened. We commissioned a logo t-shirt design, and a few other branding things, to be taken care of by a freelancer. We used Freelancer.com (which we've never had a problem with since) and found a freelancer willing to do all the work. They put a bid in, just like everyone else, and we selected them. They weren't the cheapest, but they also weren't the most expensive. However, after they won the contract, they upped their price. I was furious.

> *Freelancer: Hey, I would like to complete your project for £xxx GBP.*
>
> *Me: How quickly can you turn the project around?*
>
> *Freelancer: When do you need complete this work?*
>
> *Me: Before Friday 30th?*

Freelancer: Yes. Sure will do.

Me: Can you tell me what you plan on delivering please?

Freelancer: Yes. I am sure we can finish this work by Friday and give you editable source file.

Me: What formats please?

Freelancer: I will give you AI, JPEG, and PNG.

Me: Can you do PSD as well?

Freelancer: Yes. I will do.

Me: Will the graphic be symmetrical from left to right for both the front and rear design?

Freelancer: Okay.

Me: You need t-shirt front and back and sides for sleeves.

Freelancer: Okay.

Me: I've awarded the project.

Freelancer: Can you please tell me what is your budget for this work? Yes. Thanks for awarding me.

Me: You bid XXX, that's the budget.

Freelancer: Yes, that was my basic bid. Can you increase your budget a little bit?

The project was a total disaster later on, too. The work wasn't up to par and I ended up getting a clothing designer to do everything in the United Kingdom. I thought I covered all my angles with the brief and the messages, but then I was hoodwinked. I could have just complained, I suppose, or demanded a refund, but I figured I could increase the budget a little bit and get the work done. I learned my lesson.

Never release funds until you've received the result. Also, this particular freelancer refused to hand over the files until I had completed the final payment (she also tried holding out for more money again after that). Pay only when you receive the final goods. Simple as that.

Ask for weekly "time used" updates. To keep on top of your available resources, ask for a weekly time used update and report. Most VA businesses will supply this anyway, giving you a breakdown of how many paid hours you have left, or how many you need to pay for. Most VA businesses I know will ask you to buy time up front first, then give you a certain number of hours for that sum.

After each task, ask for a report on how long it took. Then at the end of the week, ask how many hours you have left. Don't worry if you use all your hours in the first week, if you've bought a month's worth. The truth is that's pretty hard to do and if you're told what each task "cost," then you should be able to manage that.

Have a support or backup VA or team. What happens if your VA can't work and all your weekly tasks get left undone? This is a common objection I hear about why you shouldn't rely on VA staff. If you've got someone doing 10 tasks a week and they disappear (it happens, but not often), what happens with your business? Brickwork has a team of VAs and my VA herself has a backup team. This means that if she's away (holidays, sickness) another member of the team can take over. Ask if your VA has a backup team. Ask what happens if they're ill or can't complete the work.

Ask them to keep you accountable. In the same way that we mentioned in Chapter 5, people pay to be kept accountable. Use your VA in the same way! Ask them to send you an e-mail every Monday morning asking what you're going to do. Ask them on a Friday to e-mail you, asking what you've completed. You'd be amazed at how writing down and sending accountability e-mails to your VA is a productivity boost. I don't want my team to think I'm lazy or unproductive!

Ask for a weekly repetition as soon as you can. If I had to give one piece of productivity or outsourcing advice, I'd say outsource a weekly, repetitive task as soon as you can. The first job I got someone else to do was upload and schedule all my social posts. It was paramount to me being able to move off the tools I use.

I was tired of social scheduling and creating tweets. I needed to get rid of that task fast. Look at your weekly, repetitive tasks and see what you need to move off your plate. If you're not willing to do this, your business will never grow. I can promise you that. Even if you can only afford two hours a week, choose a weekly, repetitive task that should be handled by someone else. First, it'll give you your time back, the most valuable asset you have. Second, it'll give you fantastic experience managing VA staff and outsourcing. **Give freedom of intelligence.** If there is a problem that can be solved for under $100, let them solve it. As I mentioned in Chapter 8, if my team encounters a problem with a customer and they can solve it for under $100, I have them do it. This was one of my biggest takeaways from *The 4 Hour Work Week*, by Timothy Ferriss. So much time is wasted when we insist on getting involved with customer issues.

Don't get me wrong: Customer communication is a perfect time to help people and solve another problem. Just because they're unhappy doesn't mean it can't be turned around. However, calling me, texting me, messaging me, and so on, just because the customer needs something, isn't productive.

First, all refunds are guaranteed at my business. If the customer wants a refund, give it. We're not even that precious about the time period. We do have a refund process, asking what was wrong and can we move them onto another product instead. If they insist on a refund, though, we'll give it.

Note, however, that we hardly ever give refunds. In 2016, out of almost 500 sales, we gave only two refunds: one to someone who didn't understand what they were buying and another to someone who accidentally bought twice.

If there is a problem that someone is struggling with, with our software, apps, or content, and we can solve it for under $100, we'll do it. I trust that my team is smart enough not just to give $100 to every complaint. However, if someone has being trying to log into their coaching account for days and all sorts of things go wrong, we'll give them $50 back and get them something from Amazon. Small things like that go a long way.

Summary

Outsourcing your process is when your scale really begins to take off. It becomes exponential and brings its own new problems. Whenever there is a problem with an outsourcing hire, you have to accept 100% responsibility and prevent it from happening again.

- Take a cut of your revenue and invest it in outsourcing.
- Outsourcing can help run your personal life as well as your business.
- Create a management role where all your outsourcers talk to your manager and your manager talks to you.
- Accept that things will go wrong, but they can always be fixed.

CHAPTER 10

Growth Optimization

Growth is less a result of luck or tactics, but rather sheer force of will. In this chapter we're going to explore scaling your scaling, growing what is already growing in the business and achieving more every day. We're going to examine the most effective growth tactics available and explore why certain tactics don't work.

Record, Measure, and Test

You'll no doubt have hundreds of ideas on how you can grow. Some will come from this book, and some from books like *Traction* by Gabriel Weinberg, or *10x* by Grant Cardone. Whatever ideas you have, the reason some businesses grow and scale, and others don't, is because they stick with an idea and exhaust it.

First, we have a high-level, big purpose, something like, "Our business wants to help 100 businesses generate $1 million each by 2020." Then we have a mission. This is how we're going to achieve that goal at a high level: "We're going to do that through three coaching programs on sales training." Then we have goals. Goals are what we need to do to get to that mission, so we can fulfill our purpose. Goals might include the following:

- Get 100 customers.
- Build an e-mail list of 10,000 people.
- Build our social presence.

© Michael Killen 2019
M. Killen, *From Single to Scale*, https://doi.org/10.1007/978-1-4842-3814-1_10

- Write blog content every day.
- Increase traffic to our web site.
- Call five customers a day.

Finally, we have tactics. How do we achieve those goals? Now here's the hard part: Sometimes you have to pick just one goal to work on, the priority. If you have three priorities, you don't have any priorities. You need to choose a goal and brainstorm all the tactics you can think of to achieve that goal. Your priority should be to get customers, frankly.

Lots of times, though, we feel we want to do content marketing or list building. Maybe you feel you can't get customers until you do those things. Businesses don't grow without customers, though. My advice, unless you already have customers, would be to focus on getting customers before anything else. Brainstorm all the tactics you can think of to achieve your goal. Write down each step and title. For example, to get more customers, we might have to do the following:

- Start paying for traffic to come to a sales page.
- Attend more networking events.
- Call current network for referrals.
- Set up live webinars.
- Send free content to clients.
- Grow an e-mail list.

Now successful people choose a tactic and exhaust that tactic until it yields no more results. Most businesses will try and complete all tactics, or when they hear of a new tactic or method, they'll jump on that without ever exhausting their first tactic. Growth doesn't come from jumping from one idea to the next. It's about taking an idea, trying it, and running it into the ground until it doesn't give you anything more.

> "We need more back-links! Back-links are a key part of our strategy!"
> "Awesome, tell me how you're going to do that?"
>
> "We'll e-mail out every day, asking our network for back-links with a piece of structured content or pointing out a broken link on their site."

Now if I check back in a few weeks' time, most businesses will say "Yeah, we tried that, but we stopped after a few days. It was too hard." (This usually means it was boring and not exciting, so they quit.) Did they exhaust that option? Did they really push for it? Most businesses will admit that they didn't.

To keep track of all this, write down your ideas on a spreadsheet, or use a tool like growthhackers.com, and keep ideas and tactics in an "idea" column until they're being tested. Then test them and move them to the "test" column. Give yourself a time limit and do everything you can to drive that tactic. Once you've completed that test, measure the results. You can't possibly measure growth unless you know what works and what happened.

Take a look at what you wanted to achieve and if it worked. You don't have to look at complicated metrics or numbers; just determine if it worked or not. Did it move the needle on the speedometer? That's all we're interested in. You can put in some numbers if you want. For example, $1,000 spent on PPC advertising got you 500 e-mail addresses, so that cost $2 an e-mail address. Did the PPC work then? Well, if you wanted 499 e-mail addresses, then yes. You smashed it. Measure your results and keep referring back to your growth document. It'll provide proof of where you need to focus your efforts in the future. We'll go over a series of tactics that help your goal and mission in this chapter.

Find influencers who your customers look up to. Shared influencers are a powerful, fast, and easy way to find more of an audience. We're going to start by making a list of all the people your customers look up to. Getting in front of a brand new customer who doesn't know you exist is difficult. However, getting in front of a shared influencer is much easier. Often we don't really know where our customers are, but we can see who they look up to. Shared influencersThey might be on Twitter or YouTube; they could be book authors, business owners, celebrities, businesses, Facebook groups, or podcasters. You need to make a list of those influencers and write down where they are. You also need to record as much contact information as you can. You only need 20 or so, but don't skip this step. It's vital that you have a list of influencers and niche celebrities to target and use. They've built an audience of your customers already, so we're going to help them and reach more of their audience.

Read and research what those influencers produce, write, or say. You'll need to be in research mode for this exercise. Every influencer has a few stories, mantras, and viewpoints that they share over and over. In fact it's a great lesson to yourself, by observing people who are where you want to be. Most influencers who your customers look up to will share material, content, videos, products, and services that support their purpose.

If you look closely, they'll only really say a handful of things over and over. Most of them even have a slide deck with the same story on it. That story is the one they'll tell over and over. It has a hero (usually them), a driving force and need behind their journey (a catalyst), a roadblock or barrier preventing them from making that journey, a big change that changes them and the world, and finally a resolution. They'll tell this story over and over and it's your job to understand that story.

Create a list of links to the content, products, stories, videos, posts, tweets, and clips that support what your influencer says. Whatever their purpose or goal is, create a document that summarizes everything they've put out to the world. You don't have to do this for every influencer on your list of 20 right away. As you go along, though, document what they talk about and what they produce. This is going to become influencer fuel soon.

Create a list post of those influencers and their content. One of the easiest methods to gain exposure is to create a list post with influencers. You can divide this up in two ways:

- You can select a topic or viewpoint and create a list post of 7 to 10 (or more) influencers who have contributed toward that cause.

- You can select one influencer and write a list of 7 to 10 things they've done, said, published, or created.

For example, we choose a landing page design. We might select Jeff Bullas, Andy Clarke, *Smashing* magazine, Seth Godin, Ryan Deiss, Brian Gardner, Unbounce, and Russell Brunson on what they've said about landing page design. If we say we're going to show you how to increase landing page conversions, how powerful would it be if we said, "Eight experts share their advice on increasing landing page conversions"?

Find a quote, video, or resource on what those influencers say about your topic and embed the quote, tweet, or other material in the blog post. Include links to their blogs, write up a short summary of what they've said, and publish that post. Posts like this are fast to produce and easy to share, and your audience wants to read about people they look up to.

Reach out via Twitter to those influencers. Tell them they made your list. Once you've made your list, use Twitter (or any social platform) to notify your influencers of your post. Thank them for their insight and advice and tell them that they've made your post of "advice on landing pages from the experts." Use any method you can to reach out to those influencers and get them to notice your content. It's flattering to be shown that other people are quoting you, particularly if you've got a niche market where the influencers might not be that well known outside of that market.

If they retweet or thank you. Send them an e-mail with your blog post and ask them to send it to their list. If you get any response at all, thank them and keep the conversation going. This is where your research for your influencers comes in. Send an e-mail to whoever thanks or retweets or acknowledges you. Tell them you appreciate them taking the time to share your post, then send them an e-mail asking them to share it with their list. Here's an example:

> Hey Ryan,
>
> Thanks for the retweet earlier today. Your quote on blog posts acting as pages really resonated with my audience.
>
> As you did retweet my post, I thought your wider audience might like to read the post.
>
> I've included a link below. It'd mean a huge deal to me if you shared it with your list. I've even written up a paragraph for you to just copy and paste.
>
> Thanks again, love your work.
>
> Mike
>
> =====
>
> Mike at Sell Your Service has written a post about landing page design (and kindly included me as an expert!). If you want to see what the experts say about landing page conversions, you should read this post.

This is how you reach out and build an audience via influencers.

Use smoke tests. When we look at building audience growth, it's important to know what titles resonate with our audience. Web sites like Uproxx and Buzzfeed have made millions from clickbait, sugar water nonsense, sensationalist titles. However, something we can take from them is their knowledge that a title is a headline. That's what gets people interested in clicking and visiting a site.

You might have the greatest, most useful guide to money management in the world, but if your title is boring, no one is going to read it. That's why we use a *smoke test*. This practice can be used for videos, books, products, blog posts, talks, and more. Use Outbrain as a platform to perform very cheap traffic tests. Outbrain is itself a paid traffic platform. Frankly, the quality of the traffic is pretty low. You'll probably have even seen Outbrain content and advertising platforms on web sites.

Here's how it works: You choose a link from your web site, such as a blog post or page, and you tell Outbrain to promote that. As this is a smoke test, we want to keep the budget low, so $50 to $100 should be plenty to see what gets people to click. Use that same link but generate as many titles as you can—at least 10—so you can test which one gets the most clicks. What we're looking for is a variety of headlines and titles: some numbers based, some results based, and so on.

If you need an idea for headlines, check out Sumo.com/kickass-headline-generator/ for a headline generator. Choose your headlines and input them into Outbrain. Try to keep the images the same, as you want to make sure it's the headlines that people choose. Once you've run the posts for a few weeks, maybe a month, take a look and see which one got the most clicks—that's clicks per view, too. Although Outbrain should rotate the ads to show equal numbers, we want to make sure that one post that gets 1,000 clicks wasn't shown 1,000 times more than the other ads. Take the most popular titles and use those as the titles for your products, books, services, webinars, and posts. The Internet is telling you what it will read.

Join networking events. Only join events that talk to your customers or that include your customers. Networking is important to all businesses. Some of us need to join networks because we work from home and we can go a little stir crazy if we don't get out of the house. Other times, we attend networking events, lunches, and breakfasts because we're told over and over that we have to network.

I cannot stress enough how important networking at the right place is. Most serial networkers will tell you, "It's not about who you know. It's about who you know, knows." It's about growing your sphere of influence. If I talk to Mike and tell him the amazing things I do with e-commerce systems, he'll recommend me to people who are looking for that same product. Although that might be true, it requires a lot of work, repetition, and reinforcement for other people to evangelize you. Also, you can spend your entire week at networking events, talking to others and having lunch, while never really growing your business.

Networking, for many businesses, is a perfect example of busy work. Most businesses who do it religiously will tell you it's a core part of their business. I don't doubt that networking is important, but it's how we do it that matters. You're better off attending one networking event that will have your customers in it. Also, it doesn't have to be a network at a golf club or hotel. There's this thing called Facebook; it's massive. There are groups on there for everyone. Just like real life, though, you can't wander in and start selling. It's about being useful, helpful, and valuable to that community.

Does this sound like hard work? It is. You're required, on average to post on 20 threads or posts a day, within one network, group, or forum, for a month before you're even recognized. Real-life networking is exactly the same. You need to turn up week after week and always be willing to help people. Don't approach networking as a sales platform; it isn't. It's about developing relationships that make sense to continue and grow. Use that philosophy, attend fewer networking events, and get more done.

Offer free talks at universities and colleges and record them. If you're looking for some gravitas behind your name, organize a talk at a university. The goal is to be able to say, "I've spoken at Riverdale University." People will take you far more seriously after that. It's easy, too. Most universities and colleges will allow you use of their halls and lecture rooms for very reasonable rates and sometimes free if faculty and students can attend.

It doesn't have to be a presentation to hundreds of people. Invite 20 customers and a few prospects and leads, and get your colleagues to come. Tell them it's free and you're practicing for a larger talk. It doesn't hurt to have donuts or wine there, either.

Set up a camera and record your talk. Pick up a cheap lapel microphone and plug that into your phone. Record your voice from your phone and combine it with the camera footage for clearer audio. Once you've recorded that, you've got a talk at a university on record and you've got video content, too.

Use Sumo.com to see how much of a blog post people are reading. Sumo has an awesome content analytics tool that lets you see how much of a blog post people are reading. For example, if you get 100 visitors to a blog post, Sumo will tell you where people drop off. It's like a temperature gauge, showing how many people read the entire blog post. As the blog post or page goes on, the numbers drop off.

If you're getting over 50% of your readers to read 100% of the post, you're doing well. However, if you can see that 50% of people drop off after the first paragraph, you know you need to change your content structure. Insight and analytics like this are about learning how to change your business. It doesn't need to be complicated, you just need to think about how to improve readership.

If something is free, put a value on it. Increase conversions by saying "Get our free course (valued at $300)." Something you can do with lead magnets and free content is to value it. People don't value anything that's free, even if your cheat sheet is the greatest Google Doc in history. However, as soon as you mention it's worth $300, people become more interested.

Where do you use your worksheets or course material? Consulting, coaching, design, or discovery sessions? How much does that cost the customer? That's how much your worksheets are. Whatever your hourly rate is, that's how much a cheat sheet is. Be generous to yourself and value your time.

Send an "on-boarding" e-mail sequence. On-boarding e-mail sequences are key in many customer relationships after a purchase. Membership sites, software-as-a-service products, and cloud applications all use on-boarding e-mail sequences to guide the user through their new experience. The trouble is that they're hard to get right, so don't try to reinvent the wheel.

Sign up for a few services and follow their on-boarding sequence. Some of them are very in depth, with user guides, helpdesk information, and more. Take the core components of their on-boarding and apply it to your own. Even your consulting or design customers will benefit from a few e-mails telling them what's happening.

Chapter 10 | Growth Optimization

Don't ever drop your price. It's so much harder to raise it again. In the early 2000s, people were obsessed with negotiating. It was all about cutting back and scrimping on price to get the best deal. Saving $30 here and there might be fine for home shopping, but businesses don't need to work like that. Sales teams seem to keep discounts as their first resort, offering to lower the price without any resistance.

Have a conversation with a double-glazed window salesperson and they'll drop the price from $25,000 to $3,500 almost in the same breath. Do. Not. Lower. Your. Price. I could not be clearer on that. All it does is lower your value and income. If someone wants a discount, kindly say you're happy to drop the price if they tell you what it is that they want to remove from the product or service: "I'm happy to do a lower price. Just tell me what you think you could do without."

I promise you they won't want to remove anything. Stick to your pricing model. Trust yourself that you're delivering incredible value already. You shouldn't need to lower the price. Many potential customers forget there's always someone else willing to buy. They'll use every trick in the book: "Dave down the road says he'll do it for $500," "I think I could do it myself," "I don't really want to do this, I'm just being told to by my daughter." Price is price. Don't drop it.

Don't bombard people with opt-in pop-ups. I can't stress this enough. Do not listen to the opt-in, lightbox, and pop-up companies. Don't listen to the $10 marketing agencies or excitable marketing executives who tell you they increased opt-ins by 400% just by adding an opt-in. Most businesses, once they learn about opt-ins, will flood a page with them, giving a full-screen welcome mat, along with an opt-in bar, slide bar, inline form, and then a full-screen pop-up.

If you do this, people won't even bother trying to read your content; they'll just leave. You could have the world's most helpful, incredible, and well-written content, but if you're asking for e-mail addresses every 15 pixels, people will never read it. Businesses that flood their web site with opt-ins do so because they lack confidence in their content. Most businesses with lousy content feel that if they get someone's e-mail address, they'll send the good stuff later. Don't fall into this trap. Put epic content onto your web site and encourage people to learn more and get more help by giving you their contact information. It just so happens that opt-in forms are the easiest way to do that, but use them sensibly and sparingly.

Time your full-screen opt-in lightboxes. I don't think that full-screen lightboxes are the scourge of the Internet. They have a pretty good conversion rate. What you should do with them is time them, long enough so that readers can actually consume your content. Almost every opt-in form company and plug-in in the world has a % read or time delay on their lightboxes.

Let people read your content uninterrupted. If they've been on the site for over three minutes, show a lightbox. More important, test it. This might seem like a time waste and a lot of work for such a small payoff, but this is a perfect example of a task that suits a Growthhacker module or column in your growth optimization spreadsheet.

Use % of reading for scrollbars. Scrollbars and slide-ins work well, too. Instead of a time delay though, use a % read option before showing them. For example, if your opt-in box offers a cheat sheet lead magnet, show that lead magnet when you know that someone has read at least 50% of the blog post they're on. If they're getting that far, it stands to reason that they're enjoying your content. Offering the next stage makes sense.

Mention your products. I'm always staggered at how few people and businesses refer to their own products and content within their blog posts. You literally have someone's attention; they're reading about you and your company. You're helping them solve a problem and you probably have solutions to that problem. So why aren't you referring to them in your content?

I'm not talking about sales messages or pitch posts. I'm talking about the content you've got or the post you've written. Is there an example of what you're writing about that comes from your own product? I can't believe that there are no examples of your work that you can use in your content. For example, say we're talking about attracting sales to an e-commerce web site. If you've got an e-commerce web site that you've done and it's attracting sales, mention it.

This doesn't have to be a full-blown case study, just enough of a mention that shows you've got proof and experience in this area. Talk about your lead magnet, too. It's obviously helpful, so talk about that. Talk about how it's helpful to this topic and what they can do. Treat it like a conversation and mention things that are relevant.

Menus and links on landing and sales pages. It used to be that when you created a landing and sales page, you removed all links, menus, and distractions from that page. Now, apart from Google and other traffic sources requiring you to have menus and navigation items on the page no matter what, removing all links might not be the best thing to do.

The principle is that you don't give anything to distract people. There's no chance for them to click on your About page or go to your blog. You want them on that page and that's it, completing whatever action you need them to take. In tests, however, we've never seen a massive change in conversions if we've included our usual header on a sales or landing page. My advice would be to not have your usual header on a sales and landing page anyway, but make sure you do have menus and navigation in your footer.

Use social profiles on MailChimp. Follow subscribers. Most of the e-mail CRM systems have a similar feature. Make sure you're gathering as much data from your list as possible. Most systems, including MailChimp, have a feature to connect with people on social media. You can find their social profiles; if they're on Twitter or Facebook, follow them.

It's a huge connector and we've found it to be very beneficial when we follow our audience. Following their social profiles is like getting an insight into their mind. People post and share things on social media that they wouldn't necessarily say to you in person. Use that to your advantage and research what your audience are saying.

Talk to subscribers and leads. I cannot emphasize this enough. Stop using excuses like "I'm busy," or "I'm an introvert." Those are excuses: You're using labels given to you by other people to determine what you are capable of. I've got news for you: No one likes picking up the phone and talking to random strangers. We all have a fear of rejection, and if you're not willing to make calls and speak to customers, you have to ask yourself if you really deserve to scale and grow.

Your business is going to rely on people and communication if you want to grow and scale. Swallow your fear and look for ways to have conversations with your leads and customers, or someone else will. It doesn't have to be a cold call sales pitch. It just needs to be a conversation. Jason Resnick, from rezzz.com, says that you need to have small conversations with your customers and leads regularly. He knows about growing agencies, as he teaches it.

"How's business? Any problems at the moment? What are you working on? Is there anything I could be doing to help?" That's all you need to ask. Just talk to your leads and your customers. Businesses that win do so because they're willing to have conversations with their leads and customers. Do not believe what you have been told, that you can do everything online. If you're not willing to have conversations and talk with your customers, you will lose. Set up Skype calls or use Appear.in and schedule calls every week with clients and leads. Talk to them and find out what they want. Within one week of talking to my customers, I had more insight on what I needed to do than months of market research and planning could provide.

Eliminate processes and items that don't work. There's a concept called *sunk cost fallacy* whereby the time, resources, and investment into a project need to be paid off before you cancel it. It's a lot like gambling. If they bet $100 on red and lose, many people will struggle to walk away from the table until they've "won back" that lost $100.

If you've spent six days and $1,500 on a new landing page and traffic, but it isn't working, you need to get rid of it. Suck up the costs and chalk it up to experience. If it's not working, it's not working. There is a big difference between gaining traction and something not working. The same goes for processes.

Systems or steps taken to get a job done aren't always as efficient as we'd like. Some are downright horrible or broken.

For example, when we were building out our first social automation process, each blog post would produce eight tweets, which we'd copy into our posting software. I spent days building the automation and triggers, working out the copy and text for each tweet. By the end, it was overengineered and didn't work that well. The tweets usually arrived late, there were spelling errors, and the whole thing became something I dreaded every week. I persevered, though, because I chalked it up to change and growing pains. However, eventually my social media coordinator just told me it wasn't working. I was making her life and mine more difficult, so we scrapped it. Once we did it, I felt a huge weight lifted from me.

Assess whether what you're doing is really working. If it isn't, scrap it. Don't become emotionally attached or fall into the sunk cost fallacy. If it doesn't work now, it's not going to magically start working again.

Measure in cash flow, keep on profit. This simple mantra has helped me gain a real hold on my business and personal finances. Cash flow, as we often hear, is the lifeblood of a small business. It's better to have regular, repeat income predictably come into your account, rather than one-off lump sums. Others call this revenue, and at a high level they're right. It's the amount of money that customers pay you and what enters your account.

Profit is what your business keeps. We'll cover this in more detail later on. Understand, though, that what your accountant and bank manager call profit is not what we as business owners call profit. I want to see money in my account at the end of the month. We can all agree, accountants and bank managers included, that this is profit.

More often than not, though, when I submit my tax returns and I'm told I owe £20,000 of tax on the profit I've made, but there is nothing in my account to show for it, something has gone wrong. Measure your growth in cash flow. Some people call this vain (revenue is vanity), but we do need to see growth in income. We measure success in profit. Assuming we're following the other steps in this book, we'll also be growing the profit of our business.

Profit isn't enough, however. There are two types of profit: profit that shows growth (money you get to keep after paying for everything) and profit that pays for stuff. Typically, we have profit that pays for everything and we forget to keep any. That's the difference we'll cover a little later.

Think outside blog posts for social media; use quotes, images, and GIFs. Written content is awesome. It really is. I love writing, reading, and the freedom it allows us as businesses. However, you have so many options available to you—GIFs, quotes, images, videos, and so on. We've covered a few different blog post types that you can use, but always bear in mind just how many options you have when it comes to engaging, educating, and attracting customers.

With social media, use GIFs and images in your posts to draw attention. It sounds trite, and even obvious, but I so often see posts from businesses that are actively trying to grow, that just post walls of text. If you're serious about growing your audience and attracting traffic to your web site, use media other than just text. Text is great, but mix it up! The advent of live video, easy image and video posting, podcast clips, and more means you should never be short of options to engage your audience.

Test subject lines. This is still the biggest impact on your e-mail marketing. You could write the greatest e-mail sales letter in the world, or the single most incredible epic of a story that converts customers there and then. Don't let the subject line slow you down.

Test! It's easy to do. We covered the smoke test, where we try a few headlines and titles, but do the same for your subject lines. Test a variety of subject lines and send the same e-mail. Don't worry about sending the same or similar e-mails. We're testing subject lines and we want to make sure that we get the highest open rate possible. Look at the e-mails you've sent previously and analyze what's worked well. If you ever feel you're stuck in a rut, test a few subject lines. That always gets me out of a funk.

Give epic, awesome, and huge promise guarantees. I 100% guarantee, with a full 90-day, no-questions-asked refund policy, that you're going to finish reading this sentence. Recently, we've been testing a refund guarantee on a page and we discovered something really interesting. We compared a standard refund policy in the footer or a small line at the end of a page or letter with no refund policy on the page at all. The difference? Negligible. It was almost as if people who were buying either didn't care about refunds or knew they could afford the cost. Perhaps they knew they'd get a refund if it was really deficient. Instead, we then started testing with huge promise guarantees, making a big deal out of the quality of our products and our refund policy. Here is our refund example:

> Here's the deal if you aren't completely, 100% over the moon happy with what you get. If in 60 days you're not happy (in fact, even if your grandchildren told me 50 years into the future that my product sucked), I'll refund every penny of your purchase.
>
> At no point does it suit my business model to keep your money if you're unhappy.
>
> I promise that you'll generate more traffic to your web site. It's as simple as that. If you're not happy, I'm not happy. I'd rather you tell me that something isn't right, rather than stay unhappy. I'll do everything I can to help if this isn't the most useful traffic product you've ever bought.

That's our standard refund policy. We make it part of the sales process. We talk about how we're confident in our business and our service. If your business isn't willing to make a promise that you can guarantee and deliver on, what business do you have selling anything to a customer?

I've heard every excuse in the book: "If we make promises and don't deliver, customers will be unhappy," "I can't make promises, there are legal ramifications," or "If we make promises we'll be sued." Think about what you're saying: You're happy and you feel morally and ethically fine with customers gambling on your results. You don't have enough confidence in your products to make a promise. I'm not telling you to promise people they'll make $1 million in 30 days (although if you can do that, talk to me).

Don't promise on what you can't deliver. Promise on what you can deliver and then smash that goal, too. Go overboard. Kill it. Go nuts. Unless you have that kind of confidence in your product, your customers won't either. What can you promise about your business and service? What can you promise about your product? Think about what you can promise, not what you can't. Make that a part of your business. Make it obvious that you'd stake your reputation on your products. Otherwise what right do you have to have others stake their money and time on you?

Identify users who haven't logged in or opened e-mails. Segmenting your e-mail list is a big part of optimizing your growth. Most CRM and e-mail systems like MailChimp or ActiveCampaign have a lead score. It might be stars, or a percentage, but it's a rating of how often a subscriber interacts, opens, and clicks on your content. Run a report on your list of users who haven't interacted with your e-mails or web site in 60 days, or roughly two months of no activity. Set that list up as a group or tagged, or whatever helps you identify them as an inactive member. Your goal is to either get them to reengage or unsubscribe. I don't want inactive users on my list, because it damages the results that my other subscribers are helping me get.

Send a "list warmup" sequence to get them back. Once you've identified a group of users who haven't interacted much, we're going to send them a series of e-mails to either get them excited about our e-mails again or cut them from our list. It's vital that we keep subscriber hygiene. You want people to unsubscribe because it means they're data cleaning themselves. We're also going to try and unsubscribe users who we know aren't interested anymore. We're so protective of our list that we forget that spam, dead, and inactive e-mail addresses are clogging up the system. It's all well and good having a list of 8,000 people, but if that list is totally inactive, wouldn't you rather know that only 1,200 of them actually even want to receive your e-mails?

Here's the warmup sequence we use. It's paced over 60 days. It's around one e-mail sent a week, because of course, you're still also sending your regular content. Drawing attention to the fact that they are not opening your e-mails is sometimes enough for people to make sure they stay on your list.

I've Noticed ...

Subject: I've noticed you're not interested

Hey,

I just wanted to say that your e-mail address came to my attention because it looks like you're not interested in my e-mails anymore.

Is it something I said? Or is there anything I could do differently?

It's really important to me that my subscribers only get useful information and helpful resources from me. I don't want to clog up your e-mails any more than you want me to!

So, just to make sure that you're still interested in my e-mails, give the button below a click and read our killer post on How to Sell a Marketing Funnel to Any Customer.

It's our most popular post and I know you'll get something from it.

Or, hit Reply and let me know what I could be doing better/different.

Speak later!

Mike

Just Because I Want You Back

Subject: I want you back, baby!

Hey,

So at some point you opted in to be on my list. I can see that you downloaded my $100K funnel guide.

But then after that. Poof! You disappeared!

Assuming you haven't been abducted by aliens, or you've run off to become an international secret agent, I want you back!

Have you seen my video on How to Grow Your List to 1,000 Subscribers?

I don't really share it with too many people because it was recorded for a customer.

Anyway, let me know that you're still interested in my e-mails and hearing from me. Just click the link and I'll know you're still around. ;)

Or feel free to e-mail me and tell me what I should do better. I'm always open to a conversation!

Speak soon.

Mike

We Miss You!

Subject: We miss you!

Hey,

We miss you!

We haven't seen you interact with our stuff in ages! Are you still there?

Let us know that you haven't mutated into a fly-man and you're having to live in the sewers. Even if you did, we'd still love you.

Click the link below to let us know you're still cool with us sending e-mails.

Mike

P.S. The link is to a free gift that we want to give you.

We're Going to Unsubscribe You

Subject: We're going to unsubscribe you.

Hey,

We've been trying to make contact with you by sending you a few e-mails. But I've been told by my e-mail team that I need to unsubscribe you.

E-mail hygiene is really important to us. So is knowing that everyone on our list wants to receive our e-mails.

So with that, if we don't hear from you in 10 days, we'll unsubscribe you.

If you want to stay on our list and keep receiving epic content helping you sell marketing funnels to customers, click on the link below to reignite your subscription.

\>>Yes I want to stay on the list

Hope to hear from you soon.

Mike

Secret Gift Inside

Subject: Secret gift FREE inside for you.

Hey,

Have you checked out our free gift yet? It's pretty awesome.

We usually charge for it, but we want to make sure everyone gets an opportunity to see it.

It's an e-book covering the 15 stages of a successful marketing funnel project sale: everything from generating and finding leads for your business, to selling them a marketing automation funnel.

Click here to download your free version.

In the meantime, speak soon.

Mike

Are You Just Not Interested?

Subject: Maybe it's us? Are we not interesting?

Hey,

I get it. Sometimes you subscribe to a list and then you're just not interested in what they have to say.

So I tell you what, if you're really not interested in our stuff, give yourself some e-mail inbox space and hit Unsubscribe.

No harsh feelings, no bad blood. I want your e-mail inbox to be a productive place. If my e-mails just aren't that important to you, hit the Unsubscribe link below.

Or, if this has all been a misunderstanding, click the link below to claim your free e-book on finding more leads for your funnel business.

Speak soon.

Mike

In Three Days, You Won't Hear from Us

Subject: No more e-mails from Sell Your Service.

Hey,

In three days we'll be automatically unsubscribing your e-mail address from our list.

You can prevent this by clicking the link below, indicating you're still interested in our e-mails.

>>Click here to stay on the list.

No bad feelings, we just need to keep our list clean.

Mike

Today Is Your Last Day

Subject: We're sorry to see you go. You're unsub'd.

Hey,

In 24 hours, we'll be unsubscribing your e-mail address from our list.

It's nothing personal, we just need to keep our list clean and you haven't interacted with our stuff in a while.

So unless you click the link below, to keep your active profile, we'll unsubscribe you in 24 hours.

>>click here to stay on the list

I'm sorry to see you go, if you have any comments or feedback, please just hit Reply and talk to me.

Mike

Cut users who don't do anything over 60 days. Subscribers who don't interact after 60 days and those eight e-mails should be automatically unsubscribed from your e-mail list. You can set a trigger in your e-mail provider software to keep users subscribed if they click a link. Don't use opens, as sometimes programs like Gmail and Outlook pretend to open an e-mail when in fact it hasn't been opened and read. If someone doesn't click a link on any of those e-mails, unsubscribe them. They're clearly not interested and I'd rather focus on people who are interested.

Offer webinars, coaching calls, and accountability tracking to customers. The biggest reason that we have so many raving fans at Sell Your Service is because the people I create content for are my customers. My agency customers are exactly the same. I create content with them in mind first. If they love it, other people who are suitable customers will love it, too.

I try to run a webinar or coaching call for all my customers once a month. I'll tell them what I've learned, then go over some tactics or skills. It's always free and the webinar content makes fantastic lead generation content. Because I'm focused on keeping my customers engaged, I naturally attract new customers and members who want to be a part of that, too. If you're making your customers happy, people who fit that customer profile will want to join.

Use other larger companies to get ideas. There are some big companies out there who know what they're doing. They also have huge marketing teams and budgets, so look to what they're doing for ideas. MailChimp has awesome e-mails, unsurprisingly. Ideas on how to improve your growth are all around you. Just spend some time researching what the other businesses that have grown do.

Ask yourself, with every new opportunity, "Does it scale?" Finally, when it comes to optimizing your growth, you'll be offered new opportunities a lot: new leads, customers, projects, collaborations, partnerships, and more. They'll start coming your way once you start to scale and grow. It's tempting to jump on every opportunity and embrace all your new ideas. It's much harder to focus and ask yourself, "Does this scale?"

Recently I was asked to deliver a series of web sites to a large organization that needed small membership sites for each of its products. They wanted me to come on board as a part-time consultant and work with them, implementing and designing the work.

The money was good. In fact, it was really good. However, I knew that this would be time I couldn't put into other projects. I offered to have my team build the sites and for me to coach them regularly, but on my terms. They insisted that the only way I'd get the project would be if I consulted with them in their business. I did remind them that they approached me, that I wasn't looking to work for them. I had to turn down the offer. The money would have been awesome. It also would have been a decent name to have in my portfolio, but I didn't take it because I knew it wasn't "true North." I didn't want to consult and work at another business. It didn't scale. I couldn't apply myself to other areas. Although it was tough at the time, I knew I had to stick to what my plan for growth was.

Summary

Growth acts in an unbiased fashion. If a process is inefficient or ineffective, it will continue to scale with the growth of the business. If we focus on tactics that do work, we can add massive momentum to our business's growth.

- Growth is a grind. Most businesses don't grow because they don't stick with a tactic until it works.
- Measure your performance and decide what success looks like for each tactic.
- Focus on one tactic at a time and get it right, then outsource it.
- Don't listen to everyone about what you "need" to do. Do what works for your business.

CHAPTER 11

Profit and Money Management to Scale

This chapter was written to make sure that businesses like yours aren't left in the dark when it comes to money management. More often than not, the closest most of us will get to money and financial coaching is our bank sending a few "How to take care of your finances" leaflets. Other than my personal crusade to better educate small and microbusinesses about money, I think it's important that everyone learns what to do with cash.

Most of the time we believe that more income will solve all our problems. If you think this, then you should know that more money won't solve your problems. If you're not managing money well already, you're not going to magically manage it better when you have a larger income. History has proven over and over again that a large income does not equal financial security. Most people make the assumption that they can't afford to plan and manage their money, and that they need more income to start managing money better.

This simply isn't the case, and this chapter is designed to start you on the path to money management for growth. I've taken what I believe works from *Profit First* by Mike Michalowicz, *Rich Dad, Poor Dad* by Robert Kiyosaki, *How to Own the World* by Andrew Craig, and many others.

What Is Your Goal for the Business?

More important than anything, what is the goal of your business? What's the purpose behind you setting up a business and bringing it to market? What's the point of your business? What does it do to make life easier, or help your customers? You should be able to complete this sentence:

> I help [type of customers] get [result].

That's all. Who do you help and what do you get them? You should be able to do something for this customer or for their result better than anyone else in your marketplace.

Warning: Harsh truth ahead! If you can't do something better, or different, within your marketplace, what business do you have being in that market? Can you imagine saying, "Yeah we do burgers, but they're not better or different than anything else out there"? What? Then what are you doing here? You should be able to say, with confidence and conviction, that you do something better than everyone else competing within this marketplace. It sounds harsh and it is, but if you can't do that, you'll never get a foothold.

For example, Sell Your Service helps funnel builders achieve their maximum income potential. We do this better than anyone because I am the world's top sales coach for funnel buidlers. So what's your business's purpose? What do you do? How do you help? Who do you help? Why does your business exist and what does it do better than anyone else?

What Is the Financial Goal of the Business?

By this stage we should be able to work out what our financial goal for the business is. We need a monthly income and an overall target. This could be yearly or monthly or a total accumulation goal. The income to the business is what's going to pay you. Believe it or not, you also need money to survive.

Most businesses think they'll start drawing a salary when the business makes enough money, but they never plan to make more revenue for the business, so every time their income increases, they don't take anything for themselves. What are your financial goals for the business? If you can't answer this now, read the rest of the chapter to see how much you need to earn. Take into account your minimum monthly requirements, the operating costs of the business, plans to grow, investments, savings, and anything else that requires income. We need a financial goal for the business.

Work out your per hour rate. First, you need to work out your per hour rate. This is not the rate that you'll charge customers per hour. This is how much each hour costs you every day. We have maybe eight working hours a day. In fact, research shows it's probably closer to three hours a day.[1] We have to complete other tasks, of course, including e-mails, reading, lunch, and so on, but the work we do that generates profit is closer to three hours a day. To understand what each hour is costing us, we have to divide our month's desired income by four, which gives us income per week. Then, divide that number by four or five (to give us our working day). Then divide that number by three to five (for number of actual productive hours per day). The number in front of you might shock you. If you don't know your desired financial income and monthly goal yet, we'll cover that later. Keep this exercise in mind. If you'd like a worksheet to help you with this exercise, head over to singletoscale.com/hour.

This is how much you need to be earning per hour to reach your goals. For example, I know our agency's goal is $10,000 a month income. Divided by four, that gives me $2,500 a week. Divided by four (working four days a week) gives us $625 per day. Divided by three working hours a day, gives us $208.3 per hour. Let's call that $210 per hour. Most designers, developers, and consultants charge one fourth of that per hour.

Don't fall into the trap of, "Well, if I have more hours that I work per day, then I can lower my hourly rate." As we've explored in the rest of this book, you doing work like that just doesn't work. It doesn't scale. The point of this number is to work out if a job, task, or project is worth at least that amount per hour. If it isn't, then how are you going to reach $10,000 a month? Or more?

Understand the goal is to work not for money or time. You should be working for income/effort. We want to make clear that our businesses should not be working per hour for income. You should be charging per project rather than per hour. Many businesses fall into the trap that charging per hour means they are more flexible, but it's a false economy. Once you've said to a customer you'll charge per hour, you're instantly a commodity that they can turn on and off like a tap.

Instead, what we're looking to create is an income/effort result. Working eight hours a day on a customer project gives you no time for working on your business. It becomes a negative cycle, as every hour you're not working on your business is eating into your future revenue streams. On the other hand, if

---

[1] See http://www.inc.com/melanie-curtin/in-an-8-hour-day-the-average-worker-is-productive-for-this-many-hours.html

we create revenue streams that allow us to focus on promotion and outreach, while other people or systems take care of the income, we're in a better position.

By putting five hours a day, for a week, into creating a system that can deliver results without you working on them, those 20 to 25 hours become infinitely more productive. Your effort becomes more and more worth it every time someone buys. I remember my first $19 e-mail template product (that still sells really well today). It took about a week with –three to four hours a day to build the templates, create the sales page, and write a few promotional e-mails. So, for 20 or so hours of work, I created something where the rate per hour can only go up. The first sale meant that each hour was worth $0.95 per hour. As soon as a second person bought, that hourly rate went up to $1.90 per hour. See what I mean? We're at roughly $10,000 for that one product, which gives me an hourly income/effort rate of $500 per hour. What's even better, is that every hour I'm not working on it, I'm doing other things. So ask yourself, the next time a task or project comes in, "Will this income/effort rate increase in time after I've completed it?"

Your minimum monthly and daily target. If you're struggling with creating a monthly target, try starting with your minimum targets. This exercise is taken from Tim Ferriss's *4 Hour Work Week*. Write down on a piece of paper all your monthly, daily, and weekly expenses. You can use Excel or Google sheets to make things easier. Write down rent, mortgages, loans, food, bills, going out, saving, and everything else you need. I cannot stress enough how important it is to write down all the things you do need. For example going out with friends and partners is critical. Otherwise what's the point? Don't reduce the cost to make yourself feel better, either. You will need food. You will need heating.

This exercise isn't about cutting back. You don't get rich by swapping to $0.99 bread. You get rich by taking control of what needs money spent on it. Write down everything you need to pay for every month, and add 30% on top. That's your buffer zone. Whatever that number is, that is your minimum income requirement. It's probably lower than you realize. What makes a budget like this work is when you stick to it. It's no good having a plan and not executing it.

Take your minimum monthly budget and divide it by 20 (four weeks a month, seven days in total but five working days = 20 working days a month). Then divide your weekly minimum budget by five. This is your daily minimum target. That is how much you need to make per day to survive. It's probably lower that you thought and should take some pressure off. If you go back to your hourly rate, you might find your hourly rate is higher than your minimum daily budget—I know mine is—so I know that if I create one profitable hour per day, I can always survive.

Profit isn't made from one-off sales. "Our garage doesn't make any profit from selling these cars." I couldn't believe what I was hearing. My stepdad is really good with money. He taught me almost everything I know about investing and saving. At the car dealership, though, he would show me the numbers of cars sold per month and what they made per sale. It was close to nothing. In some cases, they lost money per car. "How is it possible that they're still in business? How does this guy have 10 dealerships?!" I couldn't understand it. My stepdad then showed me the customer records and how much they would bring in per customer—not per sale. The garage also did servicing and repairs. This is where the money was. The car was what started the relationship. Although people only bought a car once every 10 years, they'd be in at least twice a month for servicing: tires, oil changes, brakes, exhaust repairs, the list went on.

My stepdad explained to me that the car was a way for them to buy a customer. The commission, tax, and cost of sale almost didn't make the sale worth it. Having people booked for weeks in advance for a servicing is where the profit was made. I finally understood that one-off sales don't create profit. Repeat, predictable, and outsourceable income made profit. Think to yourself about the income generated from your projects. Are they one-off projects that won't fill your income/effort ratio? Are they projects that lead to repeat and profitable work?

Market research is cheaper than experience. A short note on building products and selling them is in order. Market research is much cheaper than experience. This means that spending time on research, building an audience, and talking to customers is much cheaper than launching a product to find no one likes it. Although I agree with the concepts of failing fast, I believe it's more important to sell something before you build it.

Spending a few days and some budget on research and learning what's out there will save you money and time in the long run. A business I know spent close to $25,000 developing a brand new theme and plug-in set for WordPress. After six months of building and developing, when they launched, they found the market was saturated with almost identical products. They failed to gain any traction in the market and they ultimately shut the project down. Talk to customers and the market. Spend time learning what they want and build an audience first. It will save you money.

Can your ads pay for themselves? When spending money on advertising, be it PPC, paid social, or old-school print media, think to yourself, "Can my ads pay for themselves?" Often, media sales agencies will convince us that their readership and exposure (the same goes for online, too) will give you access to thousands of potential customers. Advertising hasn't changed in hundreds of years: It's still about getting attention and getting people to invest in your way of thinking.

If you're spending thousands on advertising, will that ad pay for itself? In many cases, that's the best scenario you could hope for. If I paid $100 per click but the customer bought $100 worth of stuff a few days later, that's worth it. If I spend $2 a click and no one buys, eventually that's a waste. Don't pretend it's all about brand exposure or awareness. Your ads all need to have a measurable return. Almost all online PPC platforms allow you to measure that, too, so make what you spend on advertising pay for itself.

What Do You Want to Do Without a Business?

Some of the most important goals you can have are the ones totally unrelated to your business. You need to have a vision for your own life. What do you want to do outside of your business? What is your business empowering you to do?

Most of the time, we have jobs that allow us to take holidays, buy nice stuff, and be financially secure. However, when we start a business we often neglect our personal visions to focus on the business. Although this might be necessary for the start, we need to remember why we started a business in the first place. What is the vision for your life, outside of your business?

If you had a spare $200,000, what would you do? Another great question to think about is if I put $200,000 in your bank account tomorrow, what would you do? If you didn't have to work, what would you do? Whatever you think about should be a good indicator for your personal vision and business goals. If you realize that you wouldn't want to spend your time consulting on network diagnostics, maybe think of something else to do.

The work that you'd still do, if you didn't need the money, is a strong indicator of what you should be doing now. I can say with confidence that if I didn't need the money, I'd be writing and talking and creating content that helps small businesses grow.

Are you making money, or are you making profit? We've talked already about profit and revenue, and about how revenue doesn't really make a difference to your long-term growth. Profit is what your business is looking for. However, real-world profit and what I call accounting profit are two very different things.

If you asked my accountant whether I made a profit in 2015, he'd have whipped out my annual report and told you that I made a few thousand pounds profit. Now part of his job is to reduce the amount of profit I made. As insane as that sounds, my accountant's job during tax time is to reduce the amount of profit I've made for me to pay less tax. When I looked at my bank account, though, I didn't feel I had made a huge profit. I was still effectively working month to month.

Instead, after reading *Profit First* by Mike Michalowicz and *Rich Dad, Poor Dad* by Robert Kiyosaki, I started forcing profit to be made from every penny I earned. We'll go into that in a minute. First, though, ask yourself if you're just making money or if you're really making a profit, because the next few sections of this book are going to make you profitable.

The Rule of Thirds for Pricing

I'm asked this question all the time: "How much should I charge for my services?" My answer is the same every time: "I don't have a soundbite answer for that."

The truth about pricing is that we often fall into the trap of thinking there is a middle ground. We'll look at our cheapest competitor and say, "Well, they're only charging $500, so I'll do higher than that." At the same time, though, we'll look at the higher cost services and say, "They charge $10,000, and I can't possibly charge that, so I'll undercut them," and we end up somewhere in the middle.

The middle of the road is the most dangerous place you can be for your pricing. The middle of the road doesn't exist with pricing, or at least it's certainly not successful. Instead, you should be working out your pricing with a very simple formula. The total price that the customer pays should roughly work out to be one third profit, one third project expenses, and one third overhead.

Profit is where we draw profit, tax, and our salary from. It's where we find growth in our business and our sales, and we pay this first. Second, project expenses are the costs associated with doing the work. Whatever it costs you to deliver the work to the customer should be around one third of the total price: hours, hiring designers or developers, plug-ins, travel, and so on, whatever you'd have to pay for just for this project.

Third, overhead is the operating costs of the business, like your rent, bills, staff, apps, and so on. These are things you'd have to pay for even if you didn't have work come in. Your total price to the customer needs to be a combination of all three of these things: profit, expenses, and overhead. Do not lie to yourself when it comes to overhead and project expenses. If you're not willing to start charging for your time, overhead, expenses, and costs now, you'll never be able to do it in the future.

You do have costs and you do have expenses. Do not undercut people just because you live at home. You'll never grow unless you're willing to start charging and acting like a larger business.

Take a cut. Don't give a cut. One of the most crippling mistakes businesses make is to think that they should give a cut to other people. They hoard income and money that comes their way, not willing to share it with other people. If they do share it, they give as small a cut as possible to get the job done. Instead, if you want to grow, if you're serious about scaling your business, you need to take a cut instead.

What sounds more profitable and productive: five projects that you have to do all the work for, with a little help from other people, or 100 projects where you do very little and everyone else does the work? Assuming both are the same service, managing 100 projects is more profitable. You need to allow yourself the time and resources to manage the business, not do the work for the customer. Think about your project income as a cut for yourself if you do less of the work, rather than taking it all for yourself and not allowing yourself the freedom to run the business.

Rules for Saving

Most small businesses don't have a pension or savings. As terrible as this sounds, we often don't think we earn enough to justify a savings account. Saving is something we should all be doing and it's easier than you might think. Of any money that comes to you personally, just put 10% of it away in another account.

That 10% doesn't sound like a lot, but that's why this works: 10% every time you pay yourself adds up over time. You could even be smart and investigate a stocks and shares account. However, I'm not experienced enough to talk about how to do that. I suggest reading Andrew Craig's *How to Own the World* if you want to learn more about creating your pension and savings fund.

The golden rule with saving, though, is to never touch your savings once they're in another account. It's tempting when we're a few pounds short of a month's bill to dip into savings, but don't do it. Let your savings grow over time, rather than keep dipping into them.

Rules for Tax

Start getting into the habit of putting 15% of all your income into a separate account for business tax. Saving for tax will be a lifesaver once you start to make enough money. You'll find you won't even notice it after a while, but when your tax bill comes through, you'll be glad you have it.

Rules for Profit

For every payment that comes your way, 5% must go to a profit account immediately. This is the difference between real-world profit and accounting profit. Your accountant will tell you you've made $1,000 or $100,000 profit, but it can be hard to use that when you can't see it in your bank account.

The problem is that profit can be measured in the past. Things you've bought and spent money on are sometimes considered profit, so even though you have nothing in the bank, the accountants see you as having made money. Instead, you should be putting 5% of everything you earn into a special profit account. Again, make it hard to get at. You don't want to dip into it every time you need to pay a bill.

Pay your profit first: It's the only way to guarantee you're growing. Once it all adds up, you can use it to invest in other things.

Build steadily. Don't jump on one-off projects. One of the big roadblocks that businesses face when they decide to start the journey of scaling their small business is the "golden opportunity" that comes their way. It doesn't sound like much of a roadblock does it? It can be a killer, though, and is often a curse disguised as a blessing. Let's say you've decided to focus on building e-commerce web sites for audio manufacturers. You've got a process and you know what you're delivering to your customers. At some point, someone who hears "web sites" will equate that to graphic design, SEO, and social media. They'll ask you to help them out and what they want is everything that your business doesn't do. The money will be extremely tempting, though. They'll ask for a one-off project cost, and they'll even challenge you when you say it's not what you do.

My advice is to hold your resolve. Hang tight and insist that you're going to stick to your plan. Customers who aren't willing to follow your process aren't customers. It'll seem like the dumbest decision you've ever made. This new person might even say that to you—that you're crazy to turn down such a huge opportunity. The thing about opportunities is that they do come around again. Your job is to build steady monthly income. Keep to your plan and sell products that generate monthly revenue. Don't jump on one-off projects because the income looks good.

Measuring return on investment is very hard. Whenever you spend time investing in ads and online activity, it can seem like there is little to no return on your efforts. The truth is that measuring return on investment is much harder than we think. Even in a world of digital metrics and online measurement, it's still hard to see what each dollar spent gets you.

With that in mind, stick to the rules that if advertising doesn't directly help you generate traffic, subscribers, leads, or customers, don't do it. Print media is a wonderful example of media agents offering you advertising and media space. They tell you it's about brand awareness, growing a brand, and getting eyeballs. Don't fall for it. Media advertising is pure vanity, and yes, it feels good to see an ad for a few days in a newspaper or magazine, but everyone is moving to online exposure. Why? Because it's easier to measure. It's still hard, but easier. I can see how much Google Adwords or Facebook PPC increases my traffic. I can see how much revenue e-mail marketing generates. But eyeballs?

Brand awareness? Don't fall for it. Publicity, on the other hand, for brand awareness and category promotion, is 100% worth your time. Advertising is for products, publicity is for brands. Publicity is you pushing a message out to the market. Advertising is dragging attention from the market to a product.

Summary

Money is what you make of it. Businesses with a firm understanding of how their money is used will have better control when they scale. If you're not profitable after one sale, you won't be profitable after 100 sales.

- Focus on the goal of the business. Profit to your business will allow you to complete that mission.
- Create rules for your money, like any other resource, and allocate it.
- Create prices for your products by understanding what it costs you and what you'll deliver.
- Split your income up into portions and watch small amounts grow over time.

CHAPTER 12

Scale and Growth Are Just Around the Corner!

You now know that you need to scale and that growth is the strongest strategy you can employ for your business. Even as a single person or microbusiness, it's critical that you allow your business to grow larger than you are.

- Does your new business sell products and services that you don't have to deliver?
- Does your new business have products and services that can sell thousands of times and not run out?
- Can the delivery be repeated over and over?

If you answered "yes" to those questions, you've got a business designed to scale. There is absolutely nothing stopping you as a single person growing a business to scale. You need processes in place, however.

© Michael Killen 2019
M. Killen, *From Single to Scale*, https://doi.org/10.1007/978-1-4842-3814-1_12

Online courses, web site design, affiliate products: There are so many options for small and microbusinesses to expand the number of products and services from which they make money. The beauty is that you already have products available to you within your current business.

The key to selling those new, scalable products is promotion and content. Are you ready to create helpful, valuable, and useful content for your customers and audience? That's how you'll gain traction. If other people can deliver the work, you can focus on finding customers.

To build an audience, you need to have a voice and an opinion. You need to be an expert and someone who has authority. To do that, we publish content, use our voice, and help people in our audience. When enough members of that audience are following you, you can connect them to a product. You can even do it with automation. Capitalize on every new visitor to your web site by asking them to access even more content. This will start them on the journey toward discovering your paid products.

Without a machine and process, your business can't scale. It would be like you being the driver, mechanic, car designer, and manufacturer: It's too much for one person. By creating a process and a repeatable protocol, your ability to scale will drastically improve because you'll be repeating a series of steps. The journey from interest to delivery for products and services becomes faster and more profitable.

At that point, you can start to ask other people to deliver certain sections of your work. Outsourcing delivery of your projects and products is the only way that you as a small or single-person microbusiness will grow. You can't do it all. Once your product is up and being delivered, you can focus on optimizing your growth by making sure that as many visitors as possible are signing up and joining your list, and making sure that your e-mail list members are buying your stuff. There's a lot to work on and we can do it over time.

Finally, with income and revenue, we want to start focusing on profit. Financial control is the mark of a true, expert business. Even single-person businesses need to work hard at controlling their income and expenses. I hope this book has helped you scale your business to grow larger and stronger than you thought you could, as a single person or small business.

I believe microbusinesses are the most sustainable source of income for the future of both the economy and us as individuals. The concept of only working in medium-sized or large companies that is reinforced by our education system telling you that your only source of secure financial income is being employed is utterly false in my opinion. Businesses like yours are the future and I look forward to seeing you surpass even my expectations for you.

Index

A

Accountability calls, 54, 85

ActiveCampaign, 143, 197

Adsense, 46

AdWords, 122

Affiliate marketing, 89

Affiliate products, 48

Amazon, 56

Anchor, 124

Appsumo, 61

Audience
- comment marketing, 127
- content and blog posts, 113
- content upgrades, 118
- e-mail lead database list, 112, 116
- killer blog post (see Killer blog post, lead magnet)
- lead magnets to blog posts, 117–118
- remarketing list, 112
- remarketing traffic to squeeze pages
  - closed group, 126–127
  - e-books to e-mail leads, 125
  - Facebook group, 126
  - podcasts, 123–124
  - SEO and keywords, 123
  - tag/mention people, 126
  - warm and cold traffic, 122–123
- speak at university, 115
- voice and opinion, 214
- webinars
  - advertising copy, 114
  - e-mail campaigns, 114–115
  - opportunities, 114
  - paid traffic, 114
  - video series, 115
  - YouTube video content, 115

Automated manufacturing, 50–51

B

Brickwork India, 170

Buzzfeed, 189

Buzzsumo, 102–103

C

Call to action (CTA)
- background, 139
- "behind the scenes" webinar, 143–144
- ego, 140
- guarantee, 139
- lead magnets
  - SEO and social media silos, 142
  - users, 143
  - withhold, 140
- pricing, 140
- product delivery page, 140–141
- sales e-mails, 142
- splinter products in newsletters, 144
- valuable e-mails, 141
- value stack e-mails, 143
- welcome e-mail, 141

Cloud-based applications, 61–62

Coaching seminars, 53

© Michael Killen 2019
M. Killen, *From Single to Scale*, https://doi.org/10.1007/978-1-4842-3814-1

Index

Comment marketing
  bloggers, 127
  description, 127
  e-mail customers, 128
  fast traction, 127
  lead magnets, 129
  networking event, breakfast and lunch, 127
  SLOs, 129–130

Content, scalable product
  blog post roundup, 94
  book review, 95
  e-commerce web site developer, 92
  e-mail marketing, 93
  explorer posts (see Explorer posts)
  how-to guide, 95–96
  interview, 97
  myths, 97–98
  repurposing
    Buzzsumo, 102
    e-mail automation, 102
    search tool, 102
    videos, 102
    welcome e-mails, 102
  sales letter style (see Sales letter style content)
  sharing, 103–104
  templates, 98–99
  testimonials, 104
  video process, 96–97
  widgets, 91
  YouTube roundup, 94

Content silos
  Beaver Builder and Divi, 133
  blog post, 134
  e-mail subscribers, 133
  faster and easier, 134
  OptinMonster, 133
  phone call with customer
    automation process, 146
    e-mail sales campaign, 146
    one-on-one Q&A session, 144
    payment, 150
    "problem" webinar, 146–147
    product sales letter, 145
    sales page, 145
    sales webinar, 148–150
    solution webinar, 147–148
    three-page microfunnel, 150
    upselling/x-selling, 144–145
  scale, automation, and growth, 133
  SEO post, 133
  splinter product creation, 134–136
  thank you page
    benefits, 139
    common sense, 136
    CTA (see Call to action (CTA))
    e-mail signup form, 137
    fake e-mail addresses, 136
    knife twist, 138
    messages, 136
    principles for webinars and blog posts, 138
    scarcity and changes, 138
    track conversions, 137
    upselling, 137–138
  web site, blog content and lead magnets, 132

Courses
  analytics and reporting, 81
  blog posts, 88
  digital marketing, 80
  educational businesses, 80
  external consultants, 83
  hire, 86
  offering subscriptions, 84–86
  reading, materials, 87
  removing yourself, 87
  SEO subscription, 88
  teaching, 82–83
  transcript selling, 83–84
  webinar recordings, 84
  worksheets, 82

D

99 Designs, 171

Digital Marketers, 104

Digital marketing, 80

Digital products, 62

E

E-commerce supplier, 55–56

E-mail courses, 49

E-mail lead database list, 112

Index

Epic killer content, 105–106
Evergreen campaign, 114
Explorer posts
  changes in industry, 100
  lead magnet, 101
  myth, 100
  people, 101
  problem, 100
  promise, 99
  sales letter, 99

F

Feast and famine cycle of projects
  chicken and egg, 21–22
  freelancers, consultants, and solo businesses, 19
  hot desking
    consultants and freelancers, 20
    income, recurring revenue, 21
    laptop, Wi-Fi, and e-mail, 20
    running costs, 20–21
    scaling and growth, 21
  income, 19–20
Financial control, 214
Fiverr, 170
Freelance business
  confidence, 27
  freelancers paradox, 27
  micromanagers, 27
  products, systems and payment methods, 28
  reliability and consistency, 27
  surrendering control, 27
  web design project, 28
Freelancer.clom, 170, 180
Freelancers, 13–14
Frequently asked questions (FAQs), 109

G

Gas station sandwiches, 12–13
Group mastermind sessions, 53–54
Growth optimization
  cash flow, 195
  content marketing, 186
  CRM and e-mail systems, 197
  drop the price, 192
  free talks at universities and colleges, 190
  full-screen light boxes, 192–193
  goals, 185
  growthhackers.com, 187
  guarantee, 196–197
  increase conversions, 191
  influencers
    e-mails, 188
    list post, 188
    read and research, 187
    shared, 187
    Twitter, 188
  "list warm up" sequence, 197–201
  MailChimp, social profiles, 194
  mention products, 193
  menus and links, landing and sales pages, 193
  networking, 190
  offer webinars, coaching calls, and accountability tracking, 201
  on-boarding e-mail sequences, 191
  opportunities, 202
  opt-in pop-ups, 192
  scroll bars, 193
  smoke tests, 189–190
  social media (quotes, images, and GIFs), 195–196
  subscribers and leads, 194
  Sumo.com, 191
  sunk cost fallacy, 194–195
  tactics, 186
  test subject lines, 196
  unsubscribe users from e-mails, 201

H, I, J

Hire coaches, 86

K

Killer blog post, lead magnet
  AdWords, 122
  content funnel creation process, 119
  PPC, 119–120
  sales letter style, 118
  SEO, 120–121
  social media, 121–122
  Sumo, 119
Kissflow, 179

Index

L
Lead qualification, 50
Learning management software (LMS), 81

M
MailChimp, 194, 197
Membership Guys, 127
Money management
  business goal, 204
  financial goals
    advertising payment, 207
    income/effort, 205–206
    market research, 207
    minimum monthly and daily target, 206
    monthly income, 204
    profit, one-off sales, 207
    work out per hour rate, 205
  outside of business, 208
  profit and revenue, 208
  Rules for
    pricing, 209–210
    profit, 210–211
    saving, 210
    tax, 210

N
Niche market, 36

O
OnlineJobs.ph, 171
OptinMonster, 133
Outbrain, 189–190
Outsourcing
  administrative services, 49
  backup VA team, 182
  Brickwork India, 170
  candidates, 172
  clear tasks, 180
  content services, 49
  day off, 169
  99 Designs, 171
  e-mails and instructions, 174
  English speakers, 173–174
  examples of results, 175
  final payment, 181
  Fiverr, 170
  freedom of intelligence, 182–183
  Freelancer.clom, 170, 180
  Google, 171
  guidance and help, 179
  interview, 171–172
  medium-level tasks, 177
  misinterpretation, 176
  one-off tasks, 177–178
  OnlineJobs.ph, 171
  pay for results, 178–179
  personal tasks, 178
  process-driven tasks, 176
  Process.st and Kissflow, 179
  Studio Envato, 171
  tasks, 172–173
  time limits, 175
  tools, 172
  Upwork.com, 170
  weekly repetition, 182
  weekly time used updates, 181
  Zapier, 179

P
Pay per click (PPC), 119–120
Podbean, 124
Podcasts, 106, 123–124
Process
  automation, 154
    referral, FAQ, and wiki pages/sites, 163
    VA teams, 162
    Zapier, 162
  booking networking events, 158–159
  booking time, speak to clients, 159
  bookkeeping and accounting, 159
  communication, 163–166
  customer e-mails and enquiries, 158
  "done work" diary, 156
  entrepreneur, 154
  freelancers, 155
  hiring staff, 156
  interviews, 155
  list posts, 160–161
  maintenance and reporting, 161
  management, 166–167
  objectives and goals, 154
  outsourcing, 163

Index

record, regular task, 156–157
social media content, 154
social media posting, 157–158
telecommunications company, 154
uploading and editing YouTube videos, 160
weekly newsletter, 159
writing up and publishing, 157, 161

Process.st, 179

Product Launch Formula (PLF), 150

Product reselling, 47–48

Q

Quitting job
attitude, 39
Facebook, 39
fancy office, 38
freelancers and consultants, 39
full-time job, 37
growth size, 38
high-rise views and young team, 38
prioritization, 37
retirement funds, 37
smartphones, 39
time, 37

Quitting policies, 18

R

Recurring revenue
busy periods, 9
car manufacturer, 1
definition, 1
limited options, 4
market, 2
profit, 4–6
quiet periods, 8
running costs, project income, 5–6
scaling, 3
single-person business, 3, 9–10
trading time for money, 6–8
work hours and income, 2

Remarketing list, 112

S, T

Sales letter style content
epic killer content, 105–106
FAQ and SAQ, 109
GIFs, 106
networking lunch, 108–109
podcast roundup, 106
presentation, 104
product demos, 107
roundup post, 106
tool roundup, 107–108
video transcription, 107
worksheets and PDFs, 105

Scalable product
affiliate marketing, 89
audio transcription, 73
benefits, 68
blog posts
  e-book, 76–77
  lead magnets, 75–76
  social media traffic, 74
  Speedlancer, 74–75
  structure in presentations, 75, 78–79
  ultimate guide, 75
  webinars, 77
courses (see Courses)
customer focus, 65–67
deliver result, 68–69
delivery process, 70–71
e-commerce web sites, 68
face-to-face meetings, 73
promoting webinar, 79–80
qualification worksheet, 72
record, interactions, 73
rewrite transcript, 74
special and unique, 69
templates and worksheets, 71–72
tools, 70
weight loss/fitness advertisements, 67

Scaling
blueprint for growth, 33
business change, 41
busy/effective, 35
complicated systems, 36
consultancy, 26
focus on results, 40
freelance business (see Freelance business)
freelancers and consultants, 33
investment, 32
large businesses, 34
losing customers and income, 32

Index

Scaling (*cont.*)
  marginal gains
    business end goal, 31
    contributing factor, 30
    creating business, 30
    Freakonomics, 29
    granite mountain, 29
    slow progress, 29
  membership businesses, 32
  money, 25–26
  niche market, 36
  opportunities, 31
  outsourcing, 34
  running/owning, 40
  self-employed people and consultants, 40
  spare funds, 29
  startups, 34
  workshops, 33
Search engine marketing (SEM), 102
Search engine optimization (SEO), 7, 120–121
Self-liquidating offers (SLOs), 89, 129–130
Should as questions (SAQs), 109
Single-person business
  accountability calls, 54
  affiliate products, 48
  Amazon to sell products, 56
  audience, 214
  automated manufacturing, 50–51
  Cloud-based applications, 61–62
  coaching seminars, 53
  coaching transcripts, 51–52
  consulting transcripts, 52
  courses, 44–45
  digital products, 62
  e-books, transcriptions, 44
  e-commerce store with suppliers, 56
  e-commerce supplier, 55–56
  education system, 214
  e-mail courses, 49
  e-mail list drops, 61
  financial control, 214
  group mastermind sessions, 53–54
  high-traffic blog, 46
  lead qualification, 50
  machine and process, 214
  options, 214
  outsourcing administrative services, 49
  outsourcing content services, 49
  outsourcing delivery, 214
  product and service types, 44
  product reselling, 47–48
  promotion and content, 214
  publishing book, 58–59
  splinter products, 60–61
  teaching course, 45
  templated content, 46–47
  training staff, 47
  video tutorials, 56–57
  webinar recordings, 55
  web site maintenance plans, 59
  white-label products, 48
  worksheet content, 52–53
Single-person enterprises
  consultancy model, 16
  consultants, 16
  development, 18
  external consultants, 16
  grateful to customers, 17–18
  growth strategy, 18
  infinite ways, growth, 19
  products and services, 17
Smoke tests, 189–190
Social media, 121–122, 142, 157–158, 195–196
Spare funds, 29
Speedlancer, 49, 74–75
Splinter products, 60–61
Studio Envato, 171
Sumo, 119
Sunk cost fallacy, 194–195

U

Unique selling point (USP), 69
Uproxx, 189
Upwork.com, 170

V

Video tutorials, 56–57

Index

W, X, Y

Webinar recordings, 55
Weekly newsletter, 159
White-label products, 48
Working in business
    afford the time, 14
    Bill Gates, 11
    budget and location, 12
    coaching and consulting, 11
    control, 11
    education system, 10
    freelancers, 13–14
    gas station sandwiches, 12–13
    income streams and options, 12
    running, 10
    scalable product, 15–16
    services and products, 10
    single-person business, 11
    skill areas, 10
    unique delivery, 11
    WordPress, 11

Z

Zapier, 179

GPSR Compliance

The European Union's (EU) General Product Safety Regulation (GPSR) is a set of rules that requires consumer products to be safe and our obligations to ensure this.

If you have any concerns about our products, you can contact us on

ProductSafety@springernature.com

In case Publisher is established outside the EU, the EU authorized representative is:

Springer Nature Customer Service Center GmbH
Europaplatz 3
69115 Heidelberg, Germany